All rights reserved
The New World African Press
P.O. Box 7071
Porter Ranch, CA 91327
Northridge, CA 91327

W9-BNL-111

ISBN 0-9768761-3-2

PRINTED IN NORTHRIDGE, CALIFORNIA
2011

DEDICATION

For Ruth Von Blum and Elizabeth Von Blum

CONTENTS

Acknowledgements
Preface

CHAPTERS

Acknowledgements

Since I published my first book in 1976, I have had the pleasure of acknowledging friends, colleagues, relatives, and others who have contributed so substantially to my efforts. This sixth time around is special because this memoir is the most personal of my books; as my wife Ruth has accurately noted, I finally had the opportunity to write about my favorite topic after spending more than 40 years teaching that topic, albeit in sometimes thinly disguised fashion. The people below (and many others I have inadvertently omitted) have made huge contributions to my work. Without them, the book simply would not exist. And more than ever, I declare absolutely and unambiguously that I alone am responsible for all the inevitable errors, inaccuracies, misinterpretations, sweeping overgeneralizations, hyperbolic assertions, self-aggrandizing conclusions, and demented ravings that have invaded the text.

For many years, my students have implored me to get these stories down in print. I have often used my political experiences in my classes as primary source material and this book has enabled me to systematize many of them. There are literally too many of these students to name. They have been huge factors in the overwhelming gratification I have had as a university teacher since 1967. I pay special tribute to those students who have regularly mobilized on my behalf in my various struggles to implement my educational vision and to protect my intermittently endangered status at the University of California. You all know who you are and how tremendously effective you have been.

I have likewise had supportive faculty colleagues over the years at the University of California. Always a small minority in a research university, they have nevertheless supported a vision of serious, student-centered interdisciplinary education as well as my own efforts to retain my marginal status within the institutional setting. At Berkeley, Fred Reif, Fritz Tubach, the late Alain Renoir, and a few others were always in my corner. At UCLA, Paul Rosenthal, the late Al Boime, Brenda Stevenson, Richard Yarborough, and Darnell Hunt, among others, have supported my instructional and research efforts vigorously. Several Lecturer colleagues, most of whom have been active members of the AFT, have also struggled with me in the seemingly endless campaign against the academic apartheid system I describe throughout these pages. Finally, I want to thank former UCLA Social Science Dean Reynaldo Macias for granting me a quarter's worth of paid leave (rare, almost unprecedented, for a Lecturer at the

University of California). I have used this time to finish the extensive revisions for this book.

My parents, Selma Von Blum (1921-1992) and Peter Von Blum (1921-1995), created a progressive family tradition that has endured for my entire life. From the time of the Henry Wallace campaign of 1948 to the Levittown crisis of 1957 to their opposition to the retrograde policies of the Reagan and first Bush administrations, my parents were always vocal about their political and social views. All my political activism described in this memoir emerges from these family roots. Its impact, I am pleased to note, has extended to all my siblings: Jon, Aimee, Carey, and Hannah. It has been an invaluable personal heritage.

Political compatriots over the years also deserve my vigorous gratitude. There are far too many to acknowledge individually. These men and women have shown remarkable courage in resisting racism, sexism, homophobia, and a huge complex of other injustices in America and throughout the world. It has been my privilege to join them in common struggle, mostly on the streets rather than in the conventional political process. As I have regularly articulated in one of my courses at UCLA, I have found agitation a more congenial and ultimately more satisfying form of political expression and moral conduct.

Various close friends have been especially supportive during the time that I wrote the bulk of this memoir, an extremely trying period as I explain in the Epilogue. Paul Rosenthal, Carole Fabricant, Bill and June Pajaud, Lisa Gerrard, Kelly Vlahakis Hanks and Erik Hanks, Bob Ehrlich, Barbara and David Lampert, and Sylvia Merschel have all provided enormous encouragement and more, fueling my desire to see this project through to completion. The large and distinguished community of African American artists in the Los Angeles area, whose lives and works I have been privileged to document in various publications during the past twenty years, have been similarly supportive.

It has been a singular pleasure to meet and work with Dr. Joseph Holloway, the Editor-in-Chief of the New World African Press. I had followed this enterprise on the Internet for some time even before finishing my book. At a particular moment, it seemed an ideal fit to publish my book with a small publisher in the Los Angeles area that focuses substantially but not exclusively on Africa and the African Diaspora. My work is not exactly diasporic, but it's closely related because I have spent much of my life in African American settings, both as an activist and as a teacher and researcher. Above all, Joe Holloway has been profoundly helpful and supportive of this project. Moreover, he and his Pan-African Studies

Department colleagues at California State University at Northridge have been especially gracious in inviting me to speak at their Black History event in 2010.

I always save the best for last in my acknowledgments section. My wife Ruth and I will have been married for almost 40 years when this book is published. As I sometimes remark to my students, in Los Angeles, this seemingly qualifies for the Guinness Book of Records. She has been involved at every stage of this effort, from initial conception to writing, revision, even more revision, design, and everything else involved in the complex tasks of producing a book. Not the least of this assistance involved her invaluable help with the physical process of actually producing the manuscript owing to my embarrassing ineptitude with computer and all other technology.

I deeply appreciate all that help, without which there would be no memoir. But that's not the major point. The real key is Ruth's huge emotional support through all the turmoil of living a life at the academic margin for the entire time of our relationship, especially during the past year, as I reveal in the Epilogue. Much of my writing was done during a time of major institutional aggravation and personal stress (an understatement, to be sure). Without Ruth, this project and all the other routine activities of life simply couldn't have been done. It's that simple. Her love has sustained us for a very long time; this is yet another reason to dedicate the book to her once again.

PREFACE

Professors are best advised, with the rarest exceptions, to forego writing memoirs. Especially American professors, because they are not likely to experience life-threatening adventures (apart from exotic restaurants) and even less likely to be asked to run for office. Apart from think-tankers who offer opinions to the powerful and sometimes actually meet with them, college teachers merely meet classes and advise students, quarrel with other faculty members and the administration, go on leave and write books destined to be read mostly by graduate students. In short, they live a normal, comfortable and dull American middle class existence.

Paul Von Blum is clearly the exception. Not only because of his life, one of living out moral and political commitments, but also because of the stormy background leading toward professordom, he has quite a tale to tell.

The hidden story of the impact of the Left—basically, the remnants of the Popular Front movement, formerly guided by the Communist Party but at the local base, far from the institutional center—upon the civil rights movement of the 1950s remains vital to an understanding of mid-century American life at large. Here, among local people who took the issues into their own hands, battling not only popular prejudice but local and national authority (notably the FBI), and set the pace for the Freedom Movement to spread and win victories unthinkable even a few years earlier.

Von Blum grew up in and around this extraordinary movement, grew *through* it, so to speak, and emerged an extraordinary scholar-teacher. One might say that he illuminated his own Jewish-American life, family background and relationships, through the prism of how Jews (or at least a significant number of left-leaning Jews) were "different" and felt differently about American racism. Soon, in his own life, they would feel differently about the emerging War in Vietnam.

By the time that much of the nation's youth caught up with the Jewish progressive view on race and the war, Paul had also become a legal scholar and activist seeking to protect and advance precious and hard-won American civil liberties. He had also become the art history scholar and teacher, not to mention the scholar/teacher of African American studies, best known to academia in the last quarter of the twentieth century and beyond.

It is a profoundly interesting life, interestingly told. Readers of all kinds will benefit from discover the writer discover himself.

Paul Buhle
Brown University

vii

A Life at the Margins: Keeping the Political Vision

Chapter 1: Introduction

Memoir writing is an inherently arrogant act. It presupposes that one's life is exceptional and engaging enough to attract others to the narrative that follows. It assumes that the author's story contains events and details that are fundamentally different from those of billions of other people who struggle to survive and seek some meaning in their lives. It also assumes that the author has the requisite skill to offer perceptive reflections about those unusual life events. A memoir, accordingly, demands a strong fusion of unusual experiences and intellectual acuity. But even so, it can scarcely be an "objective" account of a life, because it is invariably filtered through a profoundly subjective lens and tempered by the vicissitudes of personal memory.

On some level, all memoirs are essentially fictional (or at least *not* non-fiction); they are life stories that authors want others to hear. To be sure, this does not mean that they are lies or that they are even insincere. They *are* selective without being fraudulent (there are, of course, deliberately fraudulent memoirs, but those are an entirely different category). Memoirs in general are the stories that the authors believe are accurate and equally important, they themselves *need* to believe are accurate. Some facts are verifiable through family conversations, newspaper accounts, and other primary documents—the traditional sources that historians employ and that I have used in various books and articles on cultural and art history over the years.

Many of the people who played a role in my early life are dead and therefore unavailable for conversations and confirmation of my recollections. Even many of my fellow activists from the civil rights movement and other 60s protests are gone or otherwise unavailable. And a few have changed their lives so significantly, leaving their previous social commitments and moral fervor long behind, that I have no wish to contact them at this stage of my life. My disapproval of their life choices, inevitably, would color any conversation and would be both personally unpleasant and factually marginal.

But many "facts" are not verifiable. The epistemology is complex and authors must rely on their own memories and readers must rely on authors' basic honesty. I can state, honestly I believe, that any errors, misjudgments, and inaccuracies that follow are inadvertent rather than deliberate. Doubtless, errors exist in the following pages, mostly from my inability to reconstruct the exact sequence of events, especially during the 1960s, when I

1

seemed to be involved in every protest and demonstration that occurred. Fortunately, sequential error is mostly disconcerting to me and has no serious impact on the general trajectory of my narrative.

It can be said that I have a reputation for having an unusually strong memory (especially when it comes to negative life experiences and people I judge to have wronged me). But that observation, in turn, generates other serious questions about accuracy. A few examples might be helpful. During the civil rights movement a few unpleasant encounters with police authorities resulted in physical violence against me. Yet it is fair to say that some of the key oppressive police figures from the civil rights era, like Colonel Al Lingo, head of the Alabama Highway Patrol, were unambiguously evil racists, regardless of whether they were nice to their families or not. Negative memories of people like them, and their dutiful minions who carried out their nefarious policies, are entirely understandable.

But what of the more personal slights and perceived injustices, from people with no national or even local visibility? The kindergarten teacher who, 62 years ago, humiliated me in front of the other five-year olds on my first day in school? Unambiguously evil? No. Only stupid and astonishingly insensitive. Or various university administrators who sought to terminate me from my academic position or my program from its existence? They too may well have been decent family men and women and, indeed, may even have thought that they were acting in the best interest of the institution. But human reactions are profoundly subjective. I cannot shed my view of their malevolence and in any case, their actions are indelible features of my consciousness (and my unconsciousness). History, but especially personal history, is what it is: deeply, sometimes hopelessly, subjective.

So at the outset, a reasonable obligation is to justify the entire enterprise. Readers are entitled to know why the book deserves their attention and why one more memoir—out of the seemingly endless supply—is worth their effort. Unlike many memoirs, this is not a story of massive childhood trauma, although some trauma, emerging from the Holocaust and from my parents' early leftist and civil rights activities (and their perpetual and debilitating economic struggles) certainly existed. My father dealt no drugs nor engaged in any other criminal enterprises, organized or otherwise (on one level, that was too bad, because at least my family's financial picture would likely have been brighter; this is deliberately gender specific: mothers during the immediate post-war era simply did not do major crime).

My parents never abused me and they suffered from no alcohol or drug abuse. They and my four younger siblings had no debilitating diseases and I had no need to donate any personal body parts nor engage in any other form

2

of personal sacrifice or heroism. That narrative, tragically common in America and elsewhere in the world (and widely underreported), is not part of my personal story.

Excellent health has generally followed me throughout my life. My afflictions have been relatively minor. A few surgeries, but nothing more than routine: a tonsillectomy, an appendectomy, two elbow surgeries due to fancying myself a softball player into my 60s, and very little else. My biggest challenge has been my 60-year odyssey with dentistry, reminding me of John Updike's mordant comments about his dental misadventures. I have often imagined that half my life has been spent in a dental chair. Even now, when perusing the daily obituaries, I find a tinge of gratification when seeing the demise of a dentist. But what follows contains no heroic struggle to overcome any horrible diseases.

My mother and father likewise engaged in no sexual abuse. Unlike Bettina Aptheker's disturbing allegations in *Intimate Politics* about Herbert, her famous father's sexual exploitation of her as a child, I am glad to make no such accusations on behalf of my three younger sisters. My parents rarely even used corporal punishment on me and my brother and sisters except for the occasional (and, all things considered, fairly benign) whack on the ass that was relentlessly common in the United States in the late 1940s and 1950s. In fact, we had, relatively speaking, a fairly loving family environment. Moreover, my parents were married for 50 years before my mother died in 1992 at 71. To be sure, the marriage was not perfect and there were many fights, usually about money. But no divorce. *A Life At The Margins: Keeping The Political Vision* eschews the sensational and will never reach the exalted ranks of an Oprah or similar appearance for its scandalous revelations or its inspirational stirrings.

This book also has no wildly unusual narrative that can lead to temporary media interest and high popular appeal. A good friend my age, Barbara Lampert, grew up in a New York apartment house while her father worked as a professional wrestling promoter. Her childhood memories are bizarre. While other Jewish children recalled playgrounds, bar mitzvahs, and relatively stable if somewhat conventional or neurotic childhoods, she recalls seeing people like Gorgeous George, Argentine Rocca, large female wrestlers, and male midget wrestlers in the hotel—and at family dinners. That has burdened her emotionally for over 60 years and must explain, at least partially, why she became a psychotherapist.

Nothing like that follows in this text: no family circus acts, no celebrity status in entertainment, the arts, commerce, or public affairs, no solo sailboat trips around the world, no mountain conquests, no visits from outer space or abductions from aliens on flying saucers, no spiritual breakthroughs or profound insights into God or other supernatural delusions. Indeed, nothing unusually dramatic except for a powerful set of civil rights events in Levittown, Pennsylvania in 1957—events that impacted my life, my consciousness, and my political and professional activities for more than the next half century.

Even as a child I did very little of consequence. I have been delighted to know Paul Krassner, for example, for over 40 years. In his memoir, *Confession of a Raving Unconfined Nut*, he discusses his status as a violin prodigy, playing Vivaldi at Carnegie Hall as a 6-year old in 1939. I cannot play a single instrument and even in elementary school was a consummate mediocrity in playing the "sticks" during the (dreaded) music hour. All I did (other than getting into trouble at school) was play baseball. To my permanent sorrow, I realized early on that I had dramatic limitations in baseball and other sports, although they still occupy my substantial daily attention.

Likewise, I can report no especially unusual sexual adventures, conquests, or anything else in that realm. That part of my story is relentlessly typical: the usual adolescent angst, normal heterosexual relationships in college, a few emotionally difficult break-ups, a few thrilling conquests, various hopes and fantasies, and, in short, a very common personal trajectory. I have several friends and acquaintances with unusually colorful sexual histories. In a few cases, at the extreme end of this spectrum, those tales would generate their own compelling and even salacious memoirs. But that focus is not central to this narrative. Later, a very durable relationship with my wife Ruth and problems and triumphs with my daughter Elizabeth will infuse the text at key junctures. Personal stories are inseparable from political ones.

In the popular mind, the 60s were also a time of widespread drug use. I can certainly confirm that notion if living in Berkeley provides a perceptive lens. I saw the proliferation of drugs there and elsewhere for many years. And unlike President Bill Clinton, I did inhale—but not easily or well. Both my parents were smokers, but I never was, not even a single cigarette. Smoking always struck me as stupid even though most of my peers took up the habit early. I puffed on some joints when they were passed around, but more often than not, I choked more than inhaled. I dropped acid twice, finding it marginally interesting but not especially revelatory and haven't done it for more than 40 years. That's it for drugs. No addiction, no repressed drug-induced memories, no long term concern with the drug culture at all. In fact, I was at most on the extreme periphery of this phenomenon resulting in my strongly critical views about the drugs and the entire "counter culture." Many 60s memoirs are replete with powerful, sometimes agonizing personal drug issues and problems, but not this one.

This memoir, however, is a Jewish-flavored account of a highly political and intellectual life emerging in childhood, developing in the social turmoil of the 1960s era of agitation and unrest, and continuing throughout a 40-year career as a radical academic. Any one of these elements, if extensive enough, would arguably merit book-length treatment. Many accounts of 60s activities are currently available; as a university teacher, however, I have come to understand how little my students really understand that seminal period of American history. When I speak of my own civil rights movement efforts and my anti-war work, for example, they are invariably fascinated, seeing my accounts as compelling primary source material that is far more engaging than the tedious fact-heavy material they slog through in high school advanced placement classes and elsewhere.

My personal 60s activities were extensive and they molded my entire lifetime vision and activities. Though I generally sought no leadership roles, from time to time leadership responsibilities found me. I played no major national roles, although I developed a strong oratorical style that has served me especially well as a university teacher for many decades. My story is different from those of Mario Savio and Todd Gitlin, Stokley Carmichalel (Kwame Ture) and Jim Forman, Kathleen Cleaver and Bernadine Dohrn, and so many hundreds of 60s activists known nationally and internationally. By conscious choice I was a "foot soldier" in the movement, content, even eager, to be on the front lines of conflict and confrontation. I loved the action on the streets and even now, I find it constantly exhilarating when demonstrating against a grotesque war or for any cause that touches my deepest sense of personal justice and morality.

Much of this focus involves race, that perpetually touchy topic in America that has engaged me personally and professionally for most of my life. More than any other movement, my civil rights activity has molded my identity and consciousness, informing virtually every feature of my personal and professional life since that tumultuous epoch. There is plenty of room for more autobiographical accounts of that era, especially since many of us are moving, all too swiftly, from late middle age to senior citizenry.

Like many 60s radicals, my roots lay in early childhood, although I am not literally a red diaper baby. As this book reveals, my parents were non-Communist leftists, sometimes close to the Party but never rigid ideologues. That perspective, too, deserves explication and has significant educational value for younger generations, especially for those committed to a humane and progressive vision for the future. And my father's experience as the only survivor whose entire immediate family was murdered in Auschwitz inevitably adds a powerful historical and psychological dimension to this story. Holocaust memoirs also exist in abundance (we still, even now, need

5

more of them as this generation fades from existence), but second generation Holocaust survivor stories, and their colossal impact on people's lives, can add hugely to our deeper emotional understanding of that horrific experience. This also informs all that appears in the following pages. The legacy of Nazi Germany has been crucial in my emotional life and in all my political and professional activities.

A large part of this memoir concerns my more than four decades of academic life, almost all of which has been at the University of California. My own odyssey in that institution is unique; by itself, it justifies extensive treatment because of my deeply successful career both as a teacher and a scholar while working at the periphery of academic life. My teaching in well over 10 departments and programs spanning the humanities and social sciences at two major campuses (Berkeley and UCLA) of the University is probably unprecedented. My various struggles to survive both personal and institutional assaults, owing to my aggressively nontraditional, interdisciplinary intellectual focus and my commitment to teaching in a research institution, provide some strong insights into academic culture and educational politics in the late 20th and early 21st centuries.

This story, however, has more intriguing emotional origins, detailed in the early part of this memoir. Despite my success as a teacher, my professional work since January, 1967 has the most improbable origins. From the first day of kindergarten to the last day of law school (another bizarre story in itself), I had a troubled relationship with school, sometimes even loathing it. At best, I tolerated it, but I almost never found any personal or intellectual enjoyment from the formal curriculum or even from most school activities outside the classroom. I also largely disliked the vast majority of my teachers at every level, with a few conspicuous exceptions. For some I retain strong feelings of animosity towards them many decades later, although I have transformed these feelings into productive educational and political activity. At its worst, and with some frequency, school was nightmarish, causing me extreme anxiety and more, occasionally requiring professional intervention. Most of the time, I merely disliked school. I found the subject matter boring, repetitious, and oppressive and the teaching uninspired. Frankly it was a serious waste of my time. These impressions continued throughout my 12 years of elementary through high school (I mercifully skipped a grade), 4 years of undergraduate work, and 3 years of law school. Nothing since then has caused me fundamentally to change my mind, the reasons for which will become clear in the ensuing pages.

In retrospect, I have come to understand how unnerving this must have been to my parents, a reality that I never appreciated at the time. Neither of my parents graduated from college and they both had a large emotional stake in my academic success. My intermittent failures must have been deeply troubling and their repeated calls to discuss my scholastic and behavioral difficulties with various school officials must have been unpleasant and exasperating. Finally I did make it through with some academic distinction, but more often with consummately mediocre grades. I was rarely a stellar student. I have been a far better teacher than I ever was a student—another of the major ironies of my personal story.

What is surprising—indeed, astonishing to many of my students, colleagues, and friends—is that I have never left school. Since 1948, with very few interruptions, my life has been involved with the formal educational process. Education has been one of the consuming passions of my life, at least partially because of my unpleasant personal experiences in childhood, adolescence, and early adulthood. My own commitment to teaching emerges from my huge dissatisfaction with the teaching I have experienced. It is a harsh judgment, but one I maintain with vigor: my teachers from 1948 to 1967 were mostly negative role models and I have sought to model my own professional life in profound opposition to their efforts. Virtually every day in the classroom, I am reminded of my own unpleasant memories; these no longer haunt me, but candor compels an admission that they remain a powerful motivator even now. I routinely think back to the boring men and women I had as my teachers and I prepare my efforts with them in mind.

This complex interweaving of Holocaust effects, childhood poverty and family political activism and persecution, extensive 60s civil rights and other political involvements, and a unique saga of educational alienation leading to a life of teaching and scholarly distinction and serious university conflict and educational activism underlies this memoir. The story begins at birth but the writing itself commences at age 66—surely a time in life appropriate for sustained recollection and reflection, especially since I have no discernable signs of cognitive impairment. My generation, born during or in the ashes of World War II and coming to age in the repressive era of the cold war, was the heart of 60s era agitation. Many of us from those times remain fully active, both professionally and politically. Our stories are often compelling; in any case, they will surely be significant primary source material for future historians. *A Life At the Margin: Keeping The Political Vision* is one of them.

Chapter 2
Beginnings

My birth on March 30, 1943 in Philadelphia was far from ordinary. Not the circumstances: the Second World War was raging and the entire nation was on a war footing. My father, Peter Wolfgang Blum, a refugee from Nazi Germany, was a conscript in the United States Army, later serving in Army Intelligence, although I am uncertain when he received this assignment during the War. Later conversations informed me that he had planned to be with my mother either when she gave birth or shortly afterwards if at all possible.

But it was not possible. I was supposed to be born in mid to late June 1943, making me close to three months premature. My mother, Selma Blum, reported that I entered the world at slightly more than three pounds and that initially, the doctors gave me little chance to survive. They advised her to take me home and "hope for the best." With the active assistance of my maternal grandmother, my mother fed me milk and kept me warm. I grew stronger, gained weight, and, in short, made it. I like to think that my temperament played a role and that my premature birth reflected my eagerness to take on the challenges of life. This is a pleasant myth that I often jocularly pass on to my students in informal conversations, noting, of course, that it is entirely without any scientific foundation.

My mother, Selma Blum, was the eldest of two daughters of Abraham and Cecelia Eckstein. Their ordeal was typical of early 20th century Jewish immigrants from Eastern Europe. Both of my grandparents were from the Ukraine, born and raised in early life near Kiev. Whether they knew each other there or met in the United States is unclear to me. They joined thousands of others in the arduous journey to America, traveling uncomfortably in steerage and arriving on Ellis Island—a story that has been told many thousands of times. They fled both economic and political oppression of Czarist Russia and, above all, the pervasive anti-Semitism of the time.

Unfortunately, I have only the most fleeting memories of my grandparents' conversations about their lives in "the old country" because they both died while I was still very young. Their English was excellent, but they often spoke in Ukrainian/Russian or Yiddish. I do recall their speaking, in English, about pogroms and about the pervasive persecution of the Jewish population; that registered with me then and it has stayed with me throughout my life, possibly the earliest source of my lifelong hypersensitivity to anti-Semitism and racism in any form.

My grandparents were fairly ordinary Jewish immigrants. They arrived in Philadelphia, where my grandfather established a small grocery business. I recall, when I was a few years older, that my grandmother had some experience in sweatshops and some contact with labor organizing during her oppressive work in those settings. Above all, their experiences of the Depression and their extensive conversations about their sufferings had the most impact on my early consciousness. Over and over again there were stories of economic deprivation. I heard how my grandfather lost his grocery store. How my mother and aunt had to wear cardboard in their shoes. How their profound emotional desperation stemmed from the Depression. And I heard that Herbert Hoover was the devil, while Franklin Roosevelt was the savior. He was the man who put millions back to work on the WPA, including my grandfather. And more than anything, I heard that financial security was the most important thing in the world.

That is the Eastern European Jewish side of my background. The other side is more psychologically significant. Like my mother, my father was born in 1921, in Lubeck, Germany, the son of Arnold Blum (born in Berlin in 1887) and Bela Blum (born in Berlin in 1884). He was the middle son; his older sister was Hana Blum (probably born in 1914; German records are probably accurate, but not certain) and his younger brother was Rolf Blum (born in 1927). These precise dates are generally not historically significant; only the general time frame is useful in establishing a broader context for my own story. But for me, the dates are hugely important. Each of these four persons, grandfather, grandmother, aunt, and uncle, were all murdered, most likely in 1944, in Auschwitz. Their names and their dates of birth and death deserve mention and repetition. Holocaust survivors of all generations well understand how vital it is to provide a human face to the otherwise icy abstraction of "six million." Even now, more than 60 years after the murders of relatives I never knew, I find it emotionally compelling to link this reality to my continuing political consciousness and activism. It has had a huge impact on my entire psyche, including my neuroses about making a living and my feeling that many people in positions of authority are out to get me (some, including police officers, judges, and university bureaucrats have actually been in that position, as this narrative will reveal).

The full details of my father's arrival in America are still unknown to me. The only part known to me is that his parents somehow managed to get him out of Berlin, where the family relocated from Lubeck and where his father Arnold established some sort of confectionary business. How he got to Philadelphia sometime in the mid to late 1930s remains somewhat mysterious. Near the end of his life, he began to open up somewhat, but only in broad outline. It was never clear why his parents sent him away and

9

not his siblings, although there is evidence that his older sister Hana managed to get to Sweden before returning to Germany to try to rescue the family, before being captured, deported, and killed. There is also some vague evidence that his younger brother had some kind of disability, making him doubly susceptible to the lunacy of Nazi racial policies.

All I have been able to determine is that my father, through the assistance of one or more Jewish agencies, arrived in Philadelphia and lived in various foster homes. He quickly learned English and went to school. I have a large cache of letters and cards from his parents and from his brother Rolf in the late 1930s and even early 1940s, many of which have Nazi stamps with portraits of Hitler. These are heartbreaking documents. They inquire about his health and well being, ask whether he has made any Jewish friends or whether he has gone to temple, and seek information about his schooling. Most significantly, I think, the letters reflect the tragic fact that they seemingly regarded themselves as Germans, German Jews to be sure, but Germans above all. And from what I have been able to discern, they make no mention of the darkness fatally descending on the German Jewish population. I have scarcely read them all because my German is not good enough and the script is difficult to follow, but others with better German have essentially confirmed my observations.

This is relevant to my memoir, predominantly because my father, like thousands of other Holocaust refugees and survivors, refused to talk about it. But it hovered over family life all the more because of his furtiveness and silence. It was never there, yet it was always there, a seeming contradiction that nevertheless makes complete sense to many other second generation survivors with strikingly similar recollections. Even early on, for example, I realized, and resented, that I had only one set of grandparents while all the other children had two.

A word about names: My father hated his middle and last names. At some point, he abandoned both. "Wolfgang" is easy to understand. It is conspicuously Germanic and hardly fits in an American context, especially in the post-war period. The change of the last name from "Blum" to "Von Blum" is more problematic and far more interesting psychologically. I cannot recall when he changed the family name and if he actually did it formally through some official legal process. I have only vague recollections of using "Blum," perhaps in kindergarten or first grade. Thereafter it was always "Von Blum."

So why the change from a classically Jewish surname to an ersatz Germanic one with an absurd aura of nobility? I can only speculate, because it was always a taboo topic at home. My guess is that on one level, it reflects the deeper reality of his German Jewish upbringing and identity, reflected in

10

his immediate family, perhaps even as Nazi guards marched them into the gas chambers in Auschwitz. Like so many other Jews in Germany, he probably viewed himself as a European—a German, despite his recent family tragedy at the hands of other Germans. Perhaps unconsciously, the name change permitted him to regain what had been taken from him so savagely. Even more deeply, it constituted a denial of his Jewishness, an all too typical response of Holocaust survivors. For much of my life, I saw his thinking as going something like this: "If I'm of German origin, then I'm not a Jew and therefore nobody will kill me." This deep denial would play itself out in many other ways throughout his life and would affect me as well in multifaceted ways, both emotionally and politically.

Despite his ostensibly overt repudiation of his Jewish identity, my father continued to reveal a perplexing and contradictory attitude about his Jewishness, especially when it concerned the sensitive and inflammatory issue of race relations in America. This more covert expression eventually had a colossal impact on my subsequent life as a civil rights activist and as an academic teaching writing about African American culture and politics. From early childhood, I recall my father saying, with considerable regularity, that the same things that happened to his family in Germany were happening to "Negroes" in America. He understood, intuitively, that racism is the same whatever its specific manifestations. For decades, I have told my students that "racism anywhere is racism everywhere." My viewpoint reflects a lesson I learned early on from my father's comments at home in the late 1940s and the early 1950s. Later in his life, my father explicitly compared the Nazi Holocaust against the Jews with American racism against the African American population and he vigorously maintained that his rediscovered Jewish identity compelled a powerful anti-racist perspective.

His complex, lifelong Jewish odyssey has caused me to reflect more fully about the touchy issue of Jewish/African American relationships in the United States. Like everyone involved in civil rights work, I have been acutely aware of how American mass media have highlighted the growing discord and mistrust between the two groups. I have well understood throughout my life that Jews and African Americans have shared a common yet historically distinct bond of oppression. The earlier Black/Jewish alliance of the modern civil rights movement, which formed a huge part of my fundamental personal and professional identity, has changed since the sixties, sometimes dramatically. Especially on college campuses, students today from both groups sometimes express the suspicion reflected in and fostered by press and television stories. In the post-war era, millions of American Jews have achieved unprecedented affluence and have grown more conservative, identifying more fully, even completely, with the dominant white population. Their frequent support of repressive Israeli policies has exacerbated tensions between the two communities. Substantial Jewish opposition to affirmative action has also widened the gap between Blacks and Jews. Near the end of his life, these developments caused my father considerable distress. He and I agreed entirely on both issues, seeing Israeli imperialism and racism as increasingly problematic and supporting affirmative action enthusiastically.

Nevertheless, contemporary media accounts are often exaggerated, promoting public perceptions of mutual hostility that fail to grasp a deeper historical understanding of the relationship. During the modern civil rights era, thousands of Jews of my generation were active participants. Many, like me, came from family backgrounds with close contact to the Holocaust. This history catalyzed a powerful commitment to resisting American racism, which was both understood and appreciated among large segments of the African American community. Those feelings, those political commitments, and those bonds have scarcely dissipated. Thousands of African Americans and Jews retain a huge affection for each other, a reality I have experienced throughout my academic and activist careers. My black students are perfectly aware that I have a strong Jewish identity and I know that it has enhanced, not diminished, my credibility and reputation with them. That is also the case with the African American artists about whom I write; some like Charles White, Ernie Barnes, and Bill Pajaud have actually incorporated Jewish themes into their own visual works.

My experience also persuades me that African Americans, on the whole, have deep empathy for Jewish suffering during the Nazi Holocaust. The reason is simple: they have often heard stories of slavery and lynching, recognizing all too well that American racists like the Ku Klux Klan and others have targeted Jews as well as blacks. My strong impression is that millions of African Americans also know that in Nazi Germany, individuals of African descent were severely ostracized and brutalized and that American black POWs were especially ill treated. Many too have heard that African American soldiers were among the first liberators and witnesses of Nazi atrocities.

Accordingly, African Americans know that the implications of the Holocaust are dramatically obvious: *any* genocide sets the stage for all other instances of mass murder. They know, at least intuitively, that the Nazi persecution of Jews was strikingly similar to the slave trade and the horrific pattern of racism in the new world, especially in its dehumanization of millions of human beings on arbitrary and irrational grounds of race and ethnicity. My African American students and friends regularly and properly

12

compare the Nazi Holocaust not only with slavery, but also with the horrific conditions in Darfur in the early 21st century.

I have, to be sure, encountered some Jews and African Americans who participate in the bizarre and fruitless ritual of "who has suffered most." Fortunately, I have found this spectacle of competitive suffering to be fairly rare. In fact, throughout my academic career, I have been moved by the profoundly emotional responses of my black students to my accounts of Jewish suffering from 1933 to 1945. I cannot generalize, of course, about the entire African American population. I have been fortunate to spend extensive time with African Americans in intellectual and artistic communities and thus am extremely confident about my perception of their profound comprehension of the implications of the Holocaust for their own community — and for humanity in general.

When I look at my address book containing the list of my friends and associates, I find that well over 90% are Jews and African Americans, almost in equal numbers. This is no surprise. If the old civil rights alliance is frayed, it still is alive and well among members of both communities, especially those willing to transcend media hype and sensationalism. For myself, although I have experienced and understood the privilege of light skin in a racist America, I resist the designation of "white" and wish that my more of my fellow Jews would again embrace the "otherness" that has generated so much intellectual and cultural creativity and political solidarity with the oppressed. It is no accident that I call my book *A Life at the Margins*. Historically, Jews and African Americans have both lived at the margins of society, a reality often fostering an admirable vision of social criticism and political radicalism. That has been my personal perspective on Jewish/African American solidarity for well over a half century.

As I write, I am well aware that my father's attitudes and actions may well require much deeper analysis, probably psychoanalytically. But that is not my objective in this book. My own speculations, which I write and make public here for the first time ever, are intended to shed light on *my* consciousness. They don't purport to be psychologically definitive at all. And regarding name changes, my father was not unique in our family. My first name was — and remains — Warren. From early childhood, I hated it and refused to use it. For more than 60 years, I have gone by my middle name Paul. I ascribe no serious psychological significance to that decision; many people dislike their given names and use middle names or nicknames. I am merely one of them. But the last name is another matter. I have always gone by "Von Blum," and it now has a strong personal and professional cache. If I were younger, I would change it to its original "Blum," to restore its essential Jewishness. But inertia and reputational considerations have won out.

I have no very early childhood memories. My mother told me often that she spent time, with me as a baby, in Jackson, Mississippi, where my father was stationed during his Army service. I know that German prisoners of war were incarcerated there and that my father, with his native German speaking ability, had some involvement with their incarceration and interrogation. My mother repeated, frequently, that on the train trip back from Jackson to Philadelphia, I cried constantly and was always hyperactive, if not in a strictly clinical sense. Early on, I was given the nickname "Pepi," reflecting the extremely high energy level that I have exhibited throughout my entire life. I never knew who exactly originated that name, but it stuck for several years, at least until my college days.

My earliest recollections occurred probably in late 1945 when my father was discharged honorably from the Army. Later, I learned about his service in Mississippi, where he interrogated German POWs who were brought to the United States. During his time there, he actively resisted the racial segregation in the army and in the wider Jackson community. Afterwards, he was deployed to Germany, where he augmented his earlier work by interrogating captured Nazi war criminals. That was likely where he found out about his family's fate, setting the stage for the rest of his frequently tormented life. But I recall, vaguely, his return—an alien presence when I was cared for and doted on by a mother and two grandparents. To say that I was "spoiled" would be an understatement.

We lived in an apartment in the Strawberry Mansion neighborhood of Philadelphia, then a largely Jewish district and since the mid 20th century, a predominantly African American district unfortunately known mostly for its urban decay and its high crime rate. My earliest recollections are pleasant. Having accustomed myself to a new adult male presence, I enjoyed trips to nearby Fairmount Park and the noises and bustle of urban life. My parents reminded me often that I loved the sounds of buses and trolley cars and was especially fond of the trash and garbage truck that made weekly stops in front of our residence. I reportedly stated early and often that I aspired to be a trash man or garbage man when I grew up. I also remember that I loved the noises of the streets.

That early consciousness has stayed with me throughout my life. I have always been hopelessly, arrogantly urban. The country and nature leave me cold; while I can appreciate natural beauty, and while I have occasionally traveled to regions of the world with spectacular views, I always strive to make these visits relatively short. Protracted exposure to the country makes me irritable, anxious to return to the city. This is unusual, probably neurotic, but it is scarcely unique.

The year 1947 was a turning point on several levels. The family moved to the Logan district of Philadelphia, purchasing a house under my father's GI Bill on 11th Street. The major event was my mother's pregnancy and in April, 1947, she gave birth to twins, brother Jon and sister Aimee. I am only fleetingly familiar with issues of sibling rivalry, but I must have felt some shock at the arrival of *two* little interlopers into my universe. All of a sudden, I was no longer the adored center of attention, but "Nana" seemed always solicitous of my needs. So my privilege, though modified, remained largely intact, as the first son and first grandson. That attention, presumably, is one of the sources of my own well developed sense of entitlement that has persisted throughout adulthood.

Chapter 3
Early Childhood and First Memories: Money and Politics

A bigger reality, and one where I have concrete recollections even from the age of four, was the family's ever present financial precariousness, a reality that lasted throughout my parents' lives and that had dramatic consequences for my own inner turmoil for *my* whole life. There were always discussions, and especially loud, often truculent arguments, about money and bills, a problem compounded with a growing family with two new infants. This reality caused me considerable discomfort; to this day, I find the topic of money unpleasant and emotionally debilitating. I resist thinking about it as much as possible. Indeed, I dislike money a great deal. I know people, like me, who grew up with considerable economic deprivation, who have an opposite perspective. They are consumed with money and surround themselves with material goods — the contemporary versions of Thorstein's Veblin's conspicuous consumers. And there are others like me — we have no desire to be rich but *every* desire not to be poor. This deep-seated emotional perspective has profoundly affected my behavior, details of which will also pervade the text that follows.

If 1947 had a profound impact, 1948 was even more important for me. Financial considerations soon gave way to several other concerns, especially the radical political consciousness of my family that has lasted throughout my life and that has informed almost everything I have done intellectually and professionally. In summer, 1948, the insurgent Progressive Party convened in Philadelphia to mount a left-wing challenge to the Democratic and Republican parties in the 1948 national elections. That history is well known: Progressive Party presidential candidate, former Vice President Henry Wallace and vice presidential candidate Senator Glen Taylor were left-liberals who had become extremely critical of the cold war policies of Harry Truman's administration.

The Philadelphia gathering has become legendary in American leftist circles. Young idealists mixed with seasoned political operatives, many from the Communist Party and many others from left-wing labor unions throughout the country. Iconic figures, including Elmer Benson, Rexford Tugwell, Vito Marcantonio, John Abt, Paul Robeson, W.E. B. Du Bois, and many others, were in attendance. Folk singers like Pete Seeger were also present, and I distinctly recall Seeger's rendition of "I've Got a Ballot " and someone (probably not Seeger, but I'm uncertain and it's not centrally important) singing, "everyone likes Wallace, friendly Henry Wallace, friendly Henry Wallace in the White House." Though this sounds extremely implausible, I actually remember these lyrics from 1948 and only much later

16

did I learn that "Friendly Henry Wallace" was composed by leftist lyricist Yip Harburg.

By all accounts, the Progressive Party Convention was a festive affair. My parents, both 27 at the time, were deeply engaged in the local activities. While far too young to appreciate the actual political issues at stake, I have vibrant memories of the flurry of activities I observed. Many people floated in and out of our Philadelphia home. My parents reported later that members of the California delegation either stayed temporarily with us or convened in our house for various meetings. Many adults carried banners and pennants and there were plenty of spirited conversations. I knew that they were about politics without having any idea what that really meant. But I do recall specific language, even if these too seem improbable more than 60 years later: Jim Crow, class struggle, reactionaries, the "party" (I can only imagine what that meant to me at the time), and a few other terms.

My father later told me that he and my mother took me to Shibe Park, the home of the National League Philadelphia Phillies and the American League Philadelphia A's to hear the acceptance speeches of Henry Wallace and Glen Taylor. I wish that I could remember that event—it must have been exhilarating—but I simply cannot. A few other memories from that time, however, have stuck with me. There is a snapshot of me, wearing short pants, holding a Wallace/Taylor pennant in '48. I have misplaced the photo itself, but I recall the time that the picture was taken, probably by my father. And most significantly for my future academic life, my father often informed me that he (or he and my mother) introduced me to Paul Robeson at the Convention in 1948. I want to believe that I remember such an introduction vividly and that I can trace the origins of my subsequent Robeson scholarship to a fateful introduction as a five-year old boy in Philadelphia; alas, that is not the case, so I must instead rely on the veracity of my parents.

I also remember the Wallace campaign itself. My parents did the usual precinct work and organized as many Progressive Party voters as possible. Meetings in our house were frequent and telephone conversations about the campaign were likewise common. One specific conversation stands out to me. I think it occurred in our house, but it could have been elsewhere in the neighborhood. My father had an angry exchange with another Progressive Party activist. Here is what I recall, with almost word for word accuracy: " Goddammit. . . , this is the Progressive Party, not the Communist Party."

This is what fascinates me now about memory. At five, I had no idea what this meant. For all I knew, a "party" could well have meant a birthday party. But my father's anger and emotion registered with me, allowing me that level of precision. But this becomes even more interesting, I think. I also recall that his comment was directed to someone named "Klonsky." In

17

researching the matter, I have discovered that my recollection is probably accurate. Robert Klonsky was a major Communist Party figure in Philadelphia at the time. A veteran of the Spanish Civil War, he was an unregenerate Stalinist who served federal prison time in the 1950s for a Smith Act conviction during the height of the anti-communist hysteria in the United States. His son Michael Klonsky, a true red diaper baby, later became a major leader of the Students for a Democratic Society, although I never knew him during or after the turbulent 1960s. The senior Klonsky's Communist Party affiliation and the time frame, combined with my father's non-Communist leftist ideology, join to give me confidence about my recollection, though it obviously cannot be verified.

I learned later about the origins of my father's political identity as a young man. In the late 1990's, I came to know an older woman named Sari Weiss, now deceased. She had been involved in a relationship with my father in Philadelphia when they were both young; I assumed it was sexual, but owing to the recent death of both my parents and a general sense of propriety, I felt it unseemly to inquire about this aspect. I did probe into Sari's political influence. She had been a member of the Communist Party. She told me that my father, as a late teenager, who was still obviously worried about the fate of his family in Germany, had no developed social consciousness. Sari informed him that the Communists were the major opponents of fascism in Europe, an accurate perception that I have often conveyed in my teaching over the years. Sari Weiss's influence never persuaded my father to join the Party, but it clearly helped radicalize him and set the stage for his subsequent political development in the armed forces and beyond.

When my father was drafted, he was deployed eventually in Ft. Lewis, Washington. I don't know what his specific military responsibilities were, but he often noted that while in Washington State, he had some contact with Hugh DeLacy, who subsequently became a one-term Democratic member of the United States House of Representatives. DeLacy was clearly very left-wing and probably close to the Communist Party, much like Congressman Vito Marcantonio of New York. I later inquired into DeLacy's record and everything I found confirmed what made perfect sense. His subsequent political record, including his organizing for the Progressive Party in 1948 and his unfriendly testimony later before the House Un-American Activities Committee in the 50s reflects a standard leftist, pro-Communist perspective that would have been influential to my father in his early 20s.

I imagine that my father also read various Socialist classics at the time, since he made some allusions to them as well as to other leftist sources, especially literature, which I recall as well from early childhood: Jack

London, Upton Sinclair, Howard Fast, among others. These volumes were also in our house. Despite my parents' lack of formal education beyond high school, books abounded, but it took some time before they began to have any real attraction for me. My parents also always had newspapers, especially the Philadelphia Bulletin. That paper, and the occasional morning copy of the Philadelphia Inquirer, fascinated me. As soon as I could read, shortly after I was three, I devoured the paper, mostly the sports pages and the comics. My baseball passion developed early and the newspaper gave me an opportunity to follow my heroes, peruse the box scores, and check the standings. I continue this practice even now and cannot imagine a life without newspapers. As I later discovered, we also had Marxist papers, but it took longer for me to delve into those engaging documents.

Like other leftist households, there were also plenty of records, especially works of Paul Robeson, Pete Seeger, Woody Guthrie, the Almanac Singers, and an old 78 RPM recording of the anti-fascist "Six Songs for Democracy" (Discos De Las Brigadas Internacionales), which I still have. Except for the classical music my parents played incessantly, and which I despised, these recordings were regular features of life at home. They proved to be much more valuable historical source material for me, especially about such topics as labor history, the Spanish Civil War, civil rights, and other themes rarely covered, even now, in the formal school curriculum.

I cannot recall any comparable radicalization for my mother. Unfortunately, the 1940s were a time of overt patriarchy in America and men set the tone for political vision and family participation. My mother had strong feelings about justice and social class emerging from her Depression experiences. She also commented regularly about the recent genocide of the Jews in Europe—much more than my father ever did until his final years. Moreover, unlike my father who had no relatives, my mother had a small family in Philadelphia, primarily her sister Ruth and her brother-in-law, my uncle Jack. Visits to her various family members reinforced a Jewish presence, albeit one without any specifically religious trappings. Like most of the Jewish population, she despised Herbert Hoover and Republicans generally. But any deeper radicalism largely followed my father's lead. Even more important, she had virtually complete responsibility for three small children, even during the Wallace campaign. In the late 1940s, fathers played a minimal role in childcare and housekeeping. My family was no exception.

That election concluded in November, 1948, with the surprising victory of President Harry Truman over Governor Thomas Dewey. My parents appeared not to be unusually disappointed that Henry Wallace lost the election, but it made little sense to me at that age. More immediate and

19

much more troubling concerns were occupying my attention. I had begun my formal schooling, and as I earlier noted, my 19-year process of profound educational alienation started dramatically.

Chapter 4
School Days

Kindergarten at Birney Elementary School was a grotesque beginning. I have mercifully forgotten my teacher's name, but from my perspective then (and now), she was a monster. First day: I was scared, surely not an unusual reaction for a five year old child. Separation anxiety is common and I doubt that I was particularly worse than many children in their early days at school. My fear led me to pee in my pants. The result was a large wet circle that expanded in the front of my trousers, extremely visible to everyone who saw me. Many subsequent conversations with elementary school teachers have been reassuring; some children do pee in their pants, especially when anxious or frightened. But this teacher acted savagely: she yelled at me, calling me "a dirty little boy" and exhibited me in front of the other children, pointing at the stain. I was humiliated and broke into tears. Many years later, I wrote a short story I never published or even submitted. The central character was a young West Coast academic visiting Philadelphia for a week long scholarly conference. In the middle of the week, the academic makes his way to the house of a now aging kindergarten teacher, knocks on the door, puts a bullet in her head, disappears into the night, and resumes his efforts at the conference. Bad literature, revealing psychology.

I faintly recall my mother being called to school to take me home and I was mortified on being told that I would have to return. All I can recall now is my pervasive fear of the place, almost a sense of terror at being forced to stay there for a few hours each day. Once, when my mother walked me the few blocks from home to school, I asked whether one of my little friends would be there. She replied that he would not be, because he had pneumonia. My reply has been etched into my memory for more than 60 years: "Can I have pneumonia too?" I also recall it sounding like "ammonia," and of course I had no idea what it actually meant. But for me, it meant *not* being in that dreadful place.

My brief time at Birney Elementary never improved. On a few occasions, the teacher sent me to the principal, another woman I regarded then and now with considerable loathing. She also screamed at me and called for my mother to come to school, a pattern that continued for many years. My most lasting impression from that time was simple and it is extremely clear many decades later. My intuition was that these were "big people" who meant me harm. They were not my friends. I could not know enough to have any genuine conceptual judgment, but the feelings were intense and in retrospect they were accurate. I am completely certain that my continuing distrust of authority has its origins, above all, in my earliest experiences in the Philadelphia public schools.

My parents wisely decided to remove me from that environment. They arranged a suitable transfer to Logan Demonstration School, also located relatively near our house. I found the place less oppressive and my new kindergarten teacher far more humane, probably having been apprised of my previous experiences. Still, there was little there that I enjoyed and I found it impossible to avoid conflict with authorities, mostly teachers. Early on, I refused to use my first name, Warren, insisting that teachers and fellow pupils call me Paul. That was fine with the children, but at least one teacher, probably in first grade, took great offense at my stubbornness when I simply refused to answer to my formal name. Eventually I won out, revealing an even greater persistence.

The routine daily "stuff" of elementary school was mostly boring. I had learned to read at home even before starting kindergarten, so the reading lessons were, to me, mindlessly repetitive. I had several conflicts at Logan School. I detested the music hour in first and second grades and resented the fact that I was always stuck with the "sticks," while favored children had the opportunity to play the "triangle." In retrospect, I suspect I would have failed miserably with the triangle just as I had with the group singing, which I shortly and defiantly abandoned in any case. But I learned a more valuable lesson: obsequious students gained rewards and questioning students earned punishment and institutional ostracism. I never had it in me to just go along; it has simply never been part of my personal nature. My durable education in power dynamics began at about seven years old and I credit my elementary schools for their unintentional influence.

The other dramatic incident came during "rhyming" time in second grade. I suppose that there is pedagogical value in this exercise and I imagine that the other children enjoyed rhyming "cat" and "hat" and "mouse" and "house." My turn to walk to the blackboard came when the teacher instructed me to find a rhyme for the word "hit." I strode to the board and, with all the bravado of a punk seven year old, dramatically placed the letter "s" in front of "hit." Leading to another dressing down and yet another trip to the office. But it was a further sign of my growing alienation with authority in general.

One of the deeper problems, I later discovered, was the testing mania that pervaded the Philadelphia public school system in the late 1940s and early 1950s. I have since read that American schoolchildren were tested regularly at the time, especially with "IQ" scores. As it happened, I performed well on these examinations, compounding my various problems. School officials informed my parents that I had high intelligence, but that my performance in class diverged dramatically from my "potential." This label dogged me for many years, exacerbating the emotional problems I had arising out of the family's economic misfortunes and generally making childhood a huge challenge.

Not everything was terrible. My grandparents continued to spoil me as much as ever. My best memories were trips to Atlantic City, the "shore." These were magical for a child: visiting Steel Pier, walking on the famous boardwalk, swimming in the Atlantic Ocean, eating salt water taffy, and playing skeeball and pokerino in the many arcades. This was a child's vision of utopia and it was a fantastic respite from both school and family financial aggravations.

Paradise never lasts. I never learned of Nana's cancer until the very end. My parents kept her terminal illness from me, presumably to shield me from its catastrophic consequences. The twins were simply too young to understand any of this. When she died, it was devastating. And my grandfather died soon thereafter. My parents said that he died of a broken heart, which I took extremely literally. I never learned of the actual cause and I assume that his will to die probably played a role in his early demise. But there I was, probably eight, with all four grandparents dead, two of whom I never knew at all.

After their deaths, the family began a series of residential moves and school changes that lasted until my high school graduation in 1960. The primary reason was the loss of the Logan house, presumably because the family income was insufficient to maintain the payments. My parents never explicitly stated this, but no other explanation makes sense.

It is impossible for me to recall the precise sequence of each move; my brothers and sisters are also unable to identify the sequence with specificity. My father, not formally trained in any profession, drifted into construction. He and an army friend, Charles Lunkenheimer, established a company they called the Peter/Charles Company. This was to be the first of my father's several failed business ventures. Throughout his life, he did many things, but he was never a successful entrepreneur. His lack of commercial success has had a major impact on my own consciousness.

Above all, it cemented in me a desire never to become a businessman. And, I'm sure, it forms one of the key emotional sources of my continuing animosity to business and the deeper anti-capitalist ideology I have espoused throughout my adult life. There is also a moral component: I have come to believe that success in business is a natural talent that some people have and others lack. It's like athletics or music or intellectual work. An enduring American myth is that success in business is a moral virtue. For me, that is nonsense. One's moral worth is emphatically not a function of commercial

23

acumen. I can judge my father both kindly and harshly in different ways, but his poor business record to me is thoroughly irrelevant in that calculus.

I don't know exactly what kinds of projects the Peter/Charles Company undertook, but I know that its proceeds rarely covered the family bills. Tension abounded in the household. After Logan, we moved outside the city limits to suburban Montgomery County. At that point, I found myself magically in fourth grade, having started third grade and then being "skipped" a year ahead. Once again, this process involved frenetic conversations with my parents, teachers, and school officials. Subsequently, both my parents and my new teacher informed me, yet again, that my intelligence dictated that I could do more advanced school work and that they hoped I would no longer be bored at school. The subtext, not articulated, was that I would also no longer be disruptive and disdainful of authority.

The place I remember most was in Haverford, Pennsylvania, renting a part of a large mansion on the historic Main Line. The residence revealed the trappings of affluence and privilege that masked the deeper poverty that my family endured. It was the beginning of a long process of cover-ups that, I am convinced, traced emotionally to the petit bourgeois lifestyle that my father enjoyed in pre-Nazi Germany as a child. The surface gap was obvious. The Peter/Charles Company collapsed and my parents had fierce fights in their Haverford home about money and unpaid bills.

Fourth grade placed me for the first time on a school bus, not at all an unpleasant experience after having previously walked to school, braving winter weather on the East Coast. But school itself continued to be a horror show. There were more "IQ" tests. On one occasion, I deliberately performed poorly, providing incorrect answers, in the naïve hope that a lower score would get teachers and school administrators off my back. Clever idea, immature execution: once again, I was severely reprimanded for deliberately underperforming.

Other incidents exacerbated my distress in fourth grade. I refused to play a pilgrim in the Thanksgiving Play, calling the role stupid, probably reflecting my parents' political ideology about colonial conquest of indigenous peoples. At this point, however simplistically, I began thinking about how education was official brainwashing. I need to be clear. At that age, this was a mere (but still intense) feeling, which I first developed during the repetitive "patriotic" exercises I had experienced even earlier in Philadelphia schools: the Pledge of Allegiance, Bible readings and school prayers (before the United States Supreme Court, in *Engel v. Vitale* in 1962, declared the practice unconstitutional), and cold war propaganda delivered in school assemblies, classrooms, and "documentary" films. Now, as a

24

university teacher, I make this issue of uncritical educational distortion paramount in some of my courses, but the origins of my critical pedagogy trace back to my childhood educational experiences and my family's leftist ideology.

I also refused to take a shower in the school gym when the teacher told me that I was too "dirty" to participate in some class function. Fuck her, I thought, and I might well have said it at the time. Earlier, I was rebuked in Philadelphia for having dirty hands because I used to peek under rocks to look at insects on my way to school. I felt that I was penalized for my intellectual curiosity, though again I could hardly articulate my feelings in those terms. But that is my unshakable conclusion now.

Probably the most serious conflict occurred when my teacher forced me to stay after school for some breach of rules or other indiscretion. Alone in the classroom, I proceeded to barricade the entire room by moving all the desks in front of the door. Despite the pleas of the teacher to stop, I only intensified my defiance. After an hour or so, it took several custodians to remove the barricaded desks and chairs and extricate me from the class. I have forgotten the punitive consequences of my misbehavior, but they were probably severe.

Another incident at that school stands out almost 60 years later. One afternoon when classes were finished, I was waiting for my father to pick me up. A boy, not recognizable to me, came up to me and belligerently called me "a dirty Jew" and told me to "go back to the old country." He also shoved me backwards. His hostility shook me and left me bewildered. I reported this to my father, who also seemed extremely upset at the incident. But he said nothing at all to school officials.

By that time in childhood, I had thought very little about religion. I knew that the family was vaguely Jewish, but I had no idea what that meant. We went to no religious services and performed no rituals at all, Jewish or otherwise. My mother occasionally acknowledged her Jewish background; my father never did. Nazis and Germans, of course, were bad and there was this eerie feeling pervading the household about my father's family and what had happened to them in Europe—but absolutely no details were ever forthcoming.

The operative parental ideology was atheism and I had actually reached that position simplistically on my own. God was everywhere, especially in school with its mandatory bible readings, prayers, and religious songs. Even in kindergarten, when we had milk cartons and graham crackers, we were forced to say "God is good, God is great, and we thank Him for our food." I thought it was silly even then. And the more that teachers and fellow pupils talked of God, especially of the Big Guy in the Sky with the Big Beard, the

Guy who punished people all the time for their sins, the Guy we were supposed to Love, the more ridiculous it all seemed to me. Going to church on Sundays also seemed a major waste of time, especially if it interfered with baseball or other sports. My adult atheism, of course, is more intellectually sophisticated, but its origins lay in these early childhood experiences.

Chapter 5
Poverty, Politics, and a Little Psychopathology

Yet again the family moved, this time to Wayne, Pennsylvania, in neighboring Delaware County. This was around 1952 or so when I was nine; my main marker is the presidential campaign of that year, pitting Republican Dwight Eisenhower against Democrat Adlai Stevenson. By that time, I had actually become interested in politics, moving my interests somewhat beyond the fate of the Philadelphia Phillies and the Philadelphia A's, which occupied a huge amount of my personal passion and has had a powerful residual impact on my emotional life for more than 60 years.

I watched the conventions of both parties on television. While the gavel to gavel coverage often bored me, I saw my parents' consummate engagement in Adlai Stevenson's candidacy against "Ike." I overheard the discussions at home, and with leftist friends, about the need, this time, to support the Democratic Party in the presidential election, even though they liked the new Progressive Party candidate in 1952, San Francisco radical attorney Vincent Hallinan. In Wayne, many children, echoing their parents, wore "I Like Ike" buttons. Likewise, I echoed my own parents by proclaiming that I didn't like Ike. I also remember my parents saying especially nasty things about Republican Vice Presidential candidate Richard Nixon during the campaign. Their venom toward him was obvious; some years later, I came to share it. But then, I was still a few years away from a thoughtful explication of my political views, but by 1956, I could argue the case effectively.

Political excitement notwithstanding, our family's time in Wayne was essentially horrific and the memories, even now, are especially painful to recall. My father started another construction company, one that proved in time to be even more disastrous. There were constant calls from creditors and bill collectors. At various points, my parents conscripted me to answer and to lie about their whereabouts. I developed some skill at this process, but it felt deeply humiliating. Many of the bill collectors took out their aggression on me, in effect blaming me for my parents' inability to meet their financial obligations. At their worst, these predators threatened that they would take us away from our parents and make us live in foster homes. The experience left me with an abiding hatred for collection agents. In my personal *pro bono* legal practice over the years, I have taken special pleasure in working over collection agents, often with a verbal brutality that is both uncharacteristic and gratifying. I think that I well understand the psychological origins of this behavior.

27

Worse came shortly thereafter. My father's company was involved in building some houses in a nearby area. He overextended himself and ran out of funds. Once again, his lack of business acuity probably contributed to his inability to complete the houses he had promised. I am a lawyer (a story that appears much later in this memoir). This is a classic breach of contract and civil remedies are available for the injured party (of course, monetary damages are useless if the defendant is bankrupt or otherwise lacks any resources). But the events went far beyond a civil lawsuit.

One morning, as I left the apartment to walk to fifth grade, two uniformed police officers greeted me. I suspected that they were going to my home, but I wasn't sure. I proceeded to school. When I returned in the afternoon, I found out that the cops had arrested my father, on a charge of "fraudulent conversion." One of his angry customers decided to retaliate by seeking criminal charges instead of filing a civil lawsuit.

The next days were nightmarish. My father was released on bail. But I had to face my fellow students in fifth grade. And here, I discovered the incredible cruelty of children. In my class, some of the pupils circulated a local newspaper story about my father's arrest. And they pointed to me, as if I had something to do with it. I don't know if the teacher(s) knew about this at all, but they made no attempt to intervene nor offered me any sympathy at all. During that time, as I walked the four or five blocks home, a school bully, a classmate, taunted me near the school about my father the criminal and proceeded to "sucker punch" me in the stomach, causing me to double up in pain.

Criminal law moved more swiftly in the early 1950s. My father went to trial in a Delaware County Courthouse. He hired a Philadelphia attorney, I. Raymond Kremer, who I believe subsequently became a prominent judge in Philadelphia. I remember being extremely nervous when my father left for the trial. But later that day, there was elation. The trial judge directed an acquittal, in effect throwing out the case and indicating that the dispute was a civil conflict that did not belong in a criminal trial. That result generated a personal epiphany: lawyers can help people, so maybe I should become a lawyer. When I said this in school, most of my fellow students looked at me with astonishment. How could I possibly become a lawyer? You had to be smart and do well in school. I, surely, fell far short of the mark.

During this turmoil, I turned ten. Not long afterwards, in June, 1953, my mother gave birth to my sister Carey, now making it a family of four children. Carey's birth came at an especially precarious time. She was born with some kind of RH factor related blood disorder, necessitating transfusions and additional medical expenses, straining family finances even further.

In historical perspective, all of this makes considerable sense. World War II veterans came home and immediately started having babies—the post-war "baby boom." In my father's case, I think that having a large family must also have had something to do with the tragic loss of his own family in the Holocaust. I don't think that he ever articulated this vision, nor was he ever fully or even marginally conscious of the psychological origins of his need for a large family. This is a reality, once again, where I can only speculate, but I can think of little other explanation given his extreme economic inability to support such a growing family.

At this age, I began my first foray into the work world. My mother complained, literally, of not having enough money for food. After school, I headed to the A & P supermarket a few blocks away. I stationed myself outside the entrance to the store and offered to carry grocery bags to customers' cars, for whatever tips they would offer to me. This turned out to be fairly lucrative, by my minimal 1953 standards. Each day, I made a few dollars, which I turned immediately over to my mother, who bought food and baby formula. I also found other, less lawful sources of income. I stole empty soda bottles from gas stations in Wayne, redeeming them at two cents for small bottles and five cents for large bottles. Everything helped. To put this in perspective, a movie ticket at the time cost ten cents, and I often had enough left over for myself and my twin brother and sister to enjoy a matinee.

This was the origin of my continuing work ethic—really, a work compulsion. I have never feared work and have always sought to have as much work as I can manage, at times more than I could handle. My drive has occasionally been extremely neurotic, reflecting the early insecurity I felt in childhood. I remember thinking clearly that if you work and get a salary, you won't be poor and you won't have bill collectors hounding you. Well beyond the reality of such fears, these underlying emotions have played a powerful role in my attitudes and behavior throughout my life. I suspect that they will never disappear.

Somewhere during this time in Wayne, my father declared bankruptcy, which had the effect of eliminating many of my parents' debts. Certain language from that bankruptcy proceeding has remained in my mind: "trustees"; "referee"; "creditors"; "discharged"; and several other legal terms. These words, to this day, fill me with dread. In law school, I studiously avoided anything to do with bankruptcy issues precisely because of their painful memories. I wouldn't even glance at the casebooks on this topic and walked away from students whom I overheard discussing the issues. Even now, with more than 40 years of active membership in the California State Bar, I cringe internally when the word emerges in

29

conversation. And when I am asked to refer someone to a bankruptcy lawyer, I do so, but it takes some internal emotional steeling that I have become adept at concealing.

In Spring, 1953, my family moved back to Philadelphia, in a crowed row house near Fairmount Park. I stayed behind in Wayne with a single mother and her son in the same apartment building for about a month to finish fifth grade in the class I had come to hate. In June, I returned to Philadelphia, just in time, it seemed, to hear and read the news of the execution of Ethel and Julius Rosenberg on June 19. This case had been a regular topic of conversation at home. I was old enough to follow it in broad outline and my parents, like other leftists throughout the nation and the world, believed both in the Rosenbergs' innocence and in the fundamental injustice of the proceedings against them. There was some muted conversation as well about the anti-Semitism surrounding the case, especially with the fully Jewish cast of characters involved in the prosecution. My parents' loathing for Judge Irving Kaufman and prosecutor Roy Cohn was obvious and they remarked that the government was using Jews to get the Jews.

I recall their shock the day after the execution in Sing Sing's electric chair. That was the first time my father really had a serious political conversation with me. He explained the Rosenberg case in a way that a bright ten-year old could understand. What registered most was that the Rosenbergs left two orphaned sons, Michael and Robert. Michael was born, like me, in 1943 and Robert was born, like my twin brother and sister, in 1947. That made the case infinitely more human to me. Throughout my career, I have addressed this case, including more recent evidence about the probable complicity of Julius Rosenberg. But more centrally, I have discussed it in the broader context of the anti-communist hysteria of the era. Pedagogically, my childhood recollections have made a valuable contribution to both my teaching and writing on this general topic.

Except for the horror of the Rosenberg case, the summer of 1953 was relatively benign. It allowed me to indulge even more of my baseball obsession. I hung out at Fairmount Park watching various adult league baseball games, serving as batboy and collecting used baseballs and slightly cracked bats. I also participated in the enjoyable pastimes of urban street activities; wall ball, stick ball, and pick-up baseball games in the park and in nearby fields. I fancied myself an excellent athlete, a judgment that I later had to modify considerably. But the illusion was pleasant and provided immense emotional relief from the continuing financial concerns of my growing family.

I started sixth grade in yet another elementary school in the Philadelphia district system. It began acceptably, even well. I was selected for the safety patrol, which gave me a heightened sense of power. For about a month, I wore a Sam Browne belt with a badge in the middle, guiding fellow students across the street. But my brief entry into law enforcement ended badly. I was booted from the patrol for some infraction that I cannot remember any more; I cannot imagine that it was egregious, nor was it, I'm sure, any gross abuse of power. Given my proclivities, it was likely some act of insubordination, but I have no sense that my dismissal was especially traumatic.

My rebellion in sixth grade began to assume a more political direction. My teacher gave an assignment requiring us to memorize all four stanzas of the Star-Spangled Banner. In 1953, this was yet another dimension of the same set of patriotic observances I had always had in public school. But here it was even worse. Each morning, we had the Pledge of Allegiance, required bible verses, and usually a song like the National Anthem or "God Bless America" or "My Country, 'Tis of Thee"; sometimes it was a Christian hymn like "Onward Christian Soldiers." At ten, especially given my parents' influence, I found all of this ludicrous. Indeed, my parents often told me that these exercises were simply designed to make children passive and uncritical.

The teacher's assignment was the proverbial straw. I knew the first verse of the National Anthem because I heard it frequently before televised baseball games and other sporting events. I decided that I simply would not comply. With all the subtlety of a ten-year old, I told the teacher that the assignment was "stupid." This was literally the word I used. I asked her to justify the assignment. I have never forgotten her reply, which I present here literally word for word: "Because I'm the teacher. Do it."

I have used this anecdote often in my own university teaching for many decades. I am constantly dismayed, but no longer surprised, at the numbers of my students who are puzzled at my reaction. Even those who sympathize with me say that they would have done the assignment anyway. Their easy adaptation to authority, including illegitimate authority, is severely troubling. But there are some who concur with my stance and even a few with similar records of their own.

I imagine that I received a failing grade for my early act of civil disobedience. Other consequences were more pernicious from my perspective. I was referred to the school counselor following my refusal to memorize the National Anthem stanzas. I have no idea what her professional qualifications were, and I suspect that they were far below anything that would qualify in contemporary therapeutic settings. I was extremely uncommunicative, probably hostile and defiant. She asked me why I was so unhappy. I replied only that I could only be happy if the

Phillies won (I knew precisely what I was saying; this was my deliberate verbal attempt to avoid the process).

This woman, frustrated by my uncooperative conduct, arranged to bring in a school district psychologist and to include my parents. I assume that this new woman had some kind of professional credentials, but that meant nothing to me at all. Our first meeting was memorable. Taking place on the second floor of the school, she pointed to the window and said, ever so sweetly, that some children felt like jumping out. She asked me if I wanted to jump. I'll always remember my reply: "No! I want to push you out the window."

I can acknowledge more than a half century later that I was emotionally disturbed at the time, but in ways far beyond the competence or skills of these school district functionaries. My emotions were raw, a response to all that had occurred as a result of the economic turbulence, constant moves, changing schools, and everything else that had happened in our family. But I also had the strongest sense that being sent to the school psychologist was the punitive consequence of having rebellious attitudes and different views. My parents, clearly frustrated, joined the conversations and made arrangements to get me private psychological assistance. I had a few sessions that seemed friendlier and more appropriate, especially since my parents supported my basic decision to question such a stupid assignment in the first place.

One vision stands out from these early therapeutic sessions. I articulated my basic view of human nature, but with the minimal verbal sophistication of a child. Essentially, I indicated how deeply unimpressed I was with people. I noted that I disliked them a great deal; I probably said that I hated people in general. What emerged, though, was a perspective about the human condition that still remains—an essentially pessimistic vision that from time to time has put me at odds with my friends and compatriots on the political left. I know that I must have told the therapist(s) that people generally disappointed me and that I thought that most people were actually quite dumb. My intellectual view has become more complex, but I think the insights then were relatively perceptive.

Urban life, including school, continued to be harsh. Some of the larger kids, from time to time, shook me down for my lunch money, a 50s version of later gang life in Philadelphia and elsewhere. My father drove a taxicab at night to earn more money. During the course of that employment, two black men robbed him at gunpoint. I accompanied him to City Hall to meet with police and prosecutors. He pointedly told me that I could not "blame all Negroes for the acts of these two men." He made it clear that any racist generalizations arising out of the robbery were completely unacceptable.

The most enjoyable feature of life in the city in late 1953, besides sports, was the opportunity to visit the Philadelphia Museum of Art. I liked looking at the pictures without having any art historical understanding or appreciation at all. While many of the older works were boring, some of the modern examples seemed vibrant and I thought that it would be fun to learn more about them. I had no idea, at the time, that as an adult, art history would become my major scholarly focus.

Chapter 6
Race, Power, and Religious Distress

In yet one more move, the family left Philadelphia for another suburb, this time the Delaware County seat of Media. We rented a nice old house, with a quaint coal heating arrangement and adequate room for our family of six, soon to be joined by a beautiful collie named Duke. The surroundings were attractive. There were woods and creeks and ample grounds for play and recreation. Media was a town, not a city, but it had enough to occupy my attention.

The immediate neighborhood, however, was problematic. We lived on South Avenue, the last house before a fairly large black neighborhood. Many of the houses were unpainted and we referred to them as shacks. The people in the house next door had a habit of dumping their trash in their backyard down a hill. I saw rats regularly roaming amid the debris. I was not thrilled by this early vision of black life. I saw people, especially on weekends, drinking and partying raucously. I was appalled at the lack of hygiene among many of the children, although I had little personal grounds to offer accusations on this score. A little later, when I became a paperboy, I was appalled that many of my customers declined to pay me even while having open cans of beer and bottles of liquor in their residences. Again, my father admonished me not to use these impressions to make broad racial generalizations about "Negroes." I took some time to develop the conceptual foundation to understand that logic, but it has been central to my intellectual and political efforts throughout my life.

In Media, several things happened concurrently. My father worked as a construction superintendent, moving from job to job as I recall. The twins enrolled in elementary school and the baby, of course, stayed at home with my mother; no child care in those times. I developed relatively severe asthma, occasioning several trips to the doctor and causing me fears about going to bed and worrying that I would wake up gasping for breath. I assume that this was largely psychogenic in origin, but the physical symptoms were frightening and unnerving.

Two other major features if my life occurred during our time in Media. The first is even now a touchy subject for me to address. Around 1953 or 1954, my parents (I assume that it was primarily my father's initiative) became attracted to Quakerism. It is a difficult topic because I was born a Jew and I retain a strong but highly secular Jewish identity. Any deviation from that, including even the most socially progressive Christian sect, seems to me to negate the Jewish tradition. It is not an issue for me, and my parents' brief foray into Quakerism when I was a child is hardly my responsibility. Still, I regard it as vaguely shameful, a repudiation of my Jewish heritage. I think too that my siblings have wrestled with this as well, in some cases, unlike me, with less than definitive results.

During this time, my parents began attending Friends meetings and participating in other Quaker activities, especially the progressive social action efforts for which Quakers are so well regarded. My sense is that my mother merely went along. Certainly, my father was the active protagonist in this process. He *never* explained his motivation, with one exception, even near the end of his life when he vigorously reclaimed his Jewish identity, including his apparently active interest in the Holocaust. The only rationale he ever provided was that Quakers were against wars and that membership in the Religious Society of Friends would keep me and my brother Jon from having to serve in the military. Ironically, that served my brother well as a conscientious objector during the Vietnam War.

Doubtless, the Quaker vision of peace and civil rights merged well with my parents' objection to American foreign and domestic policy, especially during the Eisenhower administration and during the menacing era of McCarthyism. Quakers were excellent on these issues and have remained at the forefront of progressive causes since then. This was, moreover, the time of nuclear testing and other reactionary activities in America.

I cannot, however, accept a merely political explanation for the conversion to Quakerism, especially in my father's case. Deeper psychological factors must have played a major, even the dominant role. His ambivalence to Judaism, it seems to me, mirrored that of many Holocaust survivors: denial. After all, since Jews are always the objects of persecution, it seems perfectly reasonable to become something else: a "Not-Jew." This attitude was reinforced at home regularly, with injunctions never to say that we were Jewish or to disclose my father's German birth, much less the fate of his family in Auschwitz. The ambience of those discussions was hushed, reinforcing the attitude that there was something dirty, something that must be hidden, about Judaism. My sister Aimee confirms this impression with an unusually powerful anecdote, which probably occurred during our time in Media. She recalls telling someone that she was Jewish and reporting it later to my father. He replied angrily, directing her *never* to say that again. All of this reflects an adult psychological interpretation, because I cannot specifically recall my reaction at the time to his active concealment of his Jewish origins.

The Quaker meetings themselves were exquisitely boring, even worse than school. Aimee also confirms this reaction, noting that she could hardly wait for the meetings to end. I think they lasted about 50 minutes. People rose to speak when "the spirit moved them." I had no idea what they were talking about and most of their comments struck me as thoroughly silly. My father, curiously, continued to profess atheism at home, noting that the Quaker doctrine of "that of God in every man" was somehow not really at odds with his atheism. I saw it as contradictory then and I have no reason now to modify that impression from my childhood.

At Quaker meetings on Sundays, children were subjected to something called "First Day School," the Quaker appellation for Sunday. In general, I skipped this as much as possible, seeing no reason to add more school to my life. But on one occasion, I recall vividly taking on the teacher, indicating that a belief in god was absurd. I admire the Quaker commitment to progressive social action, but I view the theology as critically as any other religious dogma I have ever encountered.

The parallel event was the second school where I had to complete my sixth grade. This Media elementary school, if anything, was even more oppressive than its Philadelphia counterpart. I specifically remember my teacher, a Mr. Robinson, a diehard political reactionary and a vocal supporter of Senator Joseph McCarthy. By age 11, I had absorbed much of my parents' leftist views and I was savvy enough to understand what Robinson was doing in class.

Among many of his other activities (aside from teaching his regular sixth grade subject matter), he made positive comments about the popular television program "I Led Three Lives," an absurdly anti-communist drama about an undercover informer named Herbert Philbrick. When I reported this to my father, he was furious, saying that we would never watch such pernicious fare in our house. Indeed, he forbade me from watching the program, although I watched a few episodes surreptitiously and totally concurred with my father's assessment. The program had Philbrick meeting his CP comrades furtively, planning "liquidations" and other insidious acts. These TV communists always looked evil, almost like WW II movie depictions of Nazis. They certainly looked nothing like the Communist Party members I had met through my parents, who were older kindly Jewish ladies and gentlemen with good hearts and humane values.

Robinson did even more to promote his right-wing agenda to his unsuspecting sixth graders. He regularly told us that Senator McCarthy was the only man standing between America and a communist takeover. He grew angry when, on one occasion, I sought to counter his perspective. He used his superior vocabulary to browbeat me into silence. He also repeated a story that I have heard from others of my generation in their own school experiences: Russian children are sitting at their desks in a schoolhouse. They are instructed to put their heads down and close their eyes. Then the teacher comes and places candy on each desk, whereupon they are to open their eyes and see the treats. The teacher explains that Comrade Josef Stalin has provided the candy, because the children are good communists (or perhaps good Young Pioneers—I don't specifically remember). And then Robinson told us that in Russia, schools really didn't educate students, but only "brainwashed" them to be good communists. I have had a wonderful time in my own teaching using this experience as an example of the ambience of 1950s America, always noting that Robinson had no sense of irony at all.

He was, unfortunately, even more insidious. He told us that there were "bad newspapers," specifically mentioning "The Daily Worker." He said that we should be on the lookout for these papers, especially at home. He mentioned that if we were uncomfortable in talking to our parents about them, we could always talk to him. In historical retrospect, all of this seems bizarre. But these memories are seared in my memory and have stayed with me throughout my life.

Indeed, they are especially vivid because I knew the newspapers themselves. At the time, my family made various car trips to Philadelphia to visit Tillie Sklar, a longtime Communist Party member. I don't know what her exact relationship was to my father; she may have been one of his foster parents or he may have met her during his youth when he became radicalized. Each time, after dinner and before we left, my father asked Tille if she had any newspapers. Invariably, she gave him several copies of the Worker and the National Guardian, another pro-communist leftist paper. When my father finished reading them, I read them as well, finding them fascinating and informative, as well as rather adventuresome because they were apparently forbidden. Of course, my father told me never to mention this to anyone outside the family. Generally, my parents were pleased that I was reading these and conventional newspapers, because I scarcely touched any of their other books. I did, however, read plenty of baseball novels that I obtained from the local library.

This was also the time of air raid drills and "duck and cover" exercises. Early on, I participated perfunctorily at school, though my parents told me how moronic they were. Later, in junior high, I deliberately refused, generating yet additional disciplinary sanctions for my politically oriented disobedience.

More important, I learned something about the realities of power and privilege in sixth grade. I had one good friend, whom I often visited after school. He was personable, but not especially bright. I had, for one of the few times in my formal schooling, actually taken my schoolwork seriously and finally compiled a reasonable if not exemplary record. I managed to do fairly well on papers and exams, yet "Bob" always seemed to get higher grades with inferior performance. I learned that his father was a Republican member of the local school board. My parents explained to me that his father's position ensured that he would always get good grades, regardless of his particular academic performance. It was a useful lesson and its truth has played out regularly through the years.

I rarely had pleasant encounters with the African American kids in my immediate Media neighborhood. Although they were never physically threatening, I felt a major cultural divide (one I have long since bridged, to my very deep personal satisfaction). In one incident, I became especially frustrated, and I think I used the word "nigger" pejoratively for the one and only time in my life. My father was present and I cannot ever recall seeing him so angry. His ferocity at my use of that repulsive appellation has stuck with me for the rest of my life.

I also began my formal work life in Media. I became a paperboy for the Chester Times at 11, lying about my age and claiming to be 12. This minor act of dishonesty has never caused me any distress whatever. This continued my quest to look constantly for employment, clearly a response to the childhood pattern of family economic insecurity. I enlisted the assistance of my brother Jon, who insists to this day that I exploited him and provided insufficient compensation for his efforts. He is doubtless correct, but the intention was not malevolent.

Each afternoon, after school, we bundled the stack of papers and began the route. And each week, I had to make the collections from the subscribers, as I recall 35 cents per week. I owed the Chester Times representative whatever the amount he was due. I was an "independent contractor," not an employee *per se*. That meant I was financially responsible to the Times regardless of my success in my collections, a reality that the representative reiterated frequently. Unfortunately, many of my black customers were derelict in their payments, sometimes for several weeks at a time. This ate into my profit margin and some weeks, if collections were bad, I made almost nothing. I had a visceral response to this arrangement, which later became a lifelong vision about the moral degeneracy of capitalism. The only dramatic incident during the unpleasant collection days of my Chester Times paper route stint occurred when one of my female customers, a very large African American female, appeared fully naked at the door. That voyeuristic revelation was worth the 35 cents I failed to collect.

Soon I moved into junior high school, which is difficult for most youngsters under the best of circumstances. The major problem was my size. I was extremely small, making me subject to taunts like "shrimp" and "midget," providing additional insights into juvenile cruelty. This delayed development began to dominate my emotional life, causing my parents to seek medical attention. Doctors essentially told us that nothing was wrong and that time would take care of the problem. They were correct, of course, but my congenital impatience exacerbated my feelings.

The school year itself was merely distasteful rather than catastrophic, the subjective spectrum that I had developed since my disastrous kindergarten start at Birney Elementary School. At least in junior high, students had several teachers rather than only one. Most classes were forgettable. I have only two vivid memories, one bad and one good. The homeroom teacher was an old battleaxe named Miss Smyth, near retirement and likely born in the late 19th century. She clearly disliked me and the feeling was entirely mutual. I had earlier refused to duck under my desk for an air raid drill, occasioning a trip to the office. One day, while I was daydreaming, she snuck up to my desk and viciously pulled my hair. It hurt like hell. All she said was that her action would do me good and that I would remember it. She was half right. Such physical brutality—no other term is accurate—would now be totally unacceptable, but in 1954, it was commonplace. As an aside, her act only generated in me an acute, probably pathological response. I fantasized cutting off her head and shooting baskets with it. Each morning, on arriving in the classroom, I took a dozen foul shots with her head. It was a wonderful fantasy and it was, as I recall, deeply satisfying.

The good memory involved my participation in the junior high school baseball team. I was no stellar performer, but I did an acceptable job as a second baseman. My fielding was solid and I garnered enough base hits to contribute to the team's offense. I often walked, owing to my short stature. I could also run fast and was successful in stealing many bases during the season. Most important, this experience gave me substantial emotional relief from all my other problems and some validation that I had at least modest athletic prowess. I augmented this perspective by continuing to read as many baseball stories and novels as I could find. Of course I also devoured the newspapers, especially the sports section. By this time, I think that my parents became concerned. They had wanted me to read more "serious" materials, constantly imploring me to read the novels of Howard Fast—solid lefty novels, of course. Contemporary research, I think, reveals that any reading, regardless of content, is desirable for children. In due course, my reading became profoundly serious, entirely in line with parental hopes and expectations. The baseball material (and the leftist newspapers) contributed to that result.

The big political event of 1954 for me in junior high was the Army-McCarthy hearings. I eagerly watched the televised proceedings after school between March and June. With my parents' guidance, I followed the hearings closely, following such now famous figures as McCarthy himself, his counsel Roy Cohn, Senators Karl Mundt and John McClellan, and Boston attorney Robert Welch. Even though my parents' views were obvious, I had enough knowledge myself by then to know who was good and who was evil, especially McCarthy and Cohn. My parents reserved special venom for Roy Cohn, constantly reiterating his insidious role in the Rosenberg case. They frequently used the label "fascist" for McCarthy and his operatives and the description was accurate enough. It also turned out, of course, that Cohn exceeded all expectations by becoming one of the sleaziest human beings in American history before his ironic and deeply welcome death from AIDS in 1986.

I distinctly recall the malevolent visage of Senator McCarthy over and over again on our small screen back and white circular television set. He appeared visually like the thug that history has definitively shown him to be. I cannot specifically recall Joseph Welch's famous retort to Joe McCarthy when he dramatically said, "Until this moment, Senator, I think I never gauged your cruelty or recklessness. . . ." I may or may not have seen this live, but I remember once again being impressed by a courageous lawyer. It reinforced my desire to become a lawyer, because I saw that profession as stalwart defenders of justice. Later, I came to have a very different perspective, based on much closer contact with the legal education and the legal profession. The real value, for me, of the Army-McCarthy hearings was to draw me in, irrevocably for life, into a compelling political interest and eventually substantial political activism.

Chapter 7
Levittown I

The end of seventh grade also meant another family move, one that would have lifelong emotional, educational, and political implications. We moved this time to suburban lower Bucks County, approximately 20 miles north of central city Philadelphia, to a new development called Levittown. Somehow, my father managed to get a second GI mortgage to purchase our first truly roomy house, the "Jubilee" model, one of six available, which cost approximately $12,000 in 1955. It remains unclear how my parents managed to purchase this house. Their credit must have been horrible and I cannot imagine how they could manage the monthly payments, even though they must have been reasonably low more than a half-century ago.

The story of Levittown is well known. The suburban Philadelphia development was the second Levittown that builder and developer William J. Levitt constructed; the first was on Long Island, New York. He conceived the development as a completely planned community, with curved streets, and specifically designed neighborhoods. Ours was "Vermillion Hills," where every street began with the letter "V," like our street, "Village Lane." Each Levittown neighborhood was similarly constructed. "Dogwood Hollow," which became infamous in 1957 for its racist riots I will discuss in depth later in this memoir, had streets named only with the letter "D." William Levitt was a stickler for control.

He went much further than alphabetic uniformity in this new suburban utopia. Levitt donated space for religious institutions and schools and he provided major recreational amenities including Olympic-sized public swimming pools, parks, Little League baseball fields, and children's playgrounds. Levittown also had a modern shopping center that was considered one of the finest and largest in the world at the time. Among other things, Levitt insisted on several rules to ensure his totalitarian vision: no fences, no clotheslines on Sundays, laws maintained along approved lines, and other tokens of 1950s conformity. He would have thrived as a Nazi SS officer or a Soviet apparatchik.

The demographics were clear. Levittown attracted many World War II veterans moving from a working class existence to a more comfortable lower middle class lifestyle. The new city also attracted a large number of petit bourgeois citizens who reveled in the new comfortable uniformity. All the residents were white. Levitt and Sons steadfastly refused to sell to African Americans, claiming that their presence would conflict with the attitudes of the white residents, many of whom were fleeing the growing influx of minorities, mostly African Americans, in the major East Coast cities. Levitt himself maintained that he was not personally a racist, a view that revealed itself as totally preposterous just two years later. I doubt that at the time of their move, my parents realized the egregious racism of William Levitt and his corporation. They never mentioned anything about the white-only policy, so I assume they were unaware of it. Silence in the face of this policy would have been profoundly uncharacteristic.

On the surface, the move to Levittown seemed like a fine family decision. Above all, my Aunt Ruth, Uncle Jack, and cousins Jay and Craig lived there, making our very limited family contacts instantly available. This was relatively unique for us since family connections were always minimal, especially since no one on my father's side existed at all. In theory, Levittown was the classic "great place to raise children." This is obviously why so many people made the move there in the first place. It would be dishonest to say that I disliked everything. I enjoyed the swimming pools and the baseball fields. I especially liked the freedom to roam on my bicycle. I liked the relative roominess of the house. I also liked the reasonably close proximity with public transportation to both Philadelphia and nearby Trenton, New Jersey. At 12, I was old enough to take advantage of these opportunities and in 1955 parents had no concern about children by themselves on public buses and even on city streets.

I missed the city streets enormously, the hustle and bustle and the sheer energy of daily life. Even then, I felt suburban life stifling. Without being able to articulate fully my feelings and reactions, I found Levittown a cultural wasteland, especially the stultifying monotony of that planned community. Although I made some friends, most of my neighbors left me cold. I felt that they were boring and uninformed. They could discuss baseball and sports, but never politics, which became increasingly interesting to me at the threshold of adolescence.

I also resumed my working compulsion, becoming a paperboy for the Philadelphia Bulletin—the major league of the paper route world in the Philadelphia area. Now I was able to make several dollars a week, although I continued to be an independent contractor. Alas, the job didn't last. I was fired because I told a female customer who failed to pay me for several weeks to "fuck herself." I concede that my remarks were unwise, but even now I believe that I should have been given some opportunity for redemption.

My parents continued their affair with Quakerism following our move to Levittown. They joined the Monthly Meeting in Fallsington, a short distance away. My siblings, Aimee and Jon, and I felt that we were dragged along to these extremely dull affairs, having to sit once again through these almost hour-long periods of silence punctuated with rambling and incoherent mumblings. (I know that this sounds strong; it reflects my reaction at the time, and even now I can scarcely modify the verbal harshness despite my intellectual respect for Quaker social action). Occasionally, my father rose to speak; my mother never did. His comments seemed both pretentious and self-aggrandizing, but at least they were laced with radical political content reflecting, among other things, the growing civil rights consciousness in America at the time.

This was the start of the modern civil rights movement and I was following developments closely. I specifically recall being jubilant about the historic United States Supreme Court decision in *Brown v. Board of Education* decision on May 17, 1954. I read the story in the Philadelphia Bulletin word for word and shared the excitement of my parents and their left-wing friends. I watched the reports of this momentous decision on the TV news, an early start to that lifelong habit of information gathering.

I also followed, with horror, the murder of Emmett Till in Mississippi in 1955. I can no longer specifically locate my exact setting when I found out about this unspeakable crime, but I knew of it as soon as it was nationally reported. It was a huge topic of conversation at home and it resonated with me especially because Till was only slightly older than I was. That gave it a personal dimension that I would experience even more profoundly a few years later during my own civil rights activism. It is fair to conclude as well, despite my disdain for the Quakers I met at the time, that they were uniformly sympathetic to the growing concern for the rights of the nation's black citizens.

I began 8th grade in the neighboring city of Fairless Hills, another planned community but one with a decidedly working class population. Ironically, Levittown residents sometimes looked down upon its contiguous neighbors, viewing them as social class inferiors because they often worked in blue collar jobs like truck driving and in the steel industry. I watched those reactions with interest. It gave me some early insights into social class and power. These divisions fascinated me. I could discern nothing different among people who appeared extremely similar in clothing, attitudes, demeanor, and just about everything else.

The school was William Penn Junior High School, a place that fills me with dread even decades later. The first year had many unpleasant emotional interludes, but the academics were largely uneventful. My teachers were predictably dull and I have only vague memories of any of the course subject matter. I'm sure that I managed to master sufficient material throughout my school days. I learned enough math to negotiate my way around the basic requirements of life, even though algebra and geometry seem entirely useless to me. But I obviously picked up my multiplication tables, because I use them effectively every day. I also know English grammar extremely well, so I must have learned some of this in school, even at William Penn, despite my resistance. My political, historical, social and cultural knowledge, however, is almost entirely independent of the formal curriculum. Junior high school, from my perspective, contributed absolutely nothing at all to that part of my knowledge. More insidiously, it did little to catalyze my intellectual curiosity.

Of course I recall that boys were compelled to endure shop classes and girls home economic classes, reflecting the sexist values and priorities of the era. No one ever thought to question that gender division, or more basically, the need for such instruction at all. Shop classes, to my mind, were moronic. We learned to saw wood and drill holes and I still remember hammering a piece of copper for a week or more into something vaguely resembling an ashtray. That memory now almost makes me giggle; five hours or so with a ball-peen hammer, probably fantasizing what I would rather have been doing, perhaps with the hammer itself. My products were pathetic. More important, I had utterly no interest in doing any of these tasks. I still think it was a pointless waste of time unless individual students themselves showed specific interest in such nonintellectual pursuits.

The only marginally enjoyable class was gym, which allowed me to use physical activity to discharge my aggression. I did reasonably well and appreciated the opportunity to participate in the various athletic events the teacher organized throughout the school year. But even here, I found some trauma. We had mandatory showers. After class, we had to appear naked at the shower room, fully exposed to everyone else. Still pre-puberty, I was acutely embarrassed. The only comfort now is that this reaction was not unique to me. Many youngsters, even now, report the same emotional response.

But I retain a hypersensitivity to other unpleasant 8th grade episodes. My music teacher demanded my full participation in every feature of her class. I had declined to engage in the ballroom dance unit, because I felt embarrassed by my short stature. Despite my general athletic skills, I found dance especially awkward. The teacher grabbed me, forcing me onto the classroom floor. A large, burly woman, she towered over me and made me hold her around her waist. To this day, I can "feel" her flab around my hands, but mostly I can recall the acute sense of humiliation.

The incident had an epilogue. My hostility towards the music teacher led me to scribble my rage about her in one of the textbooks. Ironically, I actually owned the book because I had paid for it, with my personal funds, when I had temporarily lost it. When I subsequently found it, the book technically became my property, or so I imagined. One day, I accidentally left the book in the classroom and the teacher discovered it. After reading my comments, she called the principal, who in turn brought me to his office. This was a familiar process, as was his ferocious response to my action and language. My protest that I could write whatever I wanted in my own book only infuriated him further. I cannot recall specifically if this was the incident that generated the following comment from a William Penn administrator. But sometime in either 8th or 9th grade, either the principal or the vice-principal told me that I was on track to wind up in "San Quentin." In any case, the principal contacted my parents, who yet again had to come to school to bail me out of another scrape. My parents were clearly frustrated with me *and* with the principal's reaction.

The principal's anger, interestingly, was not about any genuine concern that I would engage in violence against my music teacher. At under 5 feet and less than 70 pounds, I was no physical threat. Moreover, I had neither access to any weapons nor any record of personal violence whatever. His major focus at that "meeting" was on my written profanity, especially the word "fuck," which appeared a few times in my margin comments in the book. He lambasted me for my language, calling me the equivalent of a moral degenerate. This was another version of fifties era conservative political correctness. How times have changed. Today, one hears the word "fuck" hundreds of times daily on elementary school yards. Social conservatives decry this development as a debasement of both language and civilization. It doesn't bother me at all.

It occurs to me as an adult, especially in a post-Columbine age, that I should have some perspective about the principal's response. I can recognize that he had a large school to run and that I was, by any standard, a disruptive and troubled young student. He clearly had no clue about my difficulties at home with my parents' recurring financial problems or the deeper impact of the Holocaust on my father and on the entire family dynamics. Still, a more sophisticated and enlightened response to my scribbles ("I hate that bitch," "Fuck [Miss L.]," etc.) would have been better, especially since there had been no history of actual violence at the school. Perhaps the principal was also distressed at the sexual undertones of my hostility, but at the age, my saying "Fuck Miss L." was primarily intended as an act of verbal retaliation. I doubt that I even knew the sexual ramifications involved, and in any case, the idea would have repulsed me. Even now, however, I rarely encounter much psychological acuity among educational administrators at any level.

The school year 1955/1956, however, was politically and intellectually dynamic for external reasons. That period coincided with the famous

Montgomery Bus Boycott, which we watched with rapture on television at home. I know the events in intricate detail, because they have been part of my teaching and writing for most of my academic career. This knowledge goes far beyond the popular knowledge of Rosa Parks' December 1, 1955 arrest and the rise of Dr. Martin Luther King. In my teaching, I also deal extensively with the powerful role of E.D. Nixon and the Montgomery Improvement Association as well as the heroic efforts of women organizers during that historic moral and political struggle.

At the time, however, I watched the reports on television and read the accounts in the papers. The courage of the black residents of Montgomery engaged me emotionally and morally. My parents cheered them on and these seminal events mobilized my youthful idealism. This massive black rebelliousness also played directly into my own disdain for authority. It also helped lay the foundation for the political mobilization of my feelings, which have endured through adulthood. Unfortunately, nothing about the boycott ever reached William Penn Junior High and I can recall no students there, or anyone in my Vermillion Hills neighborhood, who seemed even remotely interested in what was happening. That reinforced my growing feeling of the ignorance, indeed the stupidity, of most people.

My major memory of the summer of 1956 was that I played a lot of informal sandlot baseball and that I followed the Democratic Party convention closely. By 13, I was politically informed and eager to see Adlai Stevenson take on Eisenhower again in the general election. The Vice Presidential battle between Senator Estes Kefauver and Senator John Kennedy was exhilarating. I supported Kefauver as the more progressive candidate and was thrilled when he won the nomination. I watched it all on television, augmenting my interest and knowledge in the formal mechanism of American politics. In due course, I would turn my personal passion to agitational politics, but I never lost my interest in elections and government.

My parents of course enthusiastically supported Stevenson again. Other family developments seemed both contradictory and fascinating. Despite my father's professed commitment to Quakerism and his occasional vehement denial of Jewishness, the hatred of Nazism remained strong in family discourse. My parents reiterated their adamant refusal to buy German products. They viewed Volkswagen cars, for example, with loud disdain. Through them, mostly in conversations with my father, I also learned about the Nazi apparatus and the key figures of that murderous regime: Hitler, Himmler, Goring, Goebbels, and scores of others. I also learned many of the details about the destruction of European Jewry, but with no specificity about my grandparents or aunt and uncle. I received almost no information about any of this in my junior high school history and social studies classes.

46

This was, I believe, about the time that my father began investigating reparation payments from the West German government for the murder of his immediate family. I knew of his uncle, Hans Blum, an international lawyer in London. Blum had escaped with his wife from Nazi Germany and, after the war, established a legal practice solely devoted to obtaining reparations for German Holocaust survivors. Initially, when I learned that Dr. Blum would get some money for my parents, this reinforced my high regard for lawyers. Later, when I discovered that he charged my father full fees for his services, I came to view him as a son-of-a-bitch. What kind of an uncle would charge his nephew, who lost his whole family in Auschwitz, any fee at all?

I have little memory of ninth grade academic life, but I have profound and precise recollections of the year leading up to the life-altering events of the racial battle in Levittown in the following summer of 1957. William Penn Jr. High was as stifling to me as ever. I continued the major disconnect between my robust intellectual curiosity and my mediocre academic interest and performance. I continued to challenge some assignments in history and social studies that seemed to me absurdly remote from the dramatic events taking place in the world.

One hilarious story is irresistible. Algebra class was about as stifling as I can ever remember. I got it and actually performed acceptably. Every day, the teacher went to the blackboard, mumbled incoherently about X's and other mathematical symbols, and then spent a majority of the class writing on the board. Mostly, we had an unflattering view of his ass. I sat in the back, with my friend Al, who shared my basic irreverence. One day, as we sat there, Al unzipped his pants, pulled out his penis, and quickly made it erect. He then took out a pipe-like wooden instrument that many of the boys had made in woodshop class on the jigsaw, which I avoided because it scared the hell out of me. The boys could dangle these wood items with belts at their end on the tips of their fingers in a balancing act that seemingly defied our common understanding of the physical world. I had no clue about the physics involved in how these wood carvings could hold the belts. But that afternoon, Al took one of these devices and placed it on the tip of his penis and proceeded to dangle his belt from it. It was the funniest thing ever in junior high. It's also what I remember most about algebra.

My basic defiance was met with more forced counseling; each Friday, students had "club time." These hour-long periods gave students the opportunity to pursue individual interests: sports, science, cars, woodworking, cooking, and similar recreational activities. I was excluded. Instead, I had to report to the office to meet with the school counselors to discuss my "attitudes" and my problems. I viewed them—and therapy in

47

general—as nothing more than a form of social control, like education in general. I saw it as punitive and I still believe that despite my immaturity, my basic view was accurate. It took me a long time to develop a more complex and mature view of the liberating potential of psychotherapy, one that utterly depended on sensitive and perceptive therapists.

I must give credit, however, where it is due. My social studies teacher, Bernard Schwartz, understood my attitudes and my emotional state extremely well. He asked me what I wanted to study. I replied that I was interested in current affairs, especially civil rights and international events. To my astonishment, he told me to proceed and investigate and present my findings to the class. I did so and I performed extremely well. This was smart pedagogy and insightful psychology, which I rarely encountered from kindergarten through law school. Schwartz's strategy revealed that an effective teacher could actually encourage students to pursue their personal intellectual interests and make it part of their formal schoolwork. This vision has influenced my own teaching for more than 40 years.

Chapter 8
The Battle of Levittown

Summer, 1957 marked the beginning of an entirely new political consciousness for me. The battle for housing integration in Levittown became an opening fight in the emerging civil rights movement and my parents were in the thick of it. I even played a peripheral role, but one that had profound implications for my future political activism and my later work as a teacher and scholar. The events in August, 1957 also left permanent emotional scars and forever reinforced my dim view of the human species.

The summer began quietly. My immediate salvation was the Connie Mack Baseball League, the next step up from Little League, involving players from 13 to 15 years old. I was ecstatic at making the team at 14 and delighted to play second base again. Our coach was Mr. Shafer (my spelling is approximate and I absolutely cannot remember his first name), who a year later would come to reveal himself as one of the vilest human beings I ever encountered. But at first, I was pleased that he put me into the lineup. He did offer some "shortcuts" on the field, primarily involving deceiving umpires and opposing teams, all of which came close to cheating. I wish that I could report my distress, but I regret that my moral consciousness was still insufficiently developed. I biked to each game, proud of my uniform. I performed adequately throughout the season, garnering a respectable batting average, collecting plenty of walks, and stealing several bases. Overall, it was a solid record that would ordinarily ensure my return for a final season as a 15 year-old.

I knew that something big was afoot at home and that it concerned race. Even before the school year ended, I had been privy to several meetings at home and at others' homes about William Levitt's policy of racial exclusion. My parents brought me along because of my professed interest in the topic, especially since it affected my own community. My siblings were too young to understand, but Aimee and Jon recall the violence that shortly ensued. There was an air of conspiracy and excitement at these meetings, which intensified as the summer progressed. Most of the participants were Jewish, including a family who had become good friends, Lew and Bea Wechsler and their children Katy and Nick. Sometime that summer, I also meet the Myers family, Daisy, Bill, and their small children, the courageous African Americans who broke the residential color line in Levittown and shattered the racist calm that had existed there since the city's inception.

Historians of post-war America have recognized various seminal events during the 1950s that gave rise to the modern civil rights movement. The battle of Levittown in August and September, 1957 was one of those events, although the well publicized struggle for integration at Central High School in Little Rock, Arkansas, which pitted the federal government against the racist resistance of Governor Orval Faubus, soon eclipsed Levittown as the national focus of racial conflict. I have published a few pieces about my personal reactions to the 1957 integration fight in Levittown, including an op-ed piece for the Philadelphia Inquirer I wrote on the 50th anniversary of the Myers' move into their house as the first black family in the city. I have also spoken often of my Levittown experiences, not only at my home campus, but in many invited lectures throughout the country.

There are also some documentary films and scholarly mentions on the events of 1957. In 2009, journalist David Kushner published the first complete book, *Levittown*, on the traumatic integration story. His book focused largely on the Levitt family and the Wechsler family, also mentioning the Von Blums, including me, throughout the text. Kushner pointedly noted that Levitt was a Jew and that the Wechslers had had associations with the Communist Party. I knew that at the time, and my reaction today mirrors that of a half century ago: Levitt as a Jewish racist was repulsive and the Wechslers as former communists were implementing their humane racial vision independent of the general CP foolishness and blindness about the crimes of Stalin. Indeed, my reaction to Levitt has intensified over the years. Having reclaimed my own Jewish identity strongly as a college undergraduate, I link it with a longer Jewish commitment to social justice. Jewish racism is the polar opposite of what the Jewish tradition means to me.

The historical background and the key facts about the battle of Levittown are an essential preface to my personal reflections about those traumatic and life-altering events. African Americans had long suffered the humiliations of residential segregation throughout the United States. Blacks and other minority groups had been denied equal access to housing for many decades through overt discrimination by realtors and bankers, often with the active complicity of local governmental officials. Realtors and landlords alike steered African Americans away from white areas and into black neighborhoods, further ghettoizing the African American population, especially in American cities. These actions were usually overt; after the passage of federal and state fair housing legislation, these actions became more subtle but no less discriminatory.

The end of World War II, ironically, exacerbated the problem. Although thousands of honorably discharged African American veterans were eligible for benefits under the GI Bill, which among other things guaranteed inexpensive mortgages, they often encountered disappointment and frustration. Real estate agents frequently refused to show these veterans homes in white neighborhoods. Rationalizing that residential integration would lower property values, they conducted their activities to reflect and extend the deeper racism of white America. The result was that African Americans were largely relegated to concentrated areas in cities that were already "redlined," a practice that designated and isolated specific minority neighborhoods, often with high crime rates, where lenders refused to lend money or extend credit. These realities were pervasive in America. In Los Angeles, African Americans were largely restricted from purchasing or renting property west of Crenshaw Boulevard, making South and South Central Los Angeles (including such communities as Inglewood, Hawthorne, Compton, and others) the historic center of black life in Southern California, especially in the post-war era.

The Levittown crisis of 1957 was hardly the first civil rights battle involving residential segregation. Civil rights groups had long protested against these insidious practices. Many African Americans likewise knew the sordid history of white violence against blacks when they sought to move into previously all white neighborhoods. Kevin Boyle wrote about one of the most dramatic examples in his 2004 prize-winning book, *Arc of Justice*, an account of an African American physician and his family who moved into a white area in Detroit in 1925, more than 30 years before the eerily similar events in Levittown. Days after Dr. Ossain Sweet's family arrived in his new home, angry white mobs congregated outside his house, throwing rocks, breaking windows, and yelling racist invectives. This case had a more tragic consequence: one of the occupants in Dr. Sweet's new home fired a shot into the racist crowd, killing one person. Dr. Sweet was indicted for homicide and was finally acquitted after the NAACP arranged for famed attorney Clarence Darrow to lead the defense.

No lives were lost in Levittown in 1957, but the historical facts revealed a continuation of racially exclusionary policies that had dominated the country since the end of the Civil War. Levitt & Sons purchased the land in Bucks County in 1951 and built affordable homes designed primarily for working and lower middle class white residents, especially white veterans and their families seeking to flee crowed cities with increasing minority populations. Levittown's first residents moved into the new development in 1952 and enjoyed lives of comfortable conformity, as I noted in the previous chapter. Critics, to be sure, found Levittown sterile and stultifying, fostering an environment that encouraged compliance to authority and discouraged all forms of individuality. That was my view as a young teenager, but I had yet to develop an adequate vocabulary and intellectual framework to articulate my growing sense of alienation.

Civil rights organizations were well aware of the racist policies of Levitt & Sons. By 1956, dramatic events including the Supreme Court decision of *Brown v. Board of Education*, the murder of Emmett Till, and the courage of the Montgomery bus boycotters made a challenge to Levittown's residential exclusion inevitable. Even before the Myers family moved into their house in August, 1957, a great deal of behind-the-scenes activity occurred, involving the Wechslers, my parents, and various progressive organizations including some labor unions, the NAACP, the Bucks County Human Relations Council, and the Quakers' Friends Service Association.

By August, everything was in place for the Myers to move to the house next door to the Wechslers. Kushner's account and Lew Wechsler's own memoir, *The First Stone*, provide compelling and specific details about the events. My recollections are personal, emotional, and impressionistic, but they are also factually accurate. Even children of 14 can serve as excellent historical sources, especially when they are first-hand witnesses and even minor participants in groundbreaking events.

Shortly before the Myers moved into their new home, the local newspaper, *The Levittown Times*, published a front-page story announcing the arrival of Levittown's first Negro family. Given the large racist sentiment among the city's population, this was tantamount to inviting a mob to gather at 39 Deepgreen Lane, the Myers' new residence. And that was exactly the result: hundreds of angry white homeowners rioted outside the home, fueled by racial hatred and abetted by alcohol consumption. The mood was vicious, reminiscent of the pictures of Southern lynch mobs I had seen. Threats of physical violence were in the air, directed both at the Myers and at their supporters, including my parents and me, who had gathered at the house.

Hateful cries of "niggers get out" floated through the air as the mob gathered and grew. I recall an unusually frightening image that I have not previously published, but have mentioned in various speeches. I observed one local police officer on the corner, a bottle of beer in his hand, egging the mob on, lending official cover to the racist explosion of August 17, 1957. I would soon see many other examples of racist police attitudes and actions and even now, in the early 21st century, I have a hard time abandoning the perception of white police officers as presumptively racist.

I also remember a barrage of rocks crashing at the Myers' home. We fled next door to the Wechslers' house. I feared that our very lives were in jeopardy. Decisive action from Pennsylvania Governor George M. Leader quelled the violence that summer night. But the racist backlash continued. Mobs of angry whites appeared outside the Myers' home for several nights in August. More insidiously, many of the neighbors formed a resistance organization called the Levittown Betterment Committee, dedicated to keeping the city all-white and free from any African American presence. This organization was headed by Jim Newell, a burly Southerner, who played the dominant role in generating racial fear and hatred and with whom I would have a personal courtroom confrontation a few months later.

This racist organization, deeply infiltrated by the Ku Klux Klan, would engage in even more nefarious activities in the next few weeks and months. After the first evening, however, I had seen, all too closely, the twisted face of bigotry. I had experienced human beings at their worst—and at their very best. Bill and Daisy Myers, Bea and Lou Wechsler, my parents, and the other anti-racist supporters who had gathered the first night, revealed the kind of courage and commitment that would shortly dominate national attention with the growing American civil rights struggle, especially in the South.

Emotionally, the viciousness and collective fury of the mob left a greater impact on me. My dim view of human nature was confirmed. I came to believe that most people were capable of truly horrific conduct under certain conditions. I had thought about this on my own when I considered what the Nazis had done to millions of people. In my mind, the Levittown mobs seemed just like the adoring crowds in Germany in the 1930s, who cheered Hitler and who turned a blind eye to mass murder. This may well be an emotional/intellectual function of second generation Holocaust survivorship. I have retained it throughout my life and have regularly brought it up in my university classes, asking students what they think they might have done when faced with overwhelming pressures to join mob actions.

I remained on the scene daily with my parents following the first night's violence and confrontation. The various Betterment Committee activities are seared in my memory. Not far from the Myers' home, that racist organization hoisted a large Confederate flag, a symbol that fills me with the same feelings as the swastika flag. At a nearby house, white racists blasted the song "Dixie" loudly and constantly from a loudspeaker. Caravans of cars drove regularly in front of the Wechslers and Meyers, and slightly later, in front of our home a few miles away. Mobs gathered for several nights, shouting racial invective, revealing their deep hatred. Various bigots walked regularly in front of the Myers' home with a small cocker spaniel, renamed "Nigger" in honor of the new black family.

Even more violence was forthcoming. The Wechslers' home was defaced with the letters "KKK." Then, on September 22, 1957, two men transported and burned a seven-foot wooden cross at my family's Vermillion Hill's home, located perhaps four or five miles away from the Myers. I awoke in the middle of the night, deeply frightened by the smoke and confusion and concerned about my parents and my three younger siblings in the house, especially 4-year old Carey, in the room adjacent to the cross. My sister

53

Aimee and I have slightly different recollections of the discovery of the cross. She believes that she was the first to discover it and I think I was the first. That reflects the problematic character of memory I noted at the outset of the memoir.

The honor of first discovery, of course, is irrelevant to the profound impact of this horror. The ensuing events were frenetic—fire trucks, police cars, curious neighbors, and news reporters. The specific details are blurry a half century later, but the general event, like all such traumas, remain for a lifetime. I can still conjure up the smoke, the confusion, and above all, the pervasive fear.

The two men who transported and burned the cross, Eldred Williams and Howard Bentcliff, were arrested and charged with malicious mischief or some minor variant of that charge and released on $500 bail. The Kushner book indicates that Williams had substantial contact with the Klan. I'm not sure about Bentcliff, but their formal organizational affiliations make little difference. Both men were vicious racists and both deserved long prison terms for their malevolent conduct. I recall their arraignment before a local Justice of the Peace. It appalled me, then and even now, that they were not charged with serious felonies, including arson and perhaps even attempted murder. The irony registered strongly with me that all of this occurred in a community located only a few miles from the signing of the Declaration of Independence.

Beyond the violence itself, life in the neighborhood changed drastically. Shortly after the Myers moved in, even before the cross burning incident, my parents were swiftly identified as part of the conspiracy—the communist conspiracy, the NAACP conspiracy, and any other conspiracy that could terrify the uninformed residents who feared the decline of their property values. These were, after all, people who had recently emerged from crowded inner cities apartments and row houses. Rumors abounded that their comfortable suburb would become a crime-ridden ghetto and that interracial marriage was right around the corner. At an extremely young age, I again saw the powerful human capacity for rumor, delusion, and irrationality.

From August 17th on, I heard the taunt of "nigger lover" regularly, indeed incessantly. Harvard law professor Randall Kennedy, in his fascinating book, *Nigger: The Strange Career of a Troublesome Word*, describes the term as "first cousin" of the pejorative word "nigger." At the time, of course, I knew nothing of its linguistic roots or implications. I did know that those who directed the label at my family and me were hostile racists. Sometime I heard it from complete strangers in the neighborhood when I merely walked down the street or rode my bicycle.

There were likewise anti–Semitic comments, but mostly directed against the Wechslers and other Jewish supporters of the Myers family. The Betterment Committee spread rumors of communist instigation of the integration activities. This was still the era of McCarthyism, despite the well-deserved demise of Joe McCarthy himself. More ominously, both the Wechslers and my family received threatening letters and phone calls, some laced with profanity and ugly racist invective. I answered the phone on some occasions and was on the receiving end of these anonymous threats. There were also some expressions of support, but it was hard to keep any sense of perspective in light of the overwhelming hostility I experienced.

A special dimension of that hatred was also directed against my siblings and me. Parents in the neighborhood instructed their children that they could no longer associate with us, lest they be tainted with ideas of racial equality. Although these were not especially close personal friends, I felt a major sense of loss and betrayal at the time. I also had some minor physical incidents, mostly shoving, from former childhood associates. Most responses were verbal, with the small racially charged vocabulary befitting an ignorant population.

Not everyone abandoned me. Across the street, an Italian-American friend, Andy, continued his friendship. He never said anything about the racial turmoil brewing in Levittown. I don't know if he had parental instructions to avoid the topic or he simply didn't follow the news. But here is what he did know. Andy, perhaps a little older, was extremely sexually curious. I am somewhat conflicted, even embarrassed to write about it now, but it is part of the narrative and he provided welcome emotional relief for me at the time. So it goes, as Kurt Vonnegut often wrote.

He taught me the meaning of all kinds of words I had heard, but didn't quite understand. Above all, he opened up my world to the multidimensional world of sex, a natural thing for a boy my age. Most important, he instructed me about masturbation, opening an extremely pleasant kingdom, one far beyond the realm of racial violence, political strife, and economic insecurity. He was, in retrospect, a fine teacher; it could well be said that he helped me to discover an effective hands-on style. Andy had a genuine commitment to the merger of theory and practice. He should have gone into education.

In the stultifying world of the 50s, sex education was nonexistent. Parents were embarrassed and said nothing, sometimes throwing a few books or pamphlets at their children. My parents were no exception. School was no different. We had a few ridiculous pseudo-documentaries warning us about venereal diseases and telling us, in effect, never to do anything sexually.

Real sex education took place on the street. Andy assisted me effectively in that function.

A very significant episode also occurred about the same time, perhaps a few weeks after the Myers moved to Levittown and after our family was identified as part of the conspiracy. A Jewish family named Stern lived directly next door. The father was plainly distressed at the events and the reactions of the neighbors. I could see it on his face, especially when he avoided contact or conversation with anyone in my family. One day, almost invisibly, the Sterns moved away. I recall my parents talking about it. However contradictorily given their own temporary Quakerism, they noted that it was only 12 years since the end of the Second World War. They remarked that many Jews were still extremely fearful of exposure, especially when charges of communism and race mixing were in the air. Of course, this affected my father also, but in different ways. His insights were correct and I still make the point that Jews should resist levels of assimilation that in effect diminish any genuine sense of Jewish identity.

By September, 1957, it was time to return to school. I was about to begin high school. The authorities at William Penn Junior High had earlier told my parents that I should leave the public schools. Actually, they meant that I would not be welcomed back, without actually saying so precisely. Drawing on their Quaker connections, my parents somehow got me into George School, a prestigious private Quaker prep school in nearby Newtown, Pennsylvania. I acknowledge, again, their desire to find me an appropriate educational setting. They certainly had no funds to pay tuition, so I am unsure what financial arrangement they were able to make.

Somewhat later in the school year, George School authorities told *me* that my parents were in arrears, strongly exacerbating my fragile emotional state. They repeated this refrain several times in my year and a half there, sometimes noting that my continued enrollment was in jeopardy. They knew of the Levittown crisis and of my parents' role in it, but clearly knew nothing of the deeper history of financial insecurity and its effect on my mental state. To me, they were just more bill collectors, filling me with the same sense of dread I had experienced earlier in Wayne.

George School enjoyed a stellar academic reputation. It was a boarding school, attracting many students from affluent East Coast families, especially New York. Many appeared to be Quakers and Jews. There were also day students like me, commuting mostly from various Bucks County locales. I was part of a carpool arrangement, which a few months later serendipitously added another crucial element to my burgeoning political education.

My immediate reaction was the huge social class gap. No one, in my recollection, explicitly disparaged me because of my Levittown residence.

Fellow students talked of vacations, even in Europe and exotic locations like Cape Cod. They skied and boated and had maids. Like privileged people throughout history, they knew instinctively how to "act well." They had all done extremely well in school. They knew things I had never heard of (I had my own substantial knowledge base, but it was one not formally recognized in traditional institutional settings; few George School students had read *The National Guardian* or *The Daily Worker*). I discerned a sense of class smugness, concealed by a rhetorical cover of social liberalism. I identify this reaction as one major source of my own leftist politics and my visceral distaste of liberalism.

I am confident in recalling that teachers and students alike viewed me as academically problematic. I know that some students saw me as a person of insufficient intelligence to be at that school. On rare occasions, when asked what I want to be, I replied that I wanted to become a lawyer. I remember the "look," the one with an upraised eyebrow suggesting that this was a ridiculous aspiration. Although my fragile state at the time doubtless intensified my daily reactions, these slights were real, not imagined.

I muddled through the formal curriculum, earning predictably mediocre grades. German class was a pleasant exception, where I responded easily to the subject and did well. Geometry struck me as absurd and the history and social studies classes were slightly better than what I had earlier experienced, only because current events like civil rights were at least acceptable parts of class discussion. I followed the Little Rock integration crisis closely and contributed my own observations about it competently if not eloquently.

Two other features of life at George School stick in my consciousness, one annoying and one more troublesome. School assemblies were mandatory and replete with Quaker rituals. This marked, I think, my first systematic rejection of that tradition. I began to see Quakerism as very specifically Christian and I rejected Christianity *per se*. I began reading atheist literature, especially Bertrand Russell, and I investigated various Jewish thinkers who were also atheists. That seemed like a good idea to me; it still does.

Physical education was mandatory at George School. This was fine, even desirable from my perspective. But life is never so simple. Each month, boys assembled in the gym for "physicals." We stood in line, wearing nothing but underpants, waiting to be weighed and measured. This was odd and distasteful. One day, however, the boys' physical education director told me to enter his inner office, had me step on the scale, and then ordered me to drop my underpants. He then carefully perused my genitals, though I don't think that he touched me at all. I was acutely embarrassed—or worse. I told no one. For the remainder of my time at the school, I avoided him, at times ducking into a building when I saw him on campus. I have repressed this memory for fifty years. As I wrote this paragraph, I used the magic of the Internet, on a lark, to look him up. I remembered his last name and, to my surprise, found a picture of him on a George School Archives site. That image generated a powerful emotion I had clearly repressed. It was profoundly disconcerting. We live in an age of many revelations of adult sexual misconduct against children. That PE teacher was no rapist, but what he did that afternoon was inexcusable and I cannot think that it was unintentional.

Every student had to participate in athletic teams or in intramurals. I made the George School wrestling team, which proved a tremendous emotional outlet for me. I wrestled in the 97-pound weight class, participating for two years. It enabled me to discharge considerable aggression. My opponents were, in my mind, everyone who had wronged me, especially the bigots I had recently encountered in the Levittown battle. My relative success in the sport was an ego-boosting bonus.

Getting to school was a regular challenge. My father drove me whenever he could. Occasionally, I took two buses and other times I hitchhiked, in an era when that mode of transportation was far less dangerous. A carpool arrangement was also sometimes effective. The key participant was Margery Larrabee, wife of Kent Larrabee. Both of the Larrabees had been involved in the Levittown crisis, on the side of the Myers. They had represented the American Friends Service Committee, a service and action arm of the Quakers. Margery Larrabee taught at the Quaker elementary school adjacent to George School, so this was convenient for me.

Once again, life is rarely simple. One morning, after my father dropped me off at the Larrabee residence, I waited in their den for the ride. Bored, I fiddled around, impatient to get on the road. I wandered over to the open file cabinet in the room and peeked in. I always tell my students, sometimes with a large grin, that this was wrong, an invasion of the Larrabees' privacy. Most files were mundane, but one grabbed my attention, marked clearly: "Communism in Lower Bucks County." I looked through the file and saw names I recognized: Wechsler and Von Blum. Others, of course, I could not recognize, but there were many in the file. I carefully placed the folder back and said nothing until I arrived home later that day. My parents' reaction was shock. I imagine they regarded the Larrabees as informers. I cannot confirm this, but it is more than strange that they would compile the list. But this was late 1957 or early 1958, and the nation was still in the grips of the Red Scare, even with Joe McCarthy dead. From then on, my only comments to the Larrabees were totally innocuous.

The discovery of a possible anti-communist informer (or, minimally, internal suspicions of "communist" involvement in the Levittown residential integration struggle) was no surprise. Throughout the summer and fall of

1957, rumors about communist direction of the Myers' move to Levittown had been prevalent in Bucks County, especially among the white racists opposing the family's move to the city. Even some local public officials fanned the flames of this pervasive hysteria, deliberately, if mindlessly, linking the Communist Party and the NAACP as part of a grand "race-mixing" conspiracy originating in Moscow. Lew and Bea Wechsler had, of course, been associated with the Party earlier in their lives and my own parents had certainly known (and sometimes admired) CP members over the years. But any notion that the Myers' purchase of a Levittown home was a communist operation was preposterous. Even Bill Myers was labeled a communist during the height of the controversy, a false and malicious label that ignored his honorable military service and his human desire to find decent housing for his growing family.

All of this reflected the deeper McCarthy-inspired persecution of leftists and liberals generally in the United States, a phenomenon that began well before the emergence of the malevolent junior senator from Wisconsin. Almost immediately after the Japanese surrender ending World War II, American political leaders and right-wing figures in entertainment, the professions, and elsewhere began an anti-communist crusade that pervaded American life through the early 1960s. Cold war liberals, including President Harry Truman, Senator Hubert Humphrey, and various anti-communist labor leaders, contributed to this cascading national irrationality. A voluminous literature on the subject exists and over the years I have recommended numerous sources to my students, not to mention how I have regularly referenced several of them in my various publications. One of the finest is David Caute's 1978 *The Great Fear*, with his unnerving line in the first paragraph of his Preface: "The wealthiest, most secure nation in the world was sweat-drenched in fear."

This disgraceful history is well known. Lists of "subversive" individuals and organizations, federal and state legislative investigatory committees, wholesale firings of teachers, government workers, and others because of past and present political activities and beliefs, blacklists of progressive Hollywood directors, screenwriters, and actors, leftist visual artists, singers, writers, and professors, censorship of foreign mail, removal of books and magazines from stores and libraries, and other repressive practices destroyed the lives of thousands of American citizens. The Federal Bureau of Investigation directed and sustained much of this persecution, under the malevolent leadership of J. Edgar Hoover, perhaps the most dangerous public official in all of American history.

An almost complete evisceration of the First Amendment guarantee of free expression and the persecution of those claiming their Fifth Amendment right against self-incrimination essentially destroyed the essence of the Bill of Rights in America. Even proclaiming fidelity to the Bill of Rights could cause people to be branded subversive or worse, exposing them to loss of employment or public ostracism. The effect was to make a mockery of constitutional government in America, ironically turning the United States into a pale replica of the Soviet totalitarianism it ostensibly opposed.

Thousands of accounts of the disastrous personal implications of this McCarthy-era persecution of leftists and other American dissenters are now widely available. They make for compelling, if unnerving reading. One of the most prominent victims of McCarthyism was the great Paul Robeson, whose life and work later became a major focus of my teaching and writing at UCLA. Highly sympathetic to the Soviet Union, and a strong believer in socialist ideals, Robeson was effectively blacklisted during the 1950s. Openly and aggressively radical, he confronted his accusers. As a result, he was unable to earn a living despite his international fame. Owners of concert halls and recording studios succumbed to pressure to deny him performances. Record stores refused to carry his recordings, cutting off his royalty income. The FBI followed him to meetings, performances in black churches, and home.

Like hundreds of other artists, he was called before the House Un-American Activities Committee. In 1950, the State Department cancelled his passport on the grounds that his travels abroad were not in America's "best interest." Exiled in his own land, Robeson lost the right to perform overseas, his only remaining source of income. This pervasive persecution also helped destroy his physical and mental heath and he never fully recovered even after his passport was restored. The persecution of Paul Robeson, in microcosm, mirrors the story of McCarthyism generally. It was no wonder that in 1957, Bill and Daisy Myers, Lew and Bea Wechsler, and Peter and Selma Von Blum would receive glancing blows from this same pernicious Red Scare that had despoiled the national landscape.

The major highlight of 10th grade occurred outside school, in December, 1957. The Commonwealth of Pennsylvania, through its progressive Attorney General Thomas McBride, filed a complaint in the Bucks County Court of Common Please in the County seat of Doylestown. I received a subpoena to testify in that proceeding. McBride's petition sought a permanent injunction barring the Betterment Committee and other racists in Levittown from cross burnings, various forms of harassment including motorcades, firecrackers, bombs and explosives, intimidating messages sent to the Myers or their supporters, or any other conduct designed to unlawfully compel the Myers family to leave the house they legally purchased.   In short, the injunction was sweeping and sought to end the violence and harassment that began in August.

Attorney General McBride conducted the case himself; this was rare for the highest state legal official to serve as a trial attorney. Before my testimony, he spoke to me in an especially sensitive way. He told me only to tell the truth and said that I should not be afraid. I remember his compassion and consideration well. Once again, it reinforced my high regard at the time for lawyers.

I held my own during my testimony. As is happens, I have the transcript of my testimony, which I often read in class presentations and lectures. It is revealing, I believe, on multiple levels. I present it in slightly abridged form:

Direct Examination

By Mr. McBride:

Q. How old are you, son?

A. I am fourteen years old.

Q. And where do you go to school?

A. I go to George School.

Q. And what grade are you in?

A. I am in the tenth grade.

Q. Do you live near the Myers and the Wechslers?

A. I live in Levittown.

Q. How far away?

A. I would say four or five miles away.

Q. Now, were you ever in the vicinity of the Wechsler house on September 8th of this year?

A. Yes, I was.

Q. What was the occasion?

A. Well, I was invited to a cook-out party.

Q. Now, did you see any cars going by there on that day?

A. Yes; when Mr. Newell went by in his car, he called out several names, "Nigger lovers."

Q. What?

A. Mr. Newell rode past in his car, and he called several names, among them, "Nigger lovers."

Q. Now, do you see Mr. Newell in court?

A. Yes, I do.

Q. Will you identify him?

A. Right over there (indicating).

Q. Yes. Is that the man who called you "Nigger lover?"

A. Yes, it is.

Q. Did any car go past your house?

61

A. Yes; there was a motorcade about every night, about the first few nights.
Q. A what?
A. Like a motorcade, cars and cars.
Q. Motorcade?
A. Yes.
Q. Did anybody in those cars speak out and call, or anyone else say any names?
A. Well, I heard some "Nigger lover" talking.
Q. From those cars passing your home?
A. Yes.
Q. Did these cars that went past your house have any flags on them?
A. Some of them did. They had Confederate flags, and "Don't tread on me" flags.
Q. And what?
A. "Don't tread on me" with a snake.
CROSS-EXAMINATION
By Mr. Houpt [Defenese Attorney]:
Q. Did you shout anything to Mr. Newell?
A. No, I did not.
Q. Did anyone else in your group shout anything to Mr. Newell?
A. Not here.
Q. Did anyone shout to Mr. Newell, "Heil Hitler?"
A. Might have been one or two.
Q. Is it not true that was shouted before Mr. Newell said anything?
A. If that was shouted, it was after Mr. Newell said something. By The Court:
Q. Well, now, did somebody shout out, or did they not?
A. Somebody stuck their hand up, like this?
Q. Indicating the arm outstretched over his head. But did anybody say those words, "Heil Hitler?"
A. No.
Q. Why did you say they did?
A. They stuck their hands up.
Q. All right. Don't agree to what Mr. Houpt suggests if it wasn't true. Don't agree to what anyone suggests if it isn't true.
A. Well, that was like indicating.
By Mr. Houpt:
Q. Indicating what?
A. Indicating, "Heil Hitler."
  I actually recall that Katy Wechsler, others, and I, gave the Nazi salute to Jim Newell and his racist minions that September afternoon. My reasoning was simple; if Newell, by calling us "Nigger lovers" and other names had

been acting like a Nazi, we would recognize his actions with an appropriate symbolic response. More significant, I began to realize a principle that I have articulated for decades, that racism anywhere, whether in Nazi Germany in the 1930s and 1940s or in Levittown, Pennsylvania in 1957, was structurally identical.

An incident occurred, to me personally, at the Doylestown trial that has never been reported in the literature about the Levittown case. During a recess in the proceedings, I made my way alone to a soda or candy machine. Two adult men, obviously a part of the racist defendant group, accosted me and shoved me to the floor. I immediately reported the incident to my parents and to Attorney General McBride. All three were furious. The men disappeared and were unavailable for identification.

The successful outcome of that litigation, which took some months to conclude, quelled some of the white anger in the city. But racial incidents against my family hardly vanished. Two middle aged women with hand grenades were found near our Vermillion Hills home. The most frightening incident occurred in 1958, when my parents were out for the evening. I was babysitting for my three younger siblings. A few hostile people gathered in front of the house and, yet again, racist language spewed forth. I called the police to inform them of the threat. Meanwhile, I gathered the kids together and hurried them upstairs. The layout of the house was significant. The steps to the second floor were directly behind the front door. As the door opened, anyone at the top of the stairs could see the person entering the house.

I stood at the top of the stairs with my brother's large bow and several arrows. I was determined to shoot the first person entering the house. I was poised to shoot as many as possible. Fortunately, it never came to that. The police arrived and dispersed the crowd. For the rest of the school year, neighborhood hostility was exclusively verbal. All these events and all the emotional fallout provided the foundation for the long, wonderful, and continuingly gratifying relationships I have forged with the African American community for fifty years. I might well have established these relationships anyway, but Levittown surely was the major catalyst for my close connections with my black friends and associates.

Our family and the Myers' other supporters received plenty of external support. Martin Luther King, Jr. had earlier sent Rev. Ralph Abernathy to visit and lend assistance. Baseball legend Jackie Robinson weighed in strongly as well. Paul Robeson himself told the Wechslers that he knew and naturally approved of their efforts in Levittown when they met him during a concert intermission at New York's Zion Baptist Church. I remember most vividly the visit to our family house of Anne Braden of Louisville. She and her husband Karl Braden, former 1948 Progressive Party activists, had been instrumental in breaking residential segregation near Louisville a few years earlier. For their efforts, they were indicted for sedition. She struck me as a powerful and courageous white supporter of black civil rights. Shortly thereafter, I read her memoir of the sedition fame-up, *The Wall Between*, a powerful critique of white racism and anti-communist hysteria.

I recall little of the remainder of the school year, during which I turned 15. I did well in German, and not especially well in the other subjects. Mostly, I looked forward to summer, especially the prospect of playing my final year on my Connie Mack league baseball team. I assumed that I would resume my efforts as the starting second baseman.

I appeared as scheduled for the tryouts, which I assumed was largely *pro forma* for me based on my decent record of the previous year. At the end of the tryouts, Mr. Shafer assembled everyone together to announce his final selections. I was nonchalant because I hit and fielded well—or at least adequately—during the practices. I was beginning to perceive my athletic limitations, but I also assumed that since I performed well before, I would probably improve in my final year.

Then came the blow. Shafer announced the "cuts" and I was among the first—perhaps even the first. It was absolutely devastating psychologically. I know that it reduced me to tears as I mounted my bicycle to ride home. My parents saw my despair. I am unsure what they did. They made several phone calls and somehow I got restored to the team. To this day, I don't know whether I was placed on the roster formally or not.

Each game, I put on my uniform and biked to the field. Throughout the entire season, I didn't play a single inning. I think Shafer let me coach 3rd base a few times, but his hostility toward me was palpable. A coach on a rival team, Mr. Gottlieb, saw my distress and offered to trade one of his players for me, apparently permissible under league rules. Shafer refused. In his most egregious act, Shafer decided that he needed a pinch runner. As it happened, I was among the fastest runners on the team. Shafer approached me on the bench, pointed to me, and as I was about to rise, he quickly moved his finger to the boy sitting next to me, also named Paul—one of the slowest runners on the team. The other Paul entered the game. I sat down, bitterly disappointed.

At the season's end, I attended the final award banquet. Since I never played, I was ineligible for any plaques or trophies. Every 15-year old, however, received a plaque for finishing the season and graduating. Each name but mine was called to the front of the banquet room.

I have played this episode over and over again in my mind throughout the years. I have always wondered if my rejection was political or really my lack of athletic and competitive ability. Whatever modest talents I had, they were adequate enough to play in that league on the basis of my prior performance. I have concluded that it was political, fueled by Shafer's fundamental racism, indeed, his cruelty toward a child because of his hostility to my parents' role in breaking the residential color line in Levittown. As I tell my students, I sometimes wish that I believed in Hell, because I fantasize a very special place there for the Mr. Shafers of the world.

In September, I returned to George School for 11th grade. That semester is entirely forgettable. At home, the familiar economic insecurity reemerged, probably a fusion of my father's inability to hold a job and some persecution and firing resulting from his highly visible presence in the Levittown affair. I contributed as much as possible through babysitting, lawn mowing, snow shoveling, and other odd jobs.

I continued my strong interest in current events, especially the growing civil rights movement. I also followed domestic and international affairs closely, both in the newspapers and on television. My parents continued their exasperation about my reading habits. They found my continued interest in sports novels unseemly, especially after all my experience with the Levittown events. But I enjoyed them immensely and they provided a much-needed escape from the realities of daily life.

But then I had a major reading epiphany. I started looking at a book in my parents' collection, entitled *Inside U.S.A.*, by John Gunther. This massive book of political reportage absorbed me completely. Its scope was huge. Gunther had traveled throughout the 48 states, interviewing thousands of people and providing a fascinating account of political history and culture. I learned more about many of the politicians I had already recognized, while discovering others I figured that I needed to know. Most compelling was the author's chapter on race relations in America, "Negro in the Woodpile," which I read several times, reflecting my growing interest in race in America. This catalyzed an intellectual engagement that has never ceased. It made me seek out other books on politics and history, finally satisfying my parents that I could go beyond my obsession with sports literature. To this day, I have that copy of Gunther's book and continue to use it as a valuable historical reference, both for my teaching and my writing.

In December, 1958, my father was doing some kind of construction work that took him to San Diego, California. My mother joined him while my siblings and I stayed temporarily with my aunt, uncle, and cousins in Levittown. Then during winter break, and with me in charge, we all flew to San Diego. It was a dramatic new world. I had never traveled except to New York and Atlantic City and once to Washington, D.C. California was magic: swimming pools, pristine beaches, sunshine, and warm weather in

65

December. Of course we had no idea about the underlying conservatism and militarism of San Diego.

My recollections of that trip are vivid. We swam in the Pacific, went to the San Diego Zoo, and saw the many fine museums in Balboa Park. The most exciting adventure was crossing the international border into Tijuana and Ensenada, Baja California. This was my first foreign travel. I had not even been to Canada, so this seemed especially exotic. I also had my first taco, for 15 cents in Tijuana, generating a durable love, even obsession for, Mexican food. Most important, that trip catalyzed a lifelong interest in foreign travel, which has served as a useful enhancement of my teaching and research for more than forty years.

At our motel, I continued watching television news and reading the local papers, which even at that age struck me, accurately, as reactionary. Fidel Castro's overthrow of the Cuban dictator Fulgencio Batista on January 1, 1959, widely reported in the television news, excited me at the time. Those events further politicized me, setting the stage for a more systematic political activity that would soon follow after the family relocated permanently to California.

After flying back to Philadelphia, I resumed 11th grade at George School. Overshadowing this were the family discussions about going to California for good. Like so many other domestic refugees, we discussed a "new start," a "new promise," and "new opportunities." These were the dreams of millions of migrants to California for many decades.

Chapter 9
Heading West

The decision made, we embarked on the automobile journey across the United States. Taking the Southern route, I noticed the Jim Crow signs everywhere: "Whites Only," "Colored Only," "We Serve White," etc. *ad nauseam*. In light of our recent Levittown experience, this was especially appalling to me I drew pictures—not very well—of "Mr. Bigot," modeled after Jim Newell, Eldred Williams, Howard Bentcliff, and many of the other racists I had recently encountered.

After an exhausting but exciting trip, where we saw a major cross section of America, we arrived in San Diego. We soon found a rental house in the Pacific Beach area, a few hundred yards from the Pacific Ocean. Almost immediately, I enrolled in La Jolla High School, which proved to be substantially better than any school I had previously attended. I made a few friends rapidly and adapted somewhat easily to the academic program. I had begun to realize that college was approaching and that I needed to consider my options fairly quickly. I also understood that I would have to select a college path because I had little skills or inclinations in any other direction.

Finishing 11th grade was surprisingly easy. Some of my teachers were reasonably engaging, and I found social studies and government especially valuable because of my growing interests in these areas. I continued my strong performance in German even though I found my teacher's Germanophile perspective distasteful. The biology teacher was frankly absurd. He continually asked students if they were "good Christians." Even in 1959, I understood that his remarks were an egregious violation of the separation clause of the First Amendment. Moreover, as an atheist, I found his overt expression of his religious beliefs offensive. Finally, however, I was smart enough to roll with his stupidity and save my public disdain for another day.

My political interests were growing strongly. I followed the news avidly. About that time, I think near the end of 11th grade, I began more serious political discussions with my father. Then came the talk. I could, in truth, call it the TALK. He began explaining to me about the differences between capitalism and socialism. That was extremely powerful to me and it catalyzed my growing intellectual consciousness. I had already seen some of the predatory practices of capitalism, so I was an easy convert. But to me, even now, the most compelling principle was the ethical superiority of socialism, its fundamental humanism, which I still believe is central to Karl Marx's fundamental social and philosophical vision.

Finally, at long last, I began serious and more systematic reading, beyond *Inside U.S.A.*, which I had read repeatedly. Now, I was ready for much more. Near the end of 11th grade, at my father's suggestion, I discovered Upton Sinclair. I started, like most readers, with *The Jungle*. It was mesmerizing. That 1906 novel transported me to the horrific world of the Chicago meatpacking industry. I identified with the working class struggles against poverty, exploitation and the pervasive hopelessness of workers during that time. Inevitably, I linked their struggles to my own emotions as a child. Sinclair's central character in *The Jungle*, Jurgis Rudkis, enveloped my life. In quick succession, I turned to many of Sinclair's other books, especially his Lanny Budd series. I got obsessed with Sinclair and his personal commitment to socialism. On a lark, I wrote to him at his residence in Upland, California. To my surprise, he graciously replied, offering me encouragement in my personal quest to learn more about socialism in America.

My parents resumed their affair with Quakerism and joined a Monthly Meeting in La Jolla. They nudged me to go a few times, but I quickly abandoned any pretense of interest and I more vigorously expressed my boredom and my atheism. I had quietly begun reading about Jewish history, but was a few years away from a more systematic rediscovery of that tradition and my role within it.

San Diego was enjoyable for its splendid but ultimately superficial attractions. I swam regularly in Mission Bay and rode my bike throughout the area, often with my brother. I continued my infatuation with baseball, adding the minor league San Diego Padres to my list of teams to follow. In March, 1959, I turned 16, and according to California law, was eligible for a drivers license. Although to my shame I flunked the exam three times, I finally passed and bought a 1937 Willys Coupe for $45. I felt the same exhilarating adolescent sense of freedom exhibited by millions before me.

The family moved to La Jolla itself for my senior year, and I drove my brother Jon and sister Aimee to the La Jolla campus, which also had a junior high school. La Jolla itself, part of municipal San Diego, was (and remains) a conservative enclave, with a well justified reputation for class privilege and anti-Semitism. That had little impact on me because I had not yet openly identified as a Jew. I was more closely involved with developing a foundation for my leftist politics. Only later, as a university student, did I begin merging my ethnic identity and my political consciousness.

As a high school senior, my work ethic and marginal family finances drove me again to part time work, this time as an advance person for the Fuller Brush Man, lining up appointments for him and distributing cosmetic samples while going door to door. This marked the start of a series of genuinely crappy jobs that allowed me to link my theoretical understanding of alienated labor with concrete personal experience. Mowing lawns and doing assorted other odd jobs took some modest financial burden off my parents and continued to promote a personal vision of self-sufficiency.

Several political currents flowed through my senior high school year. I intensified my independent radical reading, actually starting with *The Communist Manifesto*. I also read widely in other socialist literature, both classic texts and contemporary periodical literature. My fellow students perceived this as peculiar, but curiously, I discerned no unusual hostility. By then, I openly proclaimed myself a socialist and especially sought out the expressive cultural manifestations of this tradition.

The key source, as I recall, was Upton Sinclair's *The Cry for Justice*, an anthology of social protest material. I wrote a book report on it for one of my classes and, somewhat to my surprise and delight, I received the teacher's favorable response. It dawned on me that student motivation and passion led to increased academic performance. This thoroughly commonsensical pedagogical principle, which seemed to elude most of my teachers in the past, was finally implemented at least somewhat at La Jolla High School.

Sinclair's anthology contained material from the realms of literature and visual art. His examples of radical expressive culture especially galvanized my imagination. I had little idea then, of course, that this focus would occupy my professional attention for over forty years. At the time, I was fascinated how stories and pictures could give form to thoughts and emotions about powerful issues of social justice. I began pursuing this tradition on my own in the San Diego public library and finally examined the radical classics on my parents' bookshelves.

But the most intriguing feature at home was the large collection of records, especially the leftist folk songs that I had always enjoyed without paying close attention to the lyrics, their historical contexts, or political implications. That changed dramatically in 12th grade. Now I began listening to Paul Robeson, Pete Seeger, and The Weavers more carefully. Robeson became especially important, since I learned more about his life and how he had become ill and had largely retired from public life. The Loyalist songs of the Spanish Civil War had new, more intellectually sophisticated meaning for me. That intellectual and political journey, which started in 12th grade, to this day has never ended.

At school, I began to integrate my new reading into as many academic assignments as possible. Leftist writers like Mike Gold, Theodore Dreiser, John Dos Passos, and various black writers like Frederick Douglass, W. E. B. DuBois, Richard Wright and others soon became part of my personal arsenal.

That led me, in turn, to radical history, especially racial history. In high school, I began studying the history of black slave revolts (communist historian Herbert Aptheker was a respected, even revered figure at home), lynching, the Scottsboro case and others, all of which I emotionally connected to the Levittown crisis. I read newspapers even more voraciously (including, as usual, the sports), but clearly understood the reactionary bias of the San Diego dailies. I also specifically sought out radical newspapers in my senior year, including the communist *People's World*, the Trotskyite paper *The Militant*, the Socialist Labor Party paper *The People*, and whatever other radical publications I could find.

At the same time, I closely followed civil rights and international developments. The Cuban revolution exhilarated me, all the more so when the Eisenhower administration began developing hostility toward Fidel Castro and his regime. I became more outspoken in class and I had some teachers who actually encouraged my merger of academics and activism. It was fine to criticize "Ike" at school and to speak vigorously about the evils of capitalism. For me, this was a remarkable new experience in school. Another key issue that engaged me was the remnant of Cold War anti-communist hysteria, specifically the continued hearings of the House Un-American Activities Committee.

I have concluded that my single best high school academic experience, which I failed to realize at the time, was an elective I took called "creative writing." Students had to produce at least one piece of writing each day— a short story, a poem, an essay, a dairy entry, or anything else. Most of my writing, I suppose, was polemical, in retrospect little more than simplistic leftist rhetoric. But that was fine with the teacher. He assured me that the practice was important and he turned out to be spectacularly correct. He provided careful critical feedback and plenty of encouragement. His example has served me especially well as a teacher; I have done the same, as much as possible, for many thousands of students since 1967. That class gave me enormous self-confidence, which I had rarely received in my entire educational life. It also generated a view that language could be powerful, a major tool for personal liberation and social change.

Some classes, of course, were the usual fare: mindless regurgitation and transitory fact gathering with no serious conceptual foundation to link anything together into any coherent intellectual framework. Those experiences reinforced my notion, which I still articulate in my teaching, public presentations, and educational publications, that much of what passes as education is fundamentally worthless.

Sometime in 12th grade, I must have taken the SAT examination. I have repressed that experience, but I think I did well, since that was my usual result with standardized tests. It seemed less important at the time than three dramatic politically charged incidents at La Jolla High. Each 12th grade boy was required to participate in a mandatory conference with a history teacher to discuss his military obligations under the Selective Service Act. Although I have forgotten the teacher's name, I remember the discussion clearly. He instructed me about the various branches of the armed forces, the Reserves, the National Guard, tours of duty, and other dimensions of military service and noted that he thought that I was "college material." Accordingly, he said that when I finished college, I could join the military as an officer; an Ensign, as I recall, in the Navy and a Second Lieutenant in the Army. He also mentioned something about Officer Candidate School. Then, after his spiel, he inquired about my thoughts. I replied swiftly, telling him that I expected to be a draft dodger. After a moment of stunned silence, he gave me the same "look" I had frequently experienced in school. I suspect that he saw my reaction as merely an expression of adolescent bluster, but in fact it represented my serious anti-military position. Clearly, my longtime rebellious instincts had become fully political by the time I was 16.

I also challenged my high school principal after one of the interminable assemblies that students were compelled to endure. His invited guest was Marine General Victor Krulak, a reputedly legendary military leader who delivered a predictably jingoistic talk that contradicted my vision of American foreign policy. I remained silent during his speech, but approached the principal afterwards. I requested that he schedule a different assembly with another point of view, one with a contrary vision of American foreign and military policy. I offered to suggest some speakers. I will never forget his reply, which is strikingly close to his literal language: "There is no other point of view." I know, after many years as an educator, that there are some thoughtful and intelligent principals, some even my former students, in America's public schools. But not many, in my experience. Most, I believe, are careerist, risk-aversive bureaucrats with minimal vision and even less personal character.

My most dramatic political cause in 12th grade was the Caryl Chessman case, the so-called red-light bandit, whose internationally visible fight against his impending execution in San Quentin's gas chamber evoked powerful passions on both sides of his plight and on the broader issue of the death penalty. I immersed myself in the facts, reading everything I could find out, especially Chessman's own book, *Cell 2455, Death Row*, which he wrote while in prison awaiting execution. Then I also read his three other books, including one not very good novel, *The Kid Was a Killer*, also written during his stay on death row.

71

I had not had such a strong emotional involvement in any issue since the Levittown crisis. I wrote about the case and my reactions in my creative writing class, including a juvenile piece of poetic doggerel that I published in the school paper. I also spoke about the case in class and joined several demonstrations in downtown San Diego calling for a commutation of his death sentence. Then came the fateful day of his execution, May 2, 1960. I knew that a vigil would occur in downtown and I knew that I had to participate.

The day before, I had a sharp confrontation with one of my teachers. I had informed him that I would miss his class because of my commitment to the protest against the Chessman execution. His response was swift and severe, even cruel. He said that I could absolutely not leave the high school campus without permission, and especially for something like a protest demonstration. I told him that I would go anyway and of course I did.

His response was intended to frighten or intimidate me; instead, it only reinforced my will and it actually amused me given its toothless impact. He said that if I left campus without permission, he would give me a "U" for my citizenship grade. He was a man of his word. At the end of the semester, I earned an "A" for my academic performance and an "unsatisfactory" for "citizenship." My feelings at the time, not much different now, were that the teacher was a consummate asshole, merely enforcing the dominant ideological view against a person willing to confront what he thought was illegitimate authority. In fact, I believed I was actually promoting good citizenship by taking part in public political activity. The very notion of a "citizenship" grade struck me as bizarre. Even now, I enjoy telling my students that my "U" from 1960 is a small badge of honor that has had no deleterious impact on anything that I have ever done. But the teacher's stupidity also helped galvanize a deeper critique of educational institutions and their role in underpinning dominant political, social, economic, and legal priorities.

Chessman's execution itself was devastating. His death left me a permanent opponent of capital punishment, although I see some ambiguities and complexities in the issue now. I still think it brutalizes society and is a foolish exercise of collective vengeance. It was hard for me to come to grips with such a stunning political defeat after I had invested so much emotional energy into the battle to save his life. I reserved special venom for Democratic Governor Pat Brown of California, who seemed to exhibit unusual cowardice and vacillation during the Chessman affair.

I graduated from La Jolla High School at 17 and had applied only for admission to San Diego State College. I really considered nowhere else for two major reasons. The first and overriding reason was financial. I couldn't afford to go anywhere outside town and I totally rejected the notion of a loan. My parents' experiences with debt made that prospect emotionally untenable. The last thing I ever wanted was to be saddled with debt. I was resolved not to replicate my parents' experience.

The second reason was that despite my increasing political sophistication (for my age), I had absolutely no understanding of higher education stratification. I knew that Harvard and Yale and a few other colleges and universities were prestigious, but I really only knew of these institutions through football and basketball results. For my family, any college was a huge deal. Coming both from an Eastern European Jewish immigrant and a Holocaust background, college was always touted as *the* route—the path to avoiding the grinding economic hardships of my maternal grandparents and my own parents. San Diego State, accordingly, fit the bill; it was relatively cheap and I could live at home.

Chapter 10
College Days

Summer was relative peaceful. I worked another alienating job making donuts for $1 per hour. Mostly mindless and repetitive, it occupied my time until I had an injury on the job. Hot donut grease from a machinery malfunction spilled into my eye, severely burning my cornea. I almost lost the eye, but quick medical action in the emergency room saved me. The accident raised the owner's insurance rates and, angry at her increased expenses, she fired me.

I filed a claim with the California Labor Commissioner. I actually prepared the case by myself. The owner failed to appear, presumably thinking that a 17 year old kid had no chance. The hearing was reset. When she failed to appear again, I was awarded triple damages, enough to take a road trip with a school friend before school began. This affair increased my interest in becoming a lawyer, especially since my verbal talents were increasing rapidly.

I also followed political events closely during the summer of 1960. The formal process involved the heated Democratic primary battle between John Kennedy and Hubert Humphrey. I felt myself, at that point, a radical and not a liberal. Still, Humphrey seemed a bit more progressive and no one could imagine that he would be the detested pro-war Democratic presidential candidate a mere eight years down the road. The most engaging news continued to be the emerging civil rights struggles in the South. Things were stirring there and I itched to participate. The Chessman case and Levittown before it made me eager to hit the streets, a feeling I still have in my 60s. Agitational politics, confronting illegitimate policies and repressive authority, is emotionally exhilarating. I recognize many of the deeper emotional origins of those feelings, but those origins scarcely diminish the intensity of the feelings and the moral legitimacy of the conduct.

Slightly earlier, while finishing high school, I watched the accounts of the first sit-in demonstrations, which were widely reported in the national print and electronic media. The iconic Woolworth sit-in that four North Carolina Agricultural and Technical College students organized in Greensboro, North Carolina on February 1, 1960, catalyzed a wave of similar protests throughout the South. In conjunction with the Freedom Rides, I was sure that the nation was on the brink of massive change. I wanted to play my part — actually, to continue and augment my part.

The road trip across the country with a high school friend before school began was extremely enjoyable. We dipped into the South and I again saw the repulsive tokens of segregation. We also went back to Pennsylvania and I revisited Levittown, dredging up ambiguous memories of the not so distant past. Generally, we slept in the car to avoid unnecessary expenses and we ate cheaply on the trip. We took my parents' Rambler station wagon. I learned later that they allowed us to use the car so that they could avoid its repossession for not making the payments. This came as no surprise.

I entered San Diego State in September, 1960, as a freshman. The institution had approximately 14,000 students and, from my perspective, a dazzling array of courses. I immediately declared a major in political science. That seemed entirely logical given my strong political interests. I only learned later, actually longer than it should have taken me, that the academic discipline of political science had very little to do with politics. As I discovered in time, in fact, many political "scientists" (I came to regard that designation as entirely silly) were openly hostile to student political activism. Their interests were almost entirely theoretical, save for their own Machiavellian machinations in the institutional affairs of their own campuses.

I also declared my interest in something called "pre-law." Some bureaucrat assigned me to a faculty advisor who looked ancient (he was probably 55, maybe a bit younger). He suggested that I should take accounting. Dutifully, I enrolled in accounting. The first class session involved a balance sheet and homework that absolutely baffled me. I was unable to balance the balance sheet. But that was not the major problem. The topic was money, which provoked a severe and unpleasant emotional reaction. I dropped the course the next day. As it turned out, the advisor's suggestion about the value of accounting for a law school education actually made some sense conceptually, but for me, not psychologically.

I found the first year generally rough. I had rarely been a good student in a formal sense and this new experience brought back some earlier anxieties. I could not figure out how other students managed to do so well. Arrogantly, I thought I was at least as smart, or even smarter. I knew that I was much more informed, especially about the political world. My professors were largely unimpressive, with a few exceptions. The economics instructor, I thought, was senile; it may, again, have been because of my emotional aversion to the subject matter. In any case, he was insufferably dull, with the monotone delivery that millions of college students have properly come to despise for generations.

The introductory course in political science was engaging enough because the professor covered the Nixon/Kennedy election carefully and regularly. He was obviously an ardent Kennedy supporter and I began to see that professors, at least those in the social sciences and the humanities, were part

75

of a liberal orthodoxy. Initially, I found that pleasing. Much later, I came to be extremely critical of that orthodoxy, especially when I discovered that professors were apt to be mostly liberal about the affairs of others, a perspective they all too infrequently applied to their own internal departmental and campus affairs. They always wanted to change the world, but never their departments or their universities.

I recall supporting Kennedy myself in that election, but in a thoroughly lukewarm way (still 17, I was four years away in 1960 from the right to vote). My view reflected my profound disgust for Richard Nixon. I recall that Kennedy had called Martin Luther King's wife Coretta during the campaign after Dr. King had been arrested. But even then, it struck me that this was a calculated act to solicit votes for the Democrats, and that blacks in particular needed to be especially cautious about blind support for the Democratic Party. I was nervous about the whole notion of "lesser evil" politics. I have retained that feeling ever since and have frequently voted my conscience in presidential elections, opting for such leftist icons as Barry Commoner, Benjamin Spock, and Ralph Nader.

I must relate my most wonderful example of juvenile chutzpah in connection with the 1960 presidential election. I learned that Senator Kennedy would visit San Diego and make a major speech. I was curious and decided to attend. But I wanted to do more. I went to the local Democratic Party headquarters the day of his arrival and announced that I was the head of "Youth for Kennedy," a non-existent organization I made up on the spot. I then requested my identification card. Someone typed out my name and I stuck the badge on my shirt. I then proceeded to Lindbergh Field, the airport where the Senator was to land. I walked through what passed as security, with no one stopping or even questioning me. When Kennedy came off his plane, I was in the reception committee, with Governor Pat Brown, the Mayor of San Diego, and several other dignitaries. He shook my hand, mumbling something about "glad to see me." I thought to myself, "What bullshit!" I was on the platform when he delivered his clichéd remarks and I rode in a limo in the motorcade to downtown San Diego. I waved to the crowds on the street. Lots of fun. It could never happen again.

My first political science course was also illuminating in its treatment of the complexities of the formal features of American politics and government. Beyond the structure of the three branches of government, we learned how various interest groups and political parties operated. We also discussed the role of the mass media, setting the basis for my lifelong interest in mass communications in America and elsewhere. This analysis went far beyond what I had learned in high school government class and it fascinated me. It still does, but my experiences the next semester enabled me to place what I learned into a far more sophisticated and radical context.

The most intellectually and personally gratifying feature of my freshman college year was my deepening radicalization. San Diego State, in comparative terms, had a relatively mediocre college library. But for me, it was remarkably liberating. I required little scholarly specialization to pursue what I needed most. The college collections had plenty of material for me to devour. I spent many hours in the stacks, often at the expense of my formal class work and assignments. This was an autodidactic process that I believe has been the most valuable source of my intellectual development. I owe many people major debts for assisting that process, of course, but much of what I know and what I teach has very little to do with what I have learned in my formal educational experiences.

The library resources brought me into further contact with the writings of Karl Marx. I began reading Lenin and then more of the classic socialist theorists. I read substantial labor history. The biggest treasure for me was the stack of bound periodicals. I read through volumes of the *Masses*, the *New Masses*, the *Crisis*, and others, reading stories and essay editorials by some of the seminal figures of 20th century American radicalism. The *Crisis* was especially important. I read scores of essays and editorials by Dr. DuBois. In many of these magazines, I also looked closely at the radical visual imagery. That experience was one of the early foundations for my later scholarly writing and teaching on socially and politically engaged visual art.

One magazine that also caught my early attention was *The American Mercury*, edited for many years by H. L. Mencken. I enjoyed reading Mencken. I liked his acerbic view of people and society. I knew and disliked his conservative politics, but there was something about his underlying view of human nature that appealed to me. That deeper pessimism reflected what I had frequently observed in people and I simply didn't care that it appeared to be at odds with my growing radical political vision. Even now, I still don't really care.

The other great discovery was *The Devil's Dictionary* by Ambrose Bierce. I think I bought it used in the college bookstore. "Bitter Bierce," as he was dubbed, provided marvelously sardonic views of the human condition. He reflected an almost depraved, mordant wit that has appealed to me as long as I can remember. Bierce was an early entry into both literary and visual satire and I have been delighted to infuse that vision into both my teaching and into my daily life.

The one other major intellectual discovery that I began as an early college student, and that I have continued throughout life, is my investigation of the

Holocaust. Clearly reflecting my own family history, I began reading extensive historical accounts, including some now classic histories of Nazi atrocities and the destruction of European Jewry. Equally significant, I began reading memoirs and personal accounts of incarceration in grotesque places like Auschwitz, Buchenwald, Treblinka, and many other concentration and extermination camps. These were difficult to put down and at times I read several of them consecutively. Because I got no information from my father, I found these other sources invaluable. I desperately wanted to know what happened, especially to ordinary Jews caught up in a catastrophe they could barely comprehend. To this day, I feel that I should read one or two personal accounts every year, and I have largely followed through on this internal personal commitment.

I was extremely fortunate, during my second semester of college, to develop one major long term intellectual/personal relationship with a professor. I enrolled in the second class of the year long introductory political science course. I knew nothing about the instructor or his approach. That was common in a large college and it was well before student guides to professors and other informational sources to ease undergraduates into course and instructor selection.

His name was James E. Harmon. In asking around, I discovered that he had earned B.A. and M.A. degrees from San Diego State. His lack of an elite academic pedigree, including a Ph.D., meant absolutely nothing to me at that age. I knew that most professors had Ph.D. degrees, because everyone called them "Doctor." It struck me as a little silly, but I conformed to this feature of academic culture, not realizing that it assumed exaggerated psychological importance in a backwater institution like San Diego State. I discovered too that Harmon had retired from the Navy after 20 years of service. *That* actually gave me some pause, because my anti-military posture was already well established.

From the outset, his course was different. First of all, he had a wicked sense of humor, which few students appeared to pick up. His sardonic asides were terrific, appealing to that side of my consciousness. One example stands out: discussing the unit of government called special districts, like water conservation districts, he told the class that San Diego had created a "communist abatement" district. No one except me laughed. I cannot specifically recall, but he might well have been the person to recommend Ambrose Bierce to me. The deeper revelation, which occurred sometime as I was turning 18, was his inquiry into the economic foundations of political power. This resonated with me especially strongly, since it seemed compatible on many levels with what I had been reading in Marx and other socialist literature.

One other feature of his course made enormous sense. Unlike any other political science class I took subsequently, he discussed private power, especially the huge influence in the United States of major corporations. He noted that corporate power, largely unchecked in the formal political process, had profound and often negative effects on millions of human lives throughout the world. For the first and only time, Jim Harmon turned the discipline of political science into a far more comprehensive inquiry into real sources of power. For the first time, it opened the doors far beyond the realm of formal political processes—parties, branches of government, elections, public administration, and the like.

Harmon also recommended several readings, which I pursued eagerly. I cannot now recall if he was the source of my fascination with radical sociologist C. Wright Mills, who became one of the most enduring intellectual influences of my life. He encouraged my first real critique of both political science in particular and social science in general, a perspective that has permeated my entire intellectual work throughout my academic career.

Harmon's influence did not really radicalize me; that process was already well underway. But his friendship and mentorship, especially in the tough academic and personal times during my undergraduate years, meant a great deal. Throughout his academic life, which he spent subsequently (after finally earning his Ph.D.) at the Imperial Valley campus of San Diego State in Calexico, he made no scholarly waves through research and publication. He had no "visibility" in the conventional ways that academics value. Yet he certainly made a difference to me, and presumably to many other students during his career. Our friendship continued until his death in 2007.

Even as a freshman, I felt that I should become politically active on campus. I decided to start a campus chapter of the American Civil Liberties Union, because I had thought hard about the erosion of basic civil liberties in America during the era of McCarthyism and the continuing saga of congressional investigations. The right-wing character of the San Diego area also contributed to my desire to mobilize a Bill of Rights consciousness on the San Diego State College campus. As a college student, I could already discern the strong military influence in the city and the pervasive hostility to anything progressive, including a spirited defense of civil liberties. Bumper stickers like "Better Dead Than Red" and the like abounded and proto-fascist forces seemed abundant. Local conservatism was starting to irritate me and I knew that, long term, I would eventually leave the place.

I gathered faculty support, a modest list of student members, and assistance from the local and regional ACLU chapters. These efforts made me a fairly visible "liberal" presence on campus. I should hastily add that this was no major accomplishment. San Diego State students in the early

1960s were as apathetic as anywhere in the nation. They seemed perfectly content to party, to work for middling careers, and essentially to echo the uncritical views of their parents and their communities. Like any other college student, I certainly sought recreational opportunities and the usual social activities, including dating. But that was an important sideline to my major intellectual and political focus.

I was fortunate to find a job at the San Diego State Library, which provided flexible hours and enough pay to help alleviate, again, family financial pressure. That economic condition had worsened with the birth of my youngest sister Hannah, born in January, 1961, when I was already in college. The job had another powerful benefit that I had not anticipated when I first accepted it. Sorting and shelving thousands of books gave me extraordinary insights into the breadth of human knowledge. I marveled at how much knowledge really existed. This experience provided me with a serious intellectual road map, encouraging me to imagine how various fields fit together. This inclination first began with Jim Harmon's class when he insisted that politics and economics were inseparable, and that the division of academic life into these fragmented disciplines really made very little sense.

Armed with that revelation at 18, I started thinking about other close relationships. This was the origin of my *interdisciplinary* perspective that has dominated my personal academic career. It also catalyzed my growing contemptuousness for academic boundaries, which still pervade contemporary university life, although they have eroded at the margins. I had no language at the time to express my vision; that would come later, early in my own teaching career.

The April, 1961 Bay of Pigs invasion against Cuba shook me profoundly. I can recall no other students at San Diego State who shared my feelings. Even the liberal faculty I had come to know appeared primarily perturbed that President John Kennedy's invasion plans had failed. Few seem bothered by the fundamental immorality of that invasion and the audacity of the United States to invade, and attempt to overthrow, a sovereign nation because it disapproved of its ideological leanings. This reinforced my growing suspicions about liberalism. My emotions were similar to those I experienced both in Levittown and after the Chessman execution, leading me to conclude that radical opposition politics requires much higher levels of passion than convention political participation.

The paucity of protest activity in San Diego drove me to Los Angeles for some pro-Cuba vigils and demonstrations. I learned about the Fair Play for Cuba Committee and sympathized with its goals. I never joined, but through the group, I was stimulated to read C. Wright Mills' *Listen Yankee* and later other radical critics of American foreign policy, especially William Appelman Williams. I continued to feel extremely supportive of Fidel Castro, Che Guevara, and the entire Cuban revolution. As a postscript, I have visited Cuba twice in late middle age. I remain impressed by many of the revolution's accomplishments, especially in literacy and health care. But its long term disregard for civil liberties and human rights remains troublesome. I have never hesitated, in my adult years, to offer critical comments in left-wing circles.

The end of my first college year brought on a familiar set of crappy jobs: shipping clerk in a beauty supply company and later donut maker again in a neighborhood bakery. The owner, with a perfectly straight face, told me that if I worked hard, perhaps I could one day own a donut shop. Even then, I had viewed the Horatio Alger story with amused contempt; I wanted my dollar an hour and merely nodded when the owner provided me with tales of entrepreneurial inspiration.

I supplemented these gigs with free-lance gardening, cutting grass and performing similar work for several people, including a right-wing retired physician in La Jolla. He constantly informed me of his ludicrous opinions, which seemingly reflected the extreme views of the John Birch Society. With my check, he sometimes gave me Christian religious literature, apparently seeking to save my soul before he departed the world. I remember him as a splendid caricature of himself. My best lawn mowing customer was an older lady who probably had been a Communist Party member or sympathizer. I liked her enormously. She and I talked politics and she would often slip me a few issues of the *I. F. Stone Weekly*.

When I resumed my sophomore year, I was too absorbed in political concerns to pay attention to my academic work and my grades suffered accordingly, slipping from slightly above average to below average. On the whole, that year was the most problematic I had throughout my higher education. Classes, from my vantage point, were more boring than usual. I found myself especially irritated by the relentless process of factual recall. My own habits, rooted in my kindergarten through grade 12 experiences, seemed to emerge again. I sat in class thinking, "this stuff is stupid," and even worse. I turned to my old favorite, Upton Sinclair, and read his scathing critique of higher education, *The Goose Step*. His analysis was superb and its application goes far beyond its time. I have used it for years. But it only increased my personal alienation from the formal curriculum, jeopardizing my academic standing.

The worst experience was an advanced course in race relations, taught by an African American sociologist—my sole black professor as an undergraduate student. I figured this, at least, would be a breeze, given my recent past history and my present passion for civil rights. I have never been so wrong. It is erroneous to call him an "Uncle Tom," but he was extremely uneasy with my racial militancy. He avoided discussions of the current racial battles raging in the South. He discounted my paper on the Levittown crisis by asserting that it had no "scientific" value; he was, after all, a social "scientist." My mediocre grade reflected his view that I had insufficient empirical studies in the body of my text. I never thought of disputing the grade, only what I thought was his political rejection of my views, especially because I quoted Karl Marx and emphasized his analysis. I actually thought it was a good idea to link race and class issues in a Marxist perspective. Most of the class consisted of memorizing study after study from an exceedingly tedious textbook. I had a hard time seeing any connection whatsoever to "race relations." I have taken some delight, in subsequent years, in telling my students that I got a "D" in race relations.

The other curricular absurdity was the required class in public speaking. Some context: I have been an effective speaker for decades, a skill honed in the agitational trenches and perfected in the classroom and in hundreds of public presentations. As a sophomore, I was certainly not the polished speaker I have become, but I was relatively confident, extremely verbal, and definitely not nervous. Moreover I was openly political. My speeches were about censorship and police misconduct. What I, perhaps, lacked in intellectual subtlety, I made up for in passion and in effective style. I got a "C." Again, I couldn't bother to complain. But the instructor was an old (really, this time) reactionary, and I was the victim of the actual conservative political correctness of the era.

One political event dominated my consciousness during my sophomore year at San Diego State. As I recall, a liberal student group called the Committee for Student Action, which I generally supported, wanted to push the limits on the issues of free expression on campus. I liked the idea and had suggested inviting a communist leader. I thought specifically of Dorothy Healey. I didn't know her but I knew people who did. I thought she would have been an excellent choice, as a communist, but also as an internal critic of the Party (I knew because I read the *People's World*).

Alas, the invitee was George Lincoln Rockwell, the leader of the American Nazi Party. That enraged me and probably did more than anything else to galvanize me to recapture my Jewish identity. I was also beginning to think about how to manipulate a crowd. I saw the event simultaneously as an opportunity for emotional catharsis and for social experimentation, but more the former than the latter. I was angry that a Nazi would come—a Nazi whose perverse "heroes" murdered my family and millions of other Jews less than twenty years before. But I was intrigued about getting otherwise passive and apathetic students to join an angry crowd. I had, after all, seen this phenomenon in 1957 in Levittown.

March 8, 1962: I purchased a few dozen eggs and distributed them to several people, firing them up with some emotional rhetoric. Rockwell, speaking to a large audience in the College Open Air Theater, offered his usual demagogic fare: the Holocaust was a fraud, Jews and blacks were inferior, Jews were behind the communist conspiracy, and so forth. Incensed, a Jewish student, Ed Cherry, mounted the stage and landed a punch. I had hoped for such an incident, but was not responsible for it. I immediately joined the fracas by lobbing eggs and encouraging others to do the same. I found it exhilarating, both emotionally because of my hatred for Rockwell and Nazis, and intellectually because I confirmed my prediction of a mini-riot.

The incident generated both local and national media attention. I was brought up on various campus charges before a student tribunal, what I perceived as a kind of bush league kangaroo court. I also managed a television interview with Harold Keen, a leading journalist in San Diego at the time. That was my first media appearance and I discovered that I liked the exposure and that I could handle it effectively.

The tribunal hearings were perfunctory and I was found guilty of whatever infractions I had committed. I wound up with a year of "disciplinary probation" and had to appear before a Dean who solemnly admonished me on my responsibilities as a student. The College, in this era of *in loco parentis*, sent a registered letter to my parents stating, in effect, that it hoped that "Warren" would be good from now on. Its tone was patronizing and I viewed it as absurd—just another trip to the principal's office. Not surprisingly, many "liberal" professors were just as angry at me as the administration. They were, in retrospect, probably correct in their deeper views about free speech, but their specific conduct in "shunning" me (temporarily, as it turned out) reflected an immaturity I would see in abundance throughout my subsequent academic career.

The most durable personal outcome of the Rockwell affair was to make me openly Jewish. Soon I began to read about the tradition beyond the testimonies of concentration camp survivors. Once again, I found that external events, far more than any formal educational process, were responsible for my personal intellectual development.

By the end of my sophomore year, at 19, I was, I felt, a committed political radical. I was at the cusp of the era of 1960s political consciousness nationally and internationally. San Diego was at the far periphery of these developments, but I knew at this point that many other campuses and locales were becoming citadels of political rebellion. I made contact with many local civil rights organizations like the Congress of Racial Equality and radical political groups like the Socialist Workers Party. I know that I attended meetings with Communist Party members and I was always happy to accept their literature. Even then, I was critical enough to know that I would not take my direction from communist leaders like Gus Hall and I found much of the left-wing rhetoric stilted and puerile. Invited to join various groups and front organizations, I always declined. This is a personality issue. I have always been uncomfortable with organizational structures and hierarchy. I'm too much an individualist, probably too narcissistic, to be a good organizational leftist.

Moreover, there was always that fascinating disconnect when I went to meetings. I listened to people talk about the "working class" in disturbingly romanticized ways. These comments often came from seasoned political veterans of labor battles from the 30s. I respected them and their histories. I admired the notion of revolution. But more deeply, I never really believed it, and I still don't. I had seen too many working class people succumb to racism and fascism all too easily. I sometimes made sardonic comments about "the people," which evoked censorious looks and comments in return. I have continued this sardonic streak throughout my life, drawing inspiration from Mencken, Bierce, Swift, Schopenhauer, Nietzsche, and Freud, whose pessimistic views on the human condition resonated strongly with me. I have long wanted a socialist transformation of society, but my view has been that people will continue to do what they have always done throughout history.

The other major disconnect was between my personal intellectual development and my academic performance. The gap was growing and frustrating. Another talk with Jim Harmon at the start of my junior year at San Diego State turned everything around dramatically. He told me to "stop fighting the classes." He said that I was wasting my energy and that all I had to do was to figure out what the professors wanted and feed it right back to them. His personal anecdote was revealing. He told me that when he was frustrated with the absurdity of course assignments, he wrote two papers; one for the professor and one for himself. They were radically different, but they satisfied his formal requirements *and* his emotional and intellectual needs. He told me that I could do the same, although I need not go to his lengths to get similar results. Perceptively, he remarked that San Diego State professors were not very difficult to figure out.

Harmon gave me a concrete example for an upper division course I had just decided to take. He said that he had had that professor a few years back, and he remembered that the man essentially worshipped Yale political scientist Robert Dahl. So he advised me to look at Dahl's work and bring it in to my own course work, either in papers or in examination answers.

It worked like the proverbial charm. I checked out Dahl's publications, found them rather interesting, and incorporated them into the course assignments. Voila! An easy "A." With Jim Harmon's encouragement, and sometimes his specific tips, I did this in all my classes, especially in the social sciences. It was astonishingly easy and it left me a huge amount of time, as Jim predicted, to do my own reading and my own political activism.

My strategy was amazingly simple. Dissertation Abstracts gave me a sense of what my professors had done as well as their intellectual biases. I also picked up the specific vocabulary words ("poli sci" speak or "soc" speak) they liked. Then I added a little liberal orthodoxy, and all of a sudden, I became an academic star. It was cynical and it served me well. It also promoted an enduring skepticism about the entire academic enterprise.

Some classes, to be sure, had more authentic intellectual challenges. The year-long history of political theory became a major academic adventure and I did especially well because the subject matter fascinated me from start to finish. I was enthralled with the Greek political philosophers, especially Plato and Aristotle, and have used them throughout my teaching career. Later, my introduction to Machiavelli and Hobbes provided the basis for a long senior thesis I would write the following year. I wanted to add Marx, but as late as 1963/64, this was still somewhat touchy in the academy, at least at a place like San Diego State.

Most significant for me personally, the study of political theory opened the door to investigate some of the classics of Jewish thought. I found a book called, *Great Ages and Ideas of the Jewish People*, which allowed me to link Jewish thought with the Western political classics I was studying. I have since gone much beyond that initial effort, but like *Inside U.S.A.* earlier, it catalyzed a durable commitment to discovering a heritage largely denied me during childhood. I also began reading about anti-Semitism and I recall Sartre's *Anti-Semite and Jew*. It started me on the path to view *all* racism as linked and therefore worth determined resistance.

One other junior year class had a profound effect, more for its pedagogy than for its content. I had to repeat introductory biology because I had failed the course the previous academic year because I was too engaged in politics and too bored with the factual minutiae of the course. The new biology class was different from anything I had ever encountered. The professor gave students three choices: a "C" test, a "B" test," and an "A" test. For the first two, he required substantial factual knowledge of biology, with the "B" test requiring proportionately more. But the "A" test was more conceptual and philosophical, demanding knowledge of evolution and the linkage of biology

85

to broader social problems like population, the environment, and even war and peace. What a stunning approach! The resulting motivation was spectacular, propelling me to examine Darwin, and to develop an appreciation of science as a mode of inquiry instead of a random collection of facts. Office hour discussions gave me a deeper appreciation of his educational vision. It reinforced my hope that that formal education actually *could* be engaging, despite the overwhelming lack of evidence in my personal experience.

Curiously, little of my university experience led me to art history, a major focus of my teaching and research since the early 1970s. I went by myself to Balboa Park's museums and enjoyed the visual art there. I also perused art books, but it was only later that I saw artworks as part of the broader panorama of intellectual history that I had begun exploring.

The major political event of 1962 was the Cuban Missile Crisis in October. Like millions of others, I felt that this confrontation with the Soviet Union was the closest we had come to a nuclear war since Hiroshima and Nagasaki in 1945. Like people all over the globe, I was terrified as Soviet ships sailed toward Cuba and the American naval blockade. I saw President John Kennedy as a reckless warmonger whose actions threatened the very survival of the human species. I joined some small protests in downtown San Diego against the blockade. There I experienced some public hostility for opposing American policy, which I would see again on a much grander scale a few years later in opposing the war in Vietnam. I was relieved when Soviet leader Nikita Khrushchev backed down. I believed that his actions, couched in the language of diplomatic compromise and agreement, saved the world.

The crisis also left me with a permanently critical view of John Kennedy, later exacerbated during the civil rights struggle. I have often articulated this view as a university teacher, sometimes puzzling students whose view of John Kennedy is a simplistic Camelot vision fostered in various media and educational accounts they have encountered.

Chapter 11
Civil Rights Activism: My Most Enduring Political Commitment

By my junior year in college, I recognized that of all my political commitments, the developing civil rights movement in the United States exerted the most powerful emotional impact upon me. This was, in large part, related to my growing sense of Jewish identity. Even my father, despite his longtime ambivalence about his own Jewishness, often noted that the Nazi persecution of Jews was similar to American racism. That connection made perfect sense to me. It must have been influential, explicitly or implicitly, to many or even most of the young Jewish activists with whom I struggled in various civil rights activities over the next few years. I have come to hope that my specific work against racism, which has continued in my professional activities in both teaching and research, is the finest and most enduring consequence of second generation Holocaust survivorship.

I had paid extremely close attention to Southern civil rights developments during my first two years as a college student. The television age made it especially easy to track every major twist and turn in that struggle. For example, I closely followed the University of Mississippi integration battle centered on James Meredith's 1962 attempt to gain admission to that bastion of segregated higher education. I came to despise Mississippi Governor Ross Barnett and the white Southerners who rioted against the federal legal order to admit Meredith and the federal troops sent to enforce that order. They reminded me, of course, of the same racists I had encountered in Levittown in 1957. It generated the same emotional reactions and underscored my growing sense that I needed to be part of this expanding moral crusade. The Oxford, Mississippi events also increased my distaste of President Kennedy for his vacillation in this crisis, a view commonly shared among civil rights activists I knew.

Focusing on my civil rights work and its permanent consequences for my consciousness and my work has been, curiously, the most difficult part of this memoir to write. Despite my extremely strong memory, it remains impossible to reconstruct every planning meeting, every demonstration, and every confrontation with police and other upholders of white supremacy in San Diego, Atlanta, New Orleans, Phoenix, Los Angeles, San Francisco, Oakland, and elsewhere from 1962 to 1964 and beyond. After each demonstration, moreover, it was traditional to gather and sing "We Shall Overcome," linking hands in solidarity. Deeply, unforgettably emotional, this occurred scores of times, but it also further blurred the specificity of my recollections. The activities were intense, often daily, and things are, after the passage of more than 45 years, still hazy in their specific details. I have struggled with both primary and secondary civil rights materials sources in depth and I am still maddeningly unsure about the precise sequence of my civil rights activities, especially those that took place in the South.

A major point that I have made for years to my students bears repeating here. Few of us who were so thoroughly committed to the movement kept diaries or made detailed (or any) notes about our daily efforts. We were simply too engaged in the struggle. Moreover, at 19 or 20 or so, we had no real notion of such documents as valuable future historical sources. Indeed, I suspect that most young people have little deeper general historical consciousness, although most of us in the civil rights movement had some sense that we were making history with our protests. But at the time, we were truly living in the moment.

My civil rights activities were different from my other political involvements in several ways. Above all, they were scattered in several geographical regions. The Levittown affair, conversely, was concentrated in one place and I have specific documents on which to rely, like my trial transcript and various newspaper accounts. The Chessman case, similarly, occurred while I was in high school and I still have his books and my specific memories of my actions in San Diego. The UC Berkeley Free Speech Movement during Fall Semester 1964 was also confined to a singular time and place and was heavily documented. And so on and on.

Fortunately, some specific historical markers facilitate my task of autobiographical reconstruction. I attended the historic March on Washington on August 28, 1963, making it easier to locate some of my activities before and after that majestic event. On March 30, 1964, an officer from the Arizona Highway Patrol punched me in the face during a massive demonstration outside the Arizona State Capitol building. That date was my 21st birthday: extremely memorable. I'm sure that I could also access dental records following the loss of two of my teeth from that event, but that would involve far too much physical detail and bring back memories I thoroughly wish to keep submerged. On June 26, 1964, I was arrested at the main branch of the Bank of America in San Diego and charged with three misdemeanors. That too is unforgettable. I know that I am omitting some dramatic events, particularly those involving unpleasant contact with racist police officers, especially in the South, because I cannot recall their times and the places that they happened.

What follows is my best reconstruction of my multifaceted civil rights activities. I found that I had plenty of time for these efforts because I had finally figured out how to do well — exceptionally well — in school and I was becoming especially strong in time management skills. The movement work also got me away from mounting family troubles, mostly financial, and facilitated my growing personal independence. My most important goal here must be to convey the flavor and intensity of my activities and their extraordinary impact on my life. After all, there are many outstanding scholarly accounts of the civil rights movement; this effort adds but one more set of personal experiences and observations even in the absence of full chronological accuracy.

In all my classes and presentations on my civil rights efforts over the years, I make one point explicit at the outset. I always acknowledge that while thousands of white students and other volunteers, including me, deserve credit for our work, we were really supporting actors in a much broader moral struggle. I mean no rhetorical false modesty with this assertion. We encountered real dangers and some volunteers suffered serious injuries. Tragically, some died.

But the real heroes of the modern civil rights movement were the ordinary African Americans, especially in the south, who put their entire lives on the line. They often paid dearly for their courage. We from the north and the west could, and did, go back to relatively privileged and safe homes or college campuses, without fear of the Ku Klux Klan and retribution from local employers and other racist operatives. These ordinary black citizens of Georgia, Alabama, Mississippi, and Louisiana had little option other than to stay where they were and deal with the consequences of their activism. Unlike the nationally-known leaders, they had little or no opportunity to respond to police brutality and economic retaliation. When reporters and television cameras left the scene, they were on their own.

Some of these ordinary people, fortunately, have had some historical exposure through such brilliant films as Henry Hampton's iconic "Eyes on the Prize" series. Even before I accelerated my activity, I knew of Mose Wright, the uncle of Emmett Till, who testified against his nephew's killers in 1955 and Elizabeth Eckford, the young African American teenager who braved the mobs in Little Rock in 1957 as she tried to enroll in school. They reminded me of Bill and Daisy Myers and their children in Levittown. Later, I saw the same thing with the black children who were fire hosed in Birmingham, black sharecroppers who dared to register to vote in Mississippi, and black New Orleans residents who marched on picket lines against stores that refused to employ them. These were the kinds of people I usually sought out for conversations during my most vigorous activism. My only regret is that I seldom got their names and can only vaguely recall some of the outlines of their stories so many years later.

My civil rights activity stemmed from my growing recognition—and anger—of the impact of segregation on African Americans. This system of American apartheid, formal and legally mandated in the South and informal throughout much of the rest of the country, branded people with darker skin as inferior second class citizens. The inevitable result was a powerful sense of humiliation and degradation, a feeling that one's worth as a human being was deeply and irreparably devalued. Beyond the obvious and pernicious social, political and economic consequences of this discriminatory arrangement, the deepest impact was psychological, a profound and destructive diminution of a sense of self. Many blacks, having been treated so poorly, even came to see themselves as deserving of this mistreatment. Paul Robeson had called it a racial inferiority complex and argued that only militant political action could restore a sense of racial dignity and pride to the African American population.

Even at a young age, I had read extensively, as I earlier noted, about this phenomenon. John Gunther's *Inside U.S.A.* had a revealing chapter entitled "Negro in the Woodpile," which I devoured several times during the Levittown crisis. Its most compelling feature chronicled the hypothetical daily humiliations of an African American professor at Atlanta University during the Jim Crow era: in a hotel, he would have to take the freight elevator; in a train, he would sit uncomfortably in a decrepit wooden car; he would drink at an unsanitary "colored" water fountain or use the "colored" toilet, even in a state or local office building; he would give the right of way to whites on public sidewalks; he could not try on a pair of gloves or a hat in a white store; his children could not go to any state university in the entire South; and on and on.

Gunther's book directed me to other, more scholarly sources, about the impact of segregation on African Americans, especially Gunner Myrdal's 1944 iconic *An American Dilemma*, which I also read carefully. But these personal stories gripped me much more than the more historical and analytical treatments (they still do, but I always advise students to seek solid primary and secondary sources). I had heard such stories often throughout the Levittown ordeal, especially from the African American supporters of the Myers whom I met at home and elsewhere. The accounts of their encounters with segregated public facilities were chilling reminders of racial injustice in America, giving me a broader context for the specific fight against racist housing in Levittown and later for my civil rights activism during the 1960s. They have also stayed with me throughout my life and have inflenced my teaching throughout my professional career.

Their experiences mirrored those of the hypothetical Atlanta university professor, and they were just as likely experienced in the North: refusals of entry to hotels and restaurants; long delays and discourteous service in "respectable" department stores and comparable retail outlets; discriminatory treatment, overtly and covertly, by teachers and administrators at every level of the educational process; and perhaps above all, abusive language including traditional racist invective like "coon," "boogie," "jigaboo," and, all too frequently, "nigger" itself. All of this and more reflect the historical legacy of slavery and its direct progeny, segregation. Heroic African American responses to these disgraceful historical realities have powerfully impacted my consciousness and my subsequent political and professional life.

My key focus in college at San Diego involved working with the local chapter of the Congress of Racial Equality (CORE). A relatively small group, it was led by schoolteacher Hal Brown, who later became a university level educator and administrator. CORE was based in the black community of Logan Heights and drew support from some professionals and very few students, mostly people I knew at San Diego State College. We targeted several local businesses for a variety of discriminatory practices. One early focus was the San Diego real estate industry, for me an inviting object of protest because of my emotional connection to race and residential issues.

These examples of racial bias were typical for this industry, especially its failure to sell property to qualified African American buyers and its strong complicity in generating and perpetuating residential apartheid. Without having conducted extensive research, my impression is that people in real estate have hardly been at the forefront of the struggle for racial justice in America. CORE organized some picket lines around real estate offices and even some brief sit-in demonstrations. I liked the sit-ins the best. They went beyond the polite protests with signs, mimeographed leaflets and other documents to distribute to onlookers and patrons. It felt, finally, like we were, however modestly, emulating the activities of the black students and their supporters in the South. We sat quietly, without chanting or displaying any truculence whatever.

And it was exciting! I recall the adrenalin flowing as real estate office staff locked doors and made frenetic phone calls and disappeared furtively into back rooms. Police came, but merely observed. In a relatively short time, we exited in a dignified way. A few of us engaged in some "guerrilla" actions on our own, without organizational sanction, occupying individual real estate offices and displaying homemade signs. A word about the emotional gratification of these efforts: it did generate a sense of exhilaration, which I experienced often in the civil rights movement. It was fun to bond with fellow demonstrators in common cause. None of these feelings in any way negated the powerful moral commitment of the demonstrators. "Mature" adults who cavalierly dismissed young protestors as merely political versions of earlier college "panty raiders" or as mere thrill seekers fundamentally missed the point.

CORE also targeted some commercial establishments in the San Diego area, including some local supermarkets and Montgomery Ward. In each case, we had substantial evidence of discriminatory hiring policies. Their records were typical; they had black custodial workers, but few or no managerial staff from minority communities. In most cases, these firms also had no black customer service employees at all. Little of the official CORE action was particularly provocative, but again there was some independent "guerrilla" activity I participated in, even fomented. We went to Montgomery Ward, for example, conspicuously wearing CORE "Freedom Now" buttons. We took out tape measures and measured the front entrances, suggesting that we were doing advance logistic planning for imminent sit-in demonstrations. No one in CORE told us to do this, but no one told us not to do it either, and we were certainly not quiet about the activity.

Chapter 12
The South and More

Civil rights activism in San Diego was personally and politically gratifying. I continued my efforts there until I left for Berkeley in 1964 and my subsequent civil rights activism had permanent consequences for the rest of my life. My personal intensity permitted me to feel that I was a part of the national movement, even in this conservative bastion where our activity had no media coverage nationally or even locally. I knew that the major action was in the South and I was determined to be a part of it. Sometime following my junior year in college, in summer 1963 — I cannot recall precisely when — I made plans to drive south.

I went with a friend with whom I have long lost contact. He had a small inheritance and had a new car, making an auto trip a feasible option, especially for young people accustomed to furious non-stop driving with minimal sleep and fast food. I was clearly the more knowledgeable and politically savvy partner, especially on issues of black history and the intricacies of the civil rights struggles.

Our initial goal was the March on Washington (M.O.W.). That monumental event was well publicized months in advance and I was determined to participate. We arrived in Washington several days in advance, staying in housing in the black community that M.O.W. organizers had arranged. In fact, after getting settled, we returned to those headquarters and volunteered to work. My assignment, as I recall, was to help others find temporary shelter before the march. This was a simple enough task, but it was also hugely important. Mostly it involved making phone calls to local residents, asking whether they could put up a few people from Philly or New York for a day or two. Other people had to secure water, arrange for portable toilets, and perform the myriad logistic tasks without which this historic event could never have been the stupendous success it turned out to be. Bayard Rustin, one of the great organizers and agitators of American history, directed the entire production. His contributions, I believe, are still insufficiently acknowledged. But without his army of volunteers, it could not have happened. As a university teacher, I always emphasize that social protest depends on rigorous, competent behind-the-scenes work — the stuff we never see on television.

The day of the march was memorable for all 250,000 or so participants. August 28, 1963 will always be a touchstone event in their lives. If I have forgotten some of the details of my civil rights work, I can never forget that magnificent day. The spirit was infectious and exhilarating. The music was

93

inspirational: Joan Baez, Bob Dylan, Peter, Paul & Mary, Odetta, the SNCC Freedom Singers, and Josh White! These were, and remain, my favorites. Their fusion of music and their socially conscious lyrics have kept me marginally sane for decades.

The oratory was spectacular. Even the actors were wonderful. Seeing Ossie Davis and Ruby Dee speak from the stage was an astounding experience. The opening speech from A. Phillip Randolph was especially moving. I knew and admired his long work in the Brotherhood of Sleeping Car Porters and I had read of his earlier March on Washington movement in 1941. And what a magnificent orator he was. He had a tall and dignified presence, impelling me to underscore his life and work throughout my career. There also came a moment that sweltering August morning that will haunt me forever. NAACP Executive Secretary Roy Wilkins announced that Dr. W. E. B. DuBois had died in Ghana the day before. I saw thousands of people around me stand for a moment or two in silence, remembering one of the giants of American letters and social action. I grew up knowing about Dr. DuBois, and I shared that emotion.

Everyone remembers Martin Luther King's brilliant "I Have A Dream" speech. Its power and its sheer eloquence are impossible to describe. To have been there in person to hear it is one of the privileges of a lifetime. I have used it dozens of times in my teaching. I have never tired of hearing it and I have always had the same extremely powerful emotional reactions to it each time I show it in class.

The end of the march is where my memory plays tricks. I think we went briefly to New York before heading south, but I cannot be certain. It is even possible that we went south before heading to the March on Washington. So I'll just go again with Kurt Vonnegut: so it goes. Eventually, we arrived in Atlanta and headed immediately to the headquarters of the Student Non-Violent Coordinating Committee.

We knew that SNCC was the most radical and most youthful of the contemporary civil rights organizations. I knew all about Ella Baker, her work and leadership with the Southern Christian Leadership Conference, and how she helped form SNCC, serving as the "godmother" of that organization. I admired Dr. King and deeply respected the legal and other efforts of the NAACP. But I wanted front-line action, and SNCC was the group that most fit my radical perspective.

I remember the buzz of excitement in the SNCC office. I saw and spoke with some people who became iconic civil rights and political figures, especially Executive Secretary James Forman and Julian Bond, who worked as communication director and *de facto* office manager when I was in Atlanta. It's possible that other SNCC leaders like Bob Moses, Stokely Carmichael, and John Lewis floated in and out of the office, but I don't recall seeing any of these men. Their names, of course, were constantly mentioned and I certainly knew of their exploits and reputations.

More memorably, I talked with many ordinary volunteers, mostly young students from the group of historically black colleges in Atlanta and some high school students who joined their counterparts from throughout the south. Many were deeply religious. Their civil rights commitment reflected their own Christian beliefs. Despite my own personal atheism, I came to respect these people enormously. I have continued that respect with many others in the African American community who combine strong religious passions with a powerful sense of social justice. There were also some white volunteers in SNCC, but I had little more than perfunctory contact with them at the time.

Our immediate reaction on arriving was to ask, "Where's the action?" That reflected our desire to hit the streets at once, a baptism-by-fire experience. The official response, probably from SNCC director Jim Forman himself, was, in paraphrase, "Whoa, You don't just show up and join the action. You need to get situated and get trained in nonviolence." Forman seemed extremely impressive. Several years older than anyone else there, he exuded a strong adult presence. He was also exceptionally friendly, welcoming anyone who cared to join the struggle. I followed his career closely after our initial contact, and sympathized with his efforts in the Black Panther Party and other militant groups until his death in 2005.

We stayed early on with Professor Harry Steinmetz, a Jewish radical professor who taught psychology at one of the local black colleges. I had heard of Steinmetz and was eager to talk with him. He proved to be a veritable gold mine of information, resonating especially with my personal background and interests. His story was both fascinating and horrific. He had been a professor of psychology at San Diego State College from 1930 to 1954, when he was fired for "insubordination." In fact, he was the victim of a right-wing red hunt during the worst days of cold war McCarthyism. A longtime leftist activist, Steinmetz had run unsuccessfully for office and had frequently been an outspoken advocate for progressive policies—all in his capacity as a private citizen. When he related this information, I immediately realized that his efforts were all protected under the First Amendment. But in the early 1950s, and especially in San Diego, this meant nothing.

Steinmetz told us how the American Legion, the San Diego Union, and local ultra conservative legislators conducted a vendetta against him. Like many other radicals of the era, he was summoned before the House Un-American Activities Committee, where he was courageously uncooperative. All of this converged to doom him at the college, especially with a hostile San

Diego State President, Malcolm Love (the same unimpressive president I had during my student days there). After his dismissal, he drifted from job to job, landing finally in Georgia. Meeting him was an unexpected intellectual fringe benefit. It deepened my knowledge of that troubled period of history, which had also tangentially affected my family. Above all, it revealed the extraordinary value of finding first-hand historical accounts, a principle I have passed on to generations of my own university students.

At the SNCC office, we received some informal instruction about nonviolence. This consisted largely of modest role-playing activities, which I had seen in even more detail in films in San Diego. Most important, it was made explicitly clear that we had to respond nonviolently to any provocations and that we would inevitably encounter such provocations from local racists. That message was repeated strongly. SNCC had a legitimate reputation to preserve and the last thing it needed was to have any of its demonstrators depart from the focus that provided its huge moral stature throughout the nation. Its nonviolent reactions and the remarkable dignity and self-restraint of its adherents were legendary. Although I am quick-tempered and impatient, I agreed with that stance completely.

At the same time, the entire issue of nonviolence was a ubiquitous topic of discussion and debate in the office and elsewhere among the young people I met in the movement. Who could not admire Dr. Martin Luther King? Still, many people argued about whether nonviolence should be a way of life or merely an effective strategy at a given time. Many of my discussions on my first trip south focused around the latter position. Several African American college students argued that nonviolence worked and therefore we should use it. They maintained, correctly, that images of demonstrators *not* fighting back when attacked were unusually powerful in the media, especially on television. Several also claimed that they were not committed to pacifism as a personal philosophy and that they could imagine many cases where violence would be both effective and morally acceptable.

I agreed then, and it remains my position now. I have often promoted this debate in my own classes, frequently generating robust disagreement with my anti-pacifist position. I don't specifically remember when I began focusing on Malcolm X and his advocacy of the legitimacy of defensive violence. I do remember, however, reading *Negroes With Guns* by Robert Williams when it first appeared a year earlier. Williams told the story of his resistance against the Klan in Monroe, North Carolina and the necessity of armed black self-defense. My earlier knowledge of slave revolts made me doubt Dr. King's total embrace of non-violence, but I was, at the same time, fully committed to it in my work with SNCC and CORE.

The first action I recall was classic: desegregating a southern restaurant. Here, ample documentation exists. I have also been fortunate enough to draw on both printed sources and one brief conversation with Julian Bond. The restaurant was called "Charlie Leb's," owned and run by a Jewish restaurateur. I had heard, either in the SNCC office or at the picket line outside the establishment, that the Klan had called Leb "the only good Jew in Georgia," a vision that increased my personal furor. I felt that Charlie Leb, like William Levitt before him, was betraying everything that the Jewish tradition should uphold. I ruminated that it was still less than 20 years since my grandparents, aunt, and uncle had been gassed in Auschwitz. Once again, the Holocaust joined my participation in the civil rights movement.

Mostly, I remember picketing peacefully outside the restaurant. Many civil rights demonstrators were arrested and jailed, but not me. There were many verbal responses from racist whites, some directed at me including "race traitor" and the all too familiar "nigger lover." I had become very used to such taunts and it was easy to ignore them. The Atlanta Police department was out in force, regularly shoving protestors, often roughly. Then I got hit with a billy club, fortunately a glancing blow that barely hurt. It came from a black cop.

My best memories remain the informal conversations with young black protestors. Their idealism and fierce determination to change the old Jim Crow patterns were inspirational and reinforced my own desire to continue my participation. One striking memory involved their deliberate challenge to some of the most overt forms of racial humiliation. I often saw them drink openly from water fountains marked "white" and, following suit, I took a few sips from fountains marked "colored."

Returning to San Diego, I began my senior year in college, 1963 to 1964. It was crucial in my political life, and in my subsequent decision to seek an academic career, for me to finish college. By then, my courses were a breeze, thanks to Jim Harmon, because I had everything all figured out. My academic turnaround had been dramatic. I had become a bit of a star in political science and I could essentially call the shots. Several of my professors implored me to seek graduate training in the discipline and I gave it very serious consideration. Like many student activists of the time (and now), I was torn between academic work (a Ph.D.) and an activist approach (a law degree — or so I imagined). I wound up applying for both options, I recall, figuring that I would decide later. These professors had specific contacts at Berkeley and eagerly recommended that I apply there. That advice coincided with my desires, especially given the growing activist political reputation of Berkeley students. More troubling, a few professors told me that I was coming to the point in my life where I had to make some fundamental choices, especially between scholarship and activism. I have always found that view obnoxious and insulting.

The most traumatic event of fall semester, 1963, was the assassination of President Kennedy on November 22. Like everyone else, I remember precisely where I was when I heard the news. I was on campus and was shocked when fellow students began buzzing about the horrific events in Dallas. I was transfixed with the 24-hour television coverage, including the live coverage of Jack Ruby's murder of Lee Harvey Oswald two days later. No fan of the martyred President, I joined everyone else in decrying such grotesque political violence. Almost immediately, I began worrying about Lyndon Johnson. My fears turned out to be correct, but for different reasons, as I found out very soon during the escalation of the war in Vietnam. All that noted, it's important to add this: for all the shock of the Kennedy assassination (and I was never a zealous follower of conspiracy theories about it), the killings of Medgar Evers, Malcolm X, and Martin Luther King hit me in the gut far more powerfully, reflecting the deeper passions of my youthful political consciousness. Over the years, I have heard similar reactions from other civil rights movement veterans.

Violence against civil rights activists in the south generally concerned me closely, although like most young people, I was largely oblivious to the possibility of personal physical danger. I understood on some abstract level that it was always a serious threat, but my sense of commitment to the struggle overcame any real fear about adverse consequences. Later, of course, I learned that my parents were far more concerned about my safety even while fully supporting my actions in San Diego and in the south.

Throughout the modern civil rights movement, it was impossible to ignore the beating and killing of anti-racist activists. The most dramatic examples commanded national and international media attention. Even before my own forays into the south, I had paid close attention to the horrific violence that both racist mobs and police officials directed against civil rights workers. I vividly remember the Freedom Riders in 1961 who bravely challenged segregated waiting rooms in bus stations. They were beaten and jailed, and riders often suffered severe personal injuries. In my teaching, I have frequently used a dramatic photograph from Anniston, Alabama in 1961, where a white mob attacked Freedom riders with baseball bats and pipes and burned their Greyhound bus to a shell.

I had already begun working in the south when Birmingham, Alabama Public Safety Commissioner Eugene "Bull" Connor shocked the civilized world by ordering his officers to attack children with vicious police dogs and high-powered fire hoses. Two years later, an equally brutal Sheriff Jim Clark of Dallas County, Alabama was responsible for the violent arrests of civil rights demonstrators during the historic marches from Selma to Montgomery. His officers also joined Alabama state troopers in attacking protestors with horses, clubs, and tear gas at the Edmund Pettis Bridge, known as "Bloody Sunday." Almost every major history of the civil rights movement properly records these infamous events.

Even more ominous were the murders. Probably the most notorious were the 1964 killings of the three SNCC workers, James Chaney, Andrew Goodman, and Michael Schwerner, in Mississippi, to which I allude later in this memoir. Other murders at that general time, perhaps less well remembered in the early 21st century, are nevertheless significant parts of the tapestry of American domestic violence of that era. The martyrdom of Reverend James Reeb, a white Unitarian minister, attracted extensive media attention in March, 1965, when he and two colleagues in the movement were attacked in Selma and beaten by a group of white male racists. Rev. Reeb died of his injuries two days later. This egregious act and Dr. Martin Luther King's eulogy of the fallen civil rights activist helped galvanize national support for the passage of the federal Voting Rights Act. Significantly, it took the murder of a white volunteer like Rev. Reeb to catalyze this political action, even though an African American hospital worker, Jimmie Lee Jackson, had been murdered by police only two weeks earlier in nearby Marion, Alabama.

Another notable murder of a courageous white civil rights activist also occurred in March 1965 in Alabama. KKK members attacked Viola Liuzzo, a Michigan mother of five children, after the historic Selma March. Driving with a young African American—always a dangerous activity during the civil rights movement in the South—the Klansmen pulled alongside the car and opened fire, killing her instantly. Her companion luckily escaped injury. This case also generated massive publicity and contributed to the growing national mood that federal legislation was necessary to alleviate the injustices of segregation, including the incessant violence directed against African Americans and their supporters throughout the Southern states.

These and other acts were the more visible examples of violence directed against civil rights activists. Beyond these examples, however, were the daily instances of violence that went unrecorded in the media, but were no less traumatic to the victims. Every day, civil rights workers were subjected to petty harassment and physical violence from police officers and others. All too often, sit-in demonstrators, voting registration volunteers, picketers, and even civil rights office staff and logistics personnel were verbally abused, struck with fists and batons, arrested on phony charges, and subject to multiple other forms of indignities and worse. Thousands sustained injuries, many painful and some permanent. A huge specter of violence hovered over the movement, a recurring expression of the domestic terrorism that dominated the southern landscape since the end of Reconstruction. Anyone who participated during that time carries lifetime memories of this terrifying reality.

My personal life grew more complicated during that time. Again, my father's ill-conceived business ventures (another failed construction company) placed the family in severe financial peril. My parents, with my younger siblings, prepared to move to Berkeley, hoping for better opportunities. Because I was so close to graduation, I remained behind, staying at times with friends and living in a series of dumps near the San Diego State campus. The latter sometimes gave me good lessons in applied entomology.

I also dated regularly, adding a decent social life to my hectic academic and political activities. I could manage it all because of my high energy level, perhaps bordering on manic at the time. By the end of 1963 or so, I met Sherry Lee Phillips, a fellow student at the college. This developed into a genuinely serious relationship. Although it later ended badly (but fortunately as well), it became the most stable feature of my life at the time. Sometimes, after a hard day of classes, studying, and organizing or demonstrating, I would head to her place and spend the night.

Following the fall semester, I made plans to return south in January 1964 to resume my civil rights activities. I remember telling some of my college teachers that I would be returning to the movement down South. Good liberals all, they expressed admiration and support. In one instance, I even took a prospective assignment for a major political science paper, which I wrote in longhand and mailed back to San Diego State from SNCC headquarters.

In Atlanta, I reconnected with some of the SNCC people I had earlier met there. I think that we returned to Charlie Leb's restaurant for a reprise of the previous summer's demonstrations. This time, comedian Dick Gregory joined us, adding both gravitas and levity to our efforts. One "highlight" of these protests was the appearance of the Ku Klux Klan, fully bedecked in their traditional and ridiculous garb of bed sheets and pointy hats. Some of the Klansmen had long flashlights, which they occasionally used to strike SNCC demonstrators. But by 1964, the old Klan had lost its fearsome quality. While we were marching, we began chanting, "The KKK, it ain't what it used to be." That was especially gratifying, a perfectly nonviolent but aggressive response to America's oldest domestic terrorist organization.

We also attended the trials of Dick Gregory and other protestors in Atlanta's Fulton County Courthouse. SNCC supporters packed the courtroom, generating occasional angry admonishments from the Judge, a

100

man whose last name I recall was "Little," an accidental but accurate reflection of his mental and moral stature. The spectacle was predictably ridiculous. The SNCC lawyer was Howard Moore, one of the few black lawyers practicing in Georgia. Once again, I felt admiration for a "movement" attorney. My best memory was when Gregory was on the stand, being examined by the prosecutor (whom Judge Little referred to as "Colonel," apparently an endearing Southern appellation). Gregory was asked when he was arrested. He replied that he had not been arrested, but rather had been "abducted." That hilarious, mocking response, a splendid verbal form of resistance, again generated another angry judicial response. I thought, as I have so many thousands of times throughout my life, "what a schmuck!"

The drive back to San Diego was eventful. I know that we stopped in Alabama, but cannot recall the specific details or sequence. In Gadsden, a tough segregationist bastion, a large racist cop, during a modest demonstration, replied to my comment that we had a First Amendment right to protest by saying something like, "Boy, we ain't got no First Amendment down here and you better get yo' ass outta Alabama." We stayed in an African American residence in Birmingham, known widely as "Bombingham," for a night, spending a few hours awake, guarding against bomb threats toward the owners.

Somewhere else in Alabama, the Highway Patrol stopped and searched our car. We clearly looked different from ordinary Southern white teenagers and California plates were themselves a suspicious sign. When the officer found SNCC buttons and literature, he called for backup and several more patrol cars arrived immediately. We were detained for a few hours, because we "matched the description of some armed robbers." I have been many things, but never an armed robber. My mechanical incompetence is legendary. Guns and I don't go together. I value all my body parts.

I believe that our next stop was New Orleans, but it's possible that this experience occurred the previous year. But in any case, the events were similarly dramatic. In that majestic city, we joined the demonstrations on historic Canal Street. These efforts were similarly classic: picketing with signs directed to black consumers, asking them not to shop where they couldn't work. The large department stores and other commercial establishments were perfectly willing to accept African American money, but unwilling to hire African Americans for responsible, non-janitorial positions.

Protestors spread out in order to cover as much Canal Street territory as possible. This sometimes meant having only one or two pickets per block. Once, while I was the sole picket on the block, two young thugs approached me. Circling around, they began bouncing me between them, like a ping pong ball. I remained nonviolent. Frustrated, they grew more aggressive. Finally, they knocked me to the ground and began kicking me in the arms. I protected my head and ribs and was not seriously injured. After a few minutes, they desisted, totally puzzled by my reaction. Meanwhile two New Orleans policemen watched the entire spectacle. When I got up and brushed myself off, the cops asked my assailants if they were injured and wanted to press charges. This was southern street justice in action.

The final incident occurred in El Paso, Texas. Stopped again for "suspicion," we were taken to police headquarters and ordered to strip. Two cops, one white and one Latino, shoved us around, and in my case, surreptitiously landed a few painful blows to my back. After releasing us, the police picked us up at least twice, and maybe three times again, but with no further violence. Fleeing across the border to Juarez, Mexico, I felt like kissing Mexican soil.

Chapter 13
Civil Rights Battles Intensify in San Diego and Vicinity

My final semester was especially easy because I needed only a few units to meet the minimum required for graduation. I was completing a senior thesis and had another easy course or two, enabling me to devote extensive time to civil rights work in San Diego, with occasional forays elsewhere, and to my growing relationship with Sherry. I kept in touch with my family in Berkeley, telling them that I expected to be there in the fall. I think that I had promises of admission, either formal or informal, to both the law school and the political science department at UC Berkeley. I had written some of the faculty there about my interests and I had received some encouraging replies. Interestingly, my communications never involved money. I was so thoroughly used to working part-time since childhood that I merely assumed that I would do the same no matter what program I wound up pursuing. Tuition was cheap and I was very self sufficient and accustomed to living very frugally. I had slowly begun to abandon the idea of a legal career. My intellectual interests became dominant and increasingly, I thought that legal studies would not satisfy them. Still, I remained ambivalent.

Once again, CORE became my organizational focus. One target was the San Diego Gas and Electric Company, in downtown San Diego. Our litany of complaints was familiar, mostly issues of employment discrimination against blacks. Now, the actions became more militant, pleasing me tremendously. We began sit-ins in the main SD Gas and Electric Company office. Packing the lobby, we disrupted the entire operations of the firm. We continued this tactic frequently and actually garnered some modest press attention from the local conservative newspapers. Neither employees nor the public could enter or exit. Pledged as usual to nonviolence, we easily weathered the intermittent verbal barbs and shoves thrown in our direction.

Eventually, the Gas and Electric Company responded legally. One afternoon, as we sat in the lobby, several San Diego County sheriffs entered the building and began dumping thick legal documents on most of us. I was pleased to receive one of the documents from one of the officers. It was a Temporary Restraining Order that the San Diego Superior Court had issued. It named the Congress of Racial Equality and several of its known leaders as defendants. It also listed a number of "Does" to cover everyone else involved in the sit-ins and other direct action protests.

Alas, I was only a mere "Doe," but I soon overcame my disappointment. The officer brusquely told me that the court order instructed me and everyone else to leave the premises or we would be guilty of contempt:

"desist forthwith" or some other such semantic acrobatics. With the arrogance of a 20 year old, I replied that I would only obey after I had read the document, adding that I was a slow reader. I actually perused the document, finding its legal language archaic and incomprehensible, and filled with cases and citations apparently showing definitively that the Gas Company was right and that we were wrong—legally, not morally. It contained the kind of legal mumbo jumbo that still infuses so many legal documents, and that hopelessly confuses intelligent laypersons. As I recall, the Superior Court soon made the injunction permanent. It specified, I think, that we could not be within so many feet of the building without definitive proof of legitimate business. As far as I know, it is still in effect.

Our next target was a statewide effort of the Congress of Racial Equality. This series of events, in due course, would have life altering consequences for me. We went after the giant Bank of America and we had definitive evidence of its egregious employment discrimination against African Americans. At this juncture, I stepped up my participation, moving slightly from the front lines into a planning role. I had always attended CORE chapter meetings in San Diego and I actively participated. Now, I was invited to join the Direct Action Committee, my key focus throughout my civil rights efforts. In this role, I assumed some leadership activities, especially in conceiving and planning the tactics we would employ against the Bank of America.

Early in this campaign, we were in close contact with CORE chapters throughout California, especially in the Bay Area, a hotbed of civil rights activism. We targeted many local branches of the bank, hitting them in almost blitzkrieg fashion, disrupting their operations, often on busy Friday afternoons. By then, I had given a few speeches to CORE participants, developing a skill I would effectively use for the next 45 years. We kept the pressure on through March and April 1964, and I participated aggressively in thinking of ways to increase our effectiveness and our public visibility.

But a spring break interlude also had long-term personal consequences. CORE had done some organizing in Phoenix, Arizona in conjunction with other groups there. It was an easy drive to Phoenix, so two of us took off to survey the situation and join the massive demonstrations at the State Capitol. The protestors sought governmental action to address a variety of discriminatory practices in the state. Arizona was backwards and conservative, with Republican Senator and soon-to-be presidential candidate Barry Goldwater and Republican Governor Paul Fannin in charge. The large white majority, moreover, was hardly sympathetic to the problems and demands of the local black population. The national civil rights ferment had clearly left Arizona far behind.

Early in the morning, I joined several other demonstrators in twice occupying Governor Fannin's office. The first time, they carried us out of the office, with four police officers for each protestor — one for each arm and each leg. We went down the rotunda steps and shouted slogans and sang civil rights songs.

After depositing me on the capitol grounds, one policeman told me, under his breath, that if he saw me again that he would "beat the shit out of me." After removing me from the second occupation of the governor's office, he implemented his threat by taking me behind a police sedan when, in relative privacy and amidst the general turmoil, he slugged me directly in the face — a painful moment. Later that evening, at the organizational meeting in Phoenix, I felt blood in my mouth, an unwelcome 21st birthday present. After I returned to San Diego, I experienced more dental problems as a result of that assault. I won't describe the gory details, but eventually the problem became dentally terminal. I lost the bottom front teeth later while living in Berkeley. I'm always grateful for the advances in restorative dentistry. This was my only real injury during my civil rights activism.

In San Diego, the actions against the Bank of America grew more militant, with as much of my urging as possible. School was entirely secondary, although I continued to do exceptionally well. I was looking forward to getting out of San Diego and getting to Berkeley, though still undecided about a specific academic or professional direction. I missed my family, of course, but not the financial drama. I managed to avoid many personal and career issues through my intense political activity.

Our new tactics were called "change-ins," one of the most creative and enjoyable protest activities I have ever seen. The original idea was not mine, but I helped tweak it in some imaginative ways. Here, in short, is what we did. We would send several CORE members and sympathizers into Bank of America branches, often during extremely busy times, especially Friday afternoons. We waited patiently in the tellers' lines for service. Then, when it was our turn, we politely asked to change five or ten dollars worth of pennies into bills. The process was extremely time-consuming as we counted out the coins as slowly as possible. It was a deliberate and successful effort to halt the ordinary commercial activity at the bank. It was also, of course, a symbolic message that discriminatory hiring policies would have severe consequences on the business itself.

My twist was to have a fellow protestor stand nearby as I changed the pennies into ten dollar bills. As I counted, two hundred four, two hundred five, two hundred six and so forth, my CORE colleague then "accidentally" stumbled into me, scattering the pennies all over the teller's space. Then I would begin the counting again, starting from number one, thus slowing the process considerably more. Everyone, of course, knew exactly what we were doing. Obviously, many customers were perturbed or angry. Several offered their opinions of our actions in highly colorful language. I had some sympathy for them, but not much. That was the price of fighting racism. More privately, I thought to myself, "Fuck 'em."

In June, 1964, I graduated from San Diego State College with a B.A. in political science, with honors. It was a reasonably big deal; I *was* the first in the family to get this far. Psychologically, I honestly felt that in some ways, I got back against Hitler and the Nazis and all the teachers who had given me such a hard time in my earlier school days. It occurred to me again that it was still only 20 years since my father's family was gassed in Auschwitz. This reaction never quite goes away. Over the years, I have had tremendous sympathy for my own students who are the first to go to college. I have gone out of my way, hundreds of times, to help them as much as possible. I know that my parents were pleased, but they lacked the funds to come to the graduation. I think I went, but I have mercifully repressed everything about it.

By then, I had moved in with Sherry, to the chagrin of her conservative, Seventh Day Adventist parents. I had solidified a Jewish identity by then, but it was not strong enough to avoid a mixed relationship. The act seemed the right thing, or at least the convenient thing, to do at the time.

But I was still ensconced in conservative San Diego for a few more months during the summer. After graduation, I got some research positions on campus that paid reasonably well, used my intellectual skills marginally, and provided plenty of time flexibility for my political engagements. The campaign against B of A continued. At one CORE meeting, we learned of the disappearance in Mississippi of the three young SNCC workers, James Chaney, Andrew Goodman, and Michael Schwerner. We all knew that they had been murdered. The news was shocking, even devastating, and it was not lost on me that two of the men were Jews and the other was black. It was another reminder that what we were doing was serious business and it could have deadly consequences. My recollection too was that I had driven near the same location in Mississippi as the three martyred civil rights workers, and that I very well could have been one of those whose bodies had made national news.

I think my reaction was typical among civil rights workers. It only underscored my resolve to continue the struggle. On June 26, 1964, I pursued it to another level. I gave a pep talk before the action, and with several friends, associates, and, this time with Sherry, we assaulted the Bank of America again. First, we went to a branch on El Cajon Boulevard, where I actually opened an account for $10.00. Swiftly, we drove to the bank's main branch on Broadway, downtown San Diego's main thoroughfare.

Entering the bank, we began the usual change-in tactic, this time with a large number of participants. This continued for some time. When I finally reached my turn at the teller's window, I asked to withdraw $9. I thought that I was being clever. I knew that it would take some time to trace my account, since I had opened it within the hour. She would have to make phone calls to verify my account and do whatever else was necessary in those pre-computer days. This would tie up the teller even longer than changing pennies. I also believed that this particular approach would inoculate me from any legal liability, since I could verify that I was an actual Bank of American depositor.

I was, of course, entirely wrong. After some minutes, the branch manager approached me, demanding identification and other information. I was happy to comply; after all, I was a regular customer! I figured that he would give me a hard time and I assumed that he recognized me from previous change-in actions. His next action was dramatic. He put his hand around my upper arm and informed me that I was under arrest. It was a citizen's arrest and I had the dubious honor of being one of the first civil rights demonstrators in San Diego, or perhaps anywhere else in America, to be arrested by a bank manager. Even now, every time I enter a bank, I think about the possible multiple roles of the local manager and wonder if they receive law enforcement instructions as well as the latest managerial and leadership principles that business school professors grind out so prolifically.

Everything then happened rapidly. The San Diego Police stepped in at once to take me into custody. They were waiting in the wings and had obviously been in on the entire process. In rapid succession, all the other demonstrators were arrested and enough police cars were available to transport all of us to jail. Their logistics were as effective as ours.

Booked into the San Diego City Jail, I was charged with three misdemeanor offenses and released on bail several hours later. It seemed an interminable wait. The first hour was routine, with fingerprinting and photographing and the like. I have always wished that I could retain my mug shot because it would be a splendid pedagogical augmentation. Then it got worse. San Diego police officers, in charge of the jail, placed me initially in the "drunk tank," where alcoholics and old derelicts moaned and vomited throughout my "stay." It was a pathetic scene, giving me a concrete vision of the stupidity of criminalizing alcohol abuse. I didn't talk to anyone during the hour or so I was there, but it was obvious that many or most of the drunk tank inmates were "regulars," who needed treatment and compassion rather that their circular incarceration.

107

My next move was to a large cell with several aggressive homosexual prisoners. For another hour or so, I fended off various attacks, with inmates grabbing my crotch and ass every few minutes. I had no real worry that I would be more seriously sexually assaulted. I recognized that this was just another feature of police conduct informing me of the power realities of my temporary incarceration. I was fairly well known to the San Diego police by then because of my civil rights activity. Their harassment was routine. I was sometimes stopped and frisked on the way to meetings or to my classes. I got absurd traffic citations, like having a cracked lens on my taillight. In that particular incident, I actually went to court and told the judge that the crack was microscopic. I produced a photo to support my claim. He fined me $2, then suspended the fine and observed from the bench that the police should concern themselves with more important matters. A decent judge.

All of this has given me a consummate suspicion of police in general. My long association with the African American community has made me extremely sensitive to their pervasive suspicions about police racism. I have seen it so often myself that I know that their concerns have a well justified basis. As a lawyer, I have occasionally intervened in police misconduct cases, especially when racism is involved. The election of Barack Obama in 2008 has done little to affect police in front line conflicts with black citizens in America.

Before my release from jail, I was moved a few more times. Once, I shared a cell with a fellow demonstrator, a Trotskyite from the Socialist Workers Party. But the City Jail was not a conducive venue for a discussion of Marxist theory. In yet another move, I shared a cell with a sullen prisoner who asked a few questions about why I was there. I didn't answer because I was extremely anxious for the bail bondsman to arrive. I wanted to get the hell out of there.

Late in the evening, I was finally released. I hurried to pick up Sherry, who had been booked in the San Diego County Jail several blocks away. We went home and a few days later saw a CORE lawyer, who informed us that the trial would probably be held in late August. He said that the charges were minor and that there wasn't really much to worry about. He said the worst outcome would be a fine, maybe $100, and six months or a year of probation. Thus assured, I went back to my regular life, doing my research work at San Diego State and continuing my civil rights efforts.

I actually escalated my activity between my arrest and my trial. I spent some time in Los Angeles participating in various CORE actions. The one I most remember is the series of demonstrations at the Van de Kamp bakery chain, for the usual reasons of employment discrimination. The protests were typical in my experience: noisy picketing and hostile public reaction. In one instance, an irate customer grabbed my picket sign and hit me on the head with it. Perhaps she was upset that the picket line delayed her purchase of an apple pie or a loaf of bread for a minute or two. It amused me more than anything and I'm sure that my response thoroughly bewildered her.

In LA, I saw the organizational conflicts that were brewing within CORE. I have always stayed away from these internal battles. They are deadly and consume huge amounts of time and emotional energy. They also divert attention from the task at hand. I discovered that a breakaway organization was forming, dedicated to more militant action, believing that the CORE chapter was overly cautious. Called the Non-Violent Action Committee (N-VAC), it became a vigorous organization by summer, 1964 and I was eager to participate in some of its activities. I was drawn to N-VAC because its participants and leaders preferred "hitting the streets" rather than just meeting and talking. That appealed to me both politically and emotionally.

Significantly, it was based in the heart of the black community in Los Angeles. I began attending meetings and actions in Watts and learned a great deal about its heart, Central Avenue. I explored the area thoroughly, including the world famous Watts Towers. This early experience would later serve me well as a UCLA African American Studies faculty member decades later. I liked the militant tone of N-VAC and once again, I especially enjoyed speaking to the ordinary African Americans involved with the organization and those living in the surrounding community. When Watts exploded a year later, it came as no surprise to me. The alienation, the pervasive joblessness, the repeated instances of police harassment and brutality and much more—all of these and more converged in summer, 1965, to generate one of the largest urban rebellions in American history.

Before my trial, I also traveled to Berkeley with several objectives in mind. I was glad to see my family and I was especially eager to see my "baby" sister, now three years old. I also needed to explore the Berkeley campus carefully and talk to as many people as I could find. I was still (uncharacteristically) indecisive, but leaning towards law school. My arrest galvanized my will to fight back actively on the legal front. I was also eager to meet some civil rights activists in the Bay Area. I had already met several Bay Area people from the Bank of America actions. I had also monitored the other well publicized activities, including the San Francisco Sheraton Palace hotel protests, the Auto Row demonstrations, the Mel's Drive-in actions, and others.

I did manage to make one powerful demonstration. I joined a large group of protestors at the Cow Palace at the edge of San Francisco in July, protesting the nomination of Barry Goldwater as the Republican nominee for president against Lyndon Johnson in the upcoming November election. The feeling at the time was that Goldwater was a reactionary figure, almost a proto-fascist who would lead the United States into a nuclear confrontation. Few of us had any idea that Johnson, soon after his election, would be the most bellicose president of the 20th century.

In August, I stood trial along with Sherry in the San Diego Municipal Court. Our lawyer was Thad Williams, a competent African American who did as good a job as could be expected given the incredibly stacked deck we faced in that atmosphere. We actually disqualified the first judge we drew, Madge Bradley, because Williams said we wouldn't stand a chance with her. I don't know why he made that judgment. I knew nothing about her at all. Some superficial research for this memoir yielded very little except that she was the first woman judge on the San Diego bench and that she had a reputation for being "firm but fair." That was the giveaway. That term has always been code language for "she (more usually he) will kick you in the ass, but fairly."

The next judge was worse: firm and deeply unfair. Luther N. Hussey was consistently hostile, reflecting the deeper if not entirely conscious racism of his Virginian background. A physically large presence on the bench, I imagined him with a glowing red neck, which I could use to warm my hands in a cold climate. That was an expression of my irreverence then and it has remained with me ever since. It is a useful check on rage and psychosis.

Jury selection was laughable. Each time a prospective black juror was called, the prosecutor used a peremptory challenge to disqualify him or her. When Williams objected on grounds of racial bias and exclusion, Judge Hussey overruled the objection, holding that we had no standing to make such an objection, because we were white. The final jury was composed of 12 citizens reflecting the intractably conservative values of the San Diego area. Many were spouses of retired military personnel, whose views reflected the right-wing sentiments of that San Diego population. Most were retired senior citizens, for whom youthful protestors were anathema. After they were sworn in, I remarked sardonically to my lawyer that it was nice to have my peers defined. During one trial recess, I saw a juror reading a paperback copy of *None Dare Call it Treason,* a popular right-wing tract of the era claiming pervasive communist subversion in the United States.

As customary, the prosecution began the proceedings. The Bank of America manager, my arresting non-officer, testified about the circumstances of the demonstrations on June 26 at the main branch. Then the prosecutor, Mr. Brian Newman-Crawford, called another witness, a San Diego police undercover officer; my recollection is that he had been my sullen cellmate, but it's possible that it was another undercover cop. He testified that I had passionately incited the demonstrators before we left for the bank to violate the injunction ordering us not to engage in the change-ins or similarly disruptive activities. He described my speech in detail, emphasizing my conscious advocacy of breaking the law.

The problem was that none of his testimony was true. I furiously whispered to my lawyer, who calmed me down and told me that the police do this all the time. I had encountered what Harvard law professor Alan Dershowitz publicized as "testilying," when police perjure themselves in order to augment a case against criminal defendants, especially when they have some animosity against them. Once again, I found more evidence of my longtime suspicions of police misconduct, especially in matters of race.

Thad Williams decided that I alone should testify for the defense. I was verbal and could withstand any cross-examination well. Throughout my testimony, Judge Hussey intervened each time I sought to explain why CORE decided to move aggressively against the Bank of America. In one instance, he attempted to cut off my testimony by ordering me not to give "political speeches." I responded by informing him that I was giving no political speech, but merely noting the discriminatory hiring policies of the bank. It appeared that he had a growing fixation about me, possibly because I appeared unafraid, even arrogant. In another instance, prosecutor Newman-Crawford asked me whether I was now, or had ever been, a member of the Congress of Racial Equality. Incredulous, I replied by asking whether he had any idea about the McCarthy-like origins of that language. I think it occasioned another loud gavel-banging by Judge Hussey.

Defended by a black lawyer in a reactionary city with a racist judge and jury, we had no chance of acquittal. While waiting for the verdict, Newman-Crawford remarked to me that we had been courageous in taking on racial discrimination. I asked him why he was prosecuting us. He said something like that was "his duty." I thought that he sounded like a good Nazi, always following orders. The jury was out for an hour or two before returning with a guilty verdict on all counts.

Judge Hussey then delivered a diatribe directed almost entirely at me, noting among other things that I was "just another common criminal" and that he would tolerate no comments about my being a "political" defendant, somehow superior to other miscreants appearing in his courtroom. He reminded me of my junior high principal, but transported to a judicial setting. It also felt exactly my earlier disciplinary encounters to me at the time. He noted the seriousness of the offenses for which we had been convicted: two counts of trespassing (one of which involved something to do with obstructing business) and one count of contempt of court for violating the injunction against our actions at the Bank of America. Hussey, I'm sure,

111

had no idea of the actual contempt I had for him and his court and the entire legal process, which I judiciously kept to myself. He then referred us to the San Diego County probation office for a pre-sentence investigation and recommendation.

My meeting with the probation officer was frustrating. He repeatedly asked me whether I "regretted" my crime, to which I responded that I could not in conscience *regret* something I did *because* of my conscience. My explanation that I *sought* to be arrested and jailed appeared incomprehensible. I explained that this kind of civil disobedience was happening throughout the country. I probably mentioned Martin Luther King. I don't know whether he was just ignorant because he lived in San Diego or simply dumb, but that entire explanation about the broader civil rights movement sweeping the nation registered not at all. Unlike Judge Hussey, he was not hostile, but rather merely befuddled. In due course, he submitted his recommendation for probation, considering that I had been convicted of three misdemeanors and had no prior criminal record.

Soon afterwards, Hussey ordered us into his chambers, but addressed almost all of his comments to me. He agreed with the recommendation that probation was in order, an outcome I always expected even after the verdict. My lawyer assured me that this was not a case where jail time would ever occur. But then Judge Hussey added the life-altering twist to the recommendation, one with a profound impact on my future academic work and subsequent career. Instead of merely placing me on "summary probation," which required little more than staying out of trouble, he placed me on formal probation, requiring close monitoring and reporting to a Probation Officer.

That itself was excessive in light of the comparatively trivial offenses for which I was convicted. But Hussey added much more. He ordered that I also write three term papers as a condition of probation. He specified the topics with precision: the first had to be a paper entitled "The Contributions of the Bank of America to the Social and Economic Progress of California." This required me to read the book *Biography of a Bank* by Marquis and Bessie James, a work produced with the active cooperation of the Bank of America. A fawning piece of hagiography, it elevated Bank of America founder A. P. Giannini to heroic status similar to other industrial figures like J. P. Morgan, Andrew Carnegie, Henry Ford, and others I regarded as robber barons and capitalist swine. My task was to read the book and, in my paper, essentially show why I was mistaken about this venerable financial institution, especially in directing my civil rights activism against a bank that was such a remarkable social and economic asset to California residents.

The second paper was to be entitled "The Birth and Growth of Pacific Southwest Airlines." As Judge Hussey explained to me in his chambers, I was to conduct interviews with PSA corporate officials so that I could better "appreciate the benefits of the free enterprise system." This required me to interview company officials based in both San Diego and San Francisco. He spoke enthusiastically about the airline corporation, with the same simplistic and uncritical (but more pernicious) faith in capitalism that I had heard from my donut shop boss a few years previously.

The final paper reflected the judge's deepest personal political biases. He informed me that my effort had to be a much longer paper, approximately 40 pages, to show that the major discrimination against "Negroes" in America occurred because of labor union racism. Judge Hussey told me that if I were so concerned about racial discrimination, I had the responsibility to see why such discrimination really existed. He made it abundantly clear to me in this conversation that my "research" had to conform to this perspective. He mentioned too that he would appoint a "blue ribbon" committee to evaluate whether I met the appropriate intellectual standards for these papers required under my probation order. In one meeting in a judicial chamber, I had become a 1964 version of Joseph K. from Franz Kafka's *Trial*. My anxiety was growing each minute. I was on the emotional edge, but I tried to conceal it as much as possible.

These preposterous papers, however, were not the most onerous feature of my probation. The Judge asked me what my future academic plans were assuming that he would grant me probation. I answered honestly because by now, with this arrest and trial, I was completely disgusted with the law, which I prudently kept to myself. My extremely ill feelings about law, lawyers, and judges had convinced me subjectively that I wanted no part of this world. Despite my admiration for movement lawyers, I determined that I did not want to spend my life in and out of unpleasant courtrooms, full of Husseys and Newman-Crawfords, even if I could win my cases. This trial was profoundly educational for me, emotionally and intellectually.

I told him that I was interested in pursuing an academic career and that I hoped to earn a Ph.D. in political science at the University of California at Berkeley, even if I had to wait a year to begin. I also told him that I had applied to, and was accepted at, the UC Berkeley Law School (Boalt Hall). He immediately seized on my remarks, while pointedly noting that Berkeley was not a good place for me because many people there would be eager to exploit my anti-social character. He had read the news reports from Berkeley and he knew those radicals were up to no good.

He then informed me that he would add another condition to my probation terms: I would be required to attend and successfully complete law

113

school. His rationale was simple. Remarking that I had shown a "demonstrated propensity" for lawbreaking, he determined that a legal education would instill in me a greater respect for the law and make me into a "productive" and law-abiding citizen. In effect, he altered my immediate academic plans and forced me into a professional training I had decided to forego. He added a little "frosting" to his probation conditions. I could not leave the Bay Area, six or seven counties, without his written permission. Then he indicated—extremely clearly—that I had the option of refusing probation with the conditions he imposed, in which case he would sentence me to a jail term of up to six months. This was an emotionally horrific but easy choice. I had no desire to spend any additional time in a San Diego jail. If I accepted the conditions, I would be in Berkeley. I also assumed that law school would be easy enough, a hunch that was largely, but not entirely accurate.

Chapter 14
Berkeley: A New Personal, Academic, and Political Chapter

Shortly after this Kafkaesque encounter, I endured another absurd probation department appointment. This time, the officer read me the specific probation conditions, apparently not realizing that I had known how to read for about 18 years. I was aware, of course, that he probably had a large number of probationers and this was the protocol. It still seemed patronizing and insulting. Instead of asking me again whether I regretted my crimes, he became more psychological. Was I beaten as a child? What caused me to become a criminal? I surely had emotional issues, but they would scarcely be addressed in this environment. I tried to be polite, informing him that my parents actively supported my civil disobedience. Eventually, the meeting ended. I regarded him as another schmuck, perhaps well meaning, but a schmuck nevertheless.

Then we relocated to Berkeley, whereupon I made another dumb mistake, but fortunately one without huge or permanent consequences. Sherry and I got married. We had been living together, so what the hell. My parents vaguely disapproved, but were not vocal about it. Her parents disliked me, probably for several reasons, including my politics and my influence in drawing her into all this stuff with "Negroes." I was 21, in a state of great emotional anguish, upset with the recent trial, extremely resistant to law school, and deeply immature despite being intellectually advanced and politically experienced for my age. I needed, I thought, some stability, and this would provide it. Young people make dumb decisions all the time. This was my version and we settled in a dump called a studio apartment across from the Berkeley campus. The community, at least, was exciting, with plenty of political action, bookstores, cafes, and all the other features that made the city unique.

I reluctantly registered for my first year classes at Boalt Hall. Happy with the political activism at Berkeley, I was decidedly displeased with law school. Most of my fellow students seemed to be young men (only a very few women) of great privilege. I felt keenly alienated personally and intellectually. I found the curriculum fundamentally absurd and boring; early on, I concluded (like many other radicals) that legal training was little more than a socialization process designed to create talented, highly paid technicians to defend and foster class and economic privileges. Unlike my earlier critical impressions of school, *this* time I had a strong intellectual apparatus and a complex vocabulary to express my discontent. My perception is at the core of the Critical Legal Studies movement and reflected the radical political and social theory I had studied, largely independently, during my undergraduate years. Forty-five years later, my views on law and legal education are remarkably unchanged.

Utterly disenchanted with subjects like property, civil procedure, contracts, and torts, I decided on a dramatic move, not long after I started legal studies. I walked across campus to the Political Science Department and asked to be admitted to first year graduate studies, even a few weeks late. In a day or so, I received an affirmative reply and actually embarked briefly on my new program. I knew, however, that I would have to inform Judge Hussey about this academic change of direction. I wrote what I believed was a good letter, indicating a "slight" change in my academic focus.

I never anticipated the severity of his response. Soon after I sent the letter, I received his answer in a telegram sent to me at my Berkeley apartment. There was no ambiguity. He gave me 48 hours to return to law school. Failing evidence of my return, he threatened to revoke my probation and impose a jail term. This news was emotionally devastating. I considered leaving the state and enrolling elsewhere a year later, assuming that my criminal record was minor enough to avoid extradition. Jail remained out of the question. Family and personal considerations prevailed and I returned reluctantly to the law school, eventually completing the degree three years later in June, 1967.

Early in my first year, probably right after my return, the (liberal) law school Dean called me to a meeting in his spacious office. Informing me that he knew of my judicial compulsion to attend law school, he requested my pledge not to break any laws during my studies at Boalt. I flatly refused. I merely noted my belief in civil disobedience when morally compelling.

At the same time, I also had to "report" regularly to the San Diego Probation Department. I recall that one time, I actually had to fly to San Diego for another stupid and perfunctory meeting. After that, I could report through the mail by filling out a monthly form, containing some financial information and a statement, probably under oath, that I had violated no laws. I filled out about a year's worth of these forms, signed them, sealed them in stamped envelopes, and mailed them at the end of each month. It was a gratifying gesture of resistance and contempt.

The study of law was generally tedious. Occasionally stressful, it was relatively easy to master legal analysis and argumentation. After a learning curve of a year or so, the law school challenge lessened for me, probably the typical experience of American law students. I developed some interest and competence in constitutional law, jurisprudence, and criminal law, a background that has occasionally informed my subsequent teaching and research. A traditional rationale of the study of law is that it leads to precise thinking and rigorous analysis. This may be true, but my impression throughout my career is that mastery of *any* complex subject solidifies these mental skills. Likewise, law study is supposed to hone skills in public speaking and verbal expression. This too may be accurate, but my own experience persuades me that my political speaking record in the 60s, far more than anything else, has been the most significant factor in my success as a university classroom teacher.

During my first year at Boalt Hall, I completed the papers for Judge Hussey, finishing the final effort during the summer before my second year. Essentially, I gave him what I knew he wanted; I had had enough emotional distress from this criminal conviction and simply wanted to complete probation as easily as possible. My first paper, in retrospect, was almost satirical. I borrowed the absurd book on the Bank of America from the UC Berkeley library, perused it for an hour or so to get its obsequious gist and pretend that I had read it, and commenced writing the "essay."

I compared A.P. Giannini with George Washington and spoke glowingly about the social and economic accomplishments of the Bank of America. I thought about adding Jesus Christ, but that would have been over the top even for this audience. I wrote the paper in one day, fortified with several bottles of beer. The "blue ribbon" commission approved its quality. One member, a retired Admiral, wrote me glowingly of his satisfaction after reading my paper. He declared that I had found "the true path to existence." Again, I discovered an example of pure asininity, a quality that has always permeated even the highest ranks of American military, commercial, and political leadership. The second and third papers were similarly pandering. It was expensive to schlep to San Francisco and San Diego for ridiculous interviews with executives of Pacific Southwest Airlines. I also rankled at identifying unions as the chief source of American racism in my final paper.

The saving grace for me in 1964 was the culture of political rebellion at Berkeley. Almost from the moment of our arrival, we became politically engaged. One of the first activities was to participate in pickets at the *Oakland Tribune* building in downtown Oakland. This newspaper was owned and edited by former United States Senator William Knowland, an arch-conservative with an unusually harsh reputation as an employer. He was also the California manager for the Goldwater campaign, making him an especially inviting target for Berkeley activists. These demonstrations were organized on the Berkeley campus at Bancroft and Telegraph Avenues, soon to become the focus of the Berkeley Free Speech Movement, a movement that shook the nation and the world and that irrevocably changed higher education as well as the trajectory of my life.

The Oakland Tribune protests demanded that Knowland increase the number of blacks employed at the paper. Crowds were noisy, with chanting, leafleting, and speaking. The action made sense in a city with a large and growing black population. As usual, there was some civil disobedience, with several arrests. I was cautious about my activity, because an arrest would result in an immediate revocation of my probation and a swift imposition of a jail term. The Tribune protest became a regular social event and we often ended the demonstration with friends, finding an inexpensive restaurant to cap the evening.

The Free Speech Movement followed almost immediately afterwards. Its history has been well documented, both in print and in film. The UC Administration, responding to conservative political pressures from Knowland and others, imposed a ban on campus-organized off-campus political advocacy, generating powerful resistance from student groups across the political spectrum at Berkeley. Even as a first-year law student, I knew the First Amendment issues well, fully aware that the ban was an egregious violation of free expression rights on a public university campus. Above all, I understood that the administration actions were directed against civil rights groups and others for whom civil disobedience was a major political tactic. My personal background made it inevitable that I would vigorously support the Free Speech Movement, despite the personal dangers as a probationer living with potential jail time for any law violation.

I participated in virtually every FSM rally and protest, including occupations of the administration building that clearly constituted a violation of the law and that exposed me to major judicial sanctions. I was paranoid, but not so much so that it deterred me from what I knew was morally required. A few law students participated, but not many. Law students, at the time, were generally conservative, unwilling by conviction and temperament to challenge authority, especially like this. This has changed in the past 40 years, but I think not as much as progressives would like to believe.

One of the most dramatic events of the FSM occurred on October 1, 1964, when former student Jack Weinberg was arrested and placed in a campus police car. About 100 students lay down in front of the car and many more lay down behind it, chanting, "Release him." The crowd grew, listening to scores of speeches, including from Mario Savio, one of the most eloquent orators I had ever heard during that exciting era. We held the car for 32 hours and I remained there the entire time, save only for some quick bathroom and nutrition breaks. I skipped classes and did no homework and

I'm sure that each minute constituted a violation of my probation order. It was a time absolutely not to be missed.

I even joined the now famous Sproul Hall administration building takeover of December 2, 1964, following Mario Savio's stirring speech ("there's a time when the operation of the machine becomes so odious, makes you so sick at heart . . .") and Joan Baez's moving rendition of Bob Dylan's "Blowin' In The Wind," and later culminating in the arrest of over 800 students and others. I left the sit-in at approximately 2 a.m., following the FSM announcement that juveniles and persons on probation should leave in order to avoid severe consequences. That applied to me with special relevance.

Those moments are forever etched in my consciousness. Savio's words have the same emotional resonance for me as Dr. King's speech at the March on Washington a year earlier. What a stunning privilege to participate in such events. What a glorious opportunity to transcend ordinary life and dedicate one's energy to resistance that has such clear and unambiguous moral direction and purpose. I think about this often. It was, I suppose, luck that I was at both these speeches, but it was also my decisions that led me there.

Though avoiding arrest, I vigorously supported the student strike that effectively brought the University of California at Berkeley to a grinding halt. A key moment for me occurred the morning of the mass arrests, when student leaders began organizing the campus strike. I knew that Governor Pat Brown, whom I despised because of the 1960 Chessman case, had ordered the mass arrests, increasing my enmity for him. Even as my fellow students were dragged off to waiting police vans, someone handed me a microphone on the Sproul Hall steps. Spontaneously, I spoke about the need for massive student support. I called for pickets to be established at the law school and at several other major campus buildings. I was astonished at my passion in this impromptu speech. I had spoken often enough in my civil rights activities and had developed an effective public speaking style. On the morning of December 3, 1964, I found myself in a "zone," a transcendent oral experience I have had regularly both as a university teacher and as a political speaker for the past 45 years. Equally important, I saw how students responded to my pleas. Hundreds moved to the buildings I identified; I immediately recognized a speaking talent that has served me unusually well in my professional life.

The strike itself was a massive success. This unprecedented collective student action forced the university to retreat and eventually moved a reluctant faculty to line up in support of the students. I walked the picket lines at various locations on campus, mostly in front of the law school, providing me a special satisfaction to skip classes there, even though we were approaching a crucial time in the first semester. I also attended the public meeting in the Greek Theater called by President Clark Kerr and some of his sycophantic administrators and department chairmen. He and his minions gave the institutional "official story," a patronizing appeal to "reasoned debate" and similar rhetoric constructs designed to conceal their repressive attitudes and policies. The "lowlight" of the convocation occurred when Mario Savio attempted to speak. Campus police officers seized him and dragged him off the stage. It was an epiphanous moment for me. I understood that the university was no different from any other dominant institution in America; it was merely an integral feature of modern capitalism.

The UC Berkeley Free Speech Movement was the chief student movement during the 1960s social protest era in America to confront the issue of free expression on college and university campuses. Administrative censorship of controversial ideas was a problem on many campuses, but the FSM victory at Berkeley quelled much of the bureaucratic zeal to squelch student political expression, especially in California. There, public campuses at least tacitly recognized that the First Amendment was fully applicable to its grounds, subject only to reasonable time, place and manner restrictions pursuant to legitimate regulation under universally accepted principles of constitutional law. Private institutions, of course, had much greater latitude to regulate and even prohibit student political expression, because the First Amendment only operates against governmental entities.

FSM support groups arose on other UC campuses during the fall semester, 1964 and similar expressions of solidarity could be found throughout the nation. Most student protest, however, was soon directed to the growing opposition to the Vietnam War, a crusade that I eagerly joined as well. But the battle for campus free speech is continuing. The quotation attributed to Thomas Jefferson, "eternal vigilance is the price of liberty," has had an especially powerful resonance in campus free expression controversies. Throughout the 60s and early 70s, many campus administrators sought to limit on-campus expressions of anti-war protest. Resistance groups often had to confront college and university bureaucrats as part of their broader opposition to American foreign policy. These actions, naturally, diverted attention from the deeper issues of American imperialism and forced student anti-war groups to expend human and other resources merely to exercise their ostensibly protected constitutional rights.

Even in recent years, free speech controversies have been prominent on American campuses, reminding people that the Free Speech Movement had implications far beyond the immediate controversy on the Berkeley campus.

120

Many universities, including public institutions, have attempted to establish "free speech zones," in effect confining student political expression to minuscule areas and fostering *de facto* censorship of controversial ideas. Dividing campuses into small islands of free speech constitutes an appalling restriction of the First Amendment and student groups from many political perspectives have mobilized in opposition to these developments.

More troubling, some college and university officials have enacted so-called "speech codes," trying to protect minorities, women, and gays from racist, sexist, and homophobic expressions. These codes can be well meaning, but they also run afoul of First Amendment guarantees. Many progressive students' groups seem less concerned about these restrictions on free expression than they do about the more historical (and continuing) attempts to limit radical expressions. As a vigorous FSM participant, I recall well that our mission was to protect *all* student expressions, not only those with which we happened to agree. The result has been that I have found myself occasionally at odds on this issue with some of my political comrades and compatriots, but I am confident that protecting free speech for everyone on campus is ultimately the wisest policy, especially for those of us challenging the dominant political and educational order.

The Free Speech Movement at Berkeley also highlighted powerful underlying issues of educational deficiencies in major research universities. My interest and involvement in discussing such issues had the most durable impact on me. They were much more intriguing than the dry legal principles I was learning at Boalt Hall. These educational critiques catalyzed my intellectual interests, something that legal analysis rarely did. That legal work seemed like complicated puzzle solving. I could do it, but my motivation was low and consequently, my performance was middling, except for a few classes that engaged me. Of course, my bitterness at being in law school, and my general alienation there, contributed to this reaction. Through the FSM, I found other students, mostly graduate students in the social sciences and the humanities, who were more interesting and engaging than my fellow law students. With a few exceptions, they were the people with whom I associated.

The discussions about higher education were the major catalyst for my decision to pursue an academic rather than a legal career—a return to my original professional plans despite being sidetracked by the San Diego Municipal Court. Many FSM activists understood that the modern research university, labeled the "multiversity" by University of California President Clark Kerr, was primarily an institution to serve dominant corporate and governmental interests in the United States. They recognized that education in general, and undergraduate education in particular, suffered enormously

121

from a scheme of misplaced institutional priorities. Above all, they recognized that a fragmented, disciplinary-based education devoid of serious inquiry about the political, social, and ethical implications of knowledge would ill equip students to become active public citizens in the remaining decades of the 20th century. I immersed myself in these conversations and in the critical educational literature that addressed them.

This educational critique also extended to its devastating consequences for students of the American university. It was no accident that most graduates emerged from four or five years of undergraduate studies fully prepared to take their "rightful" places in corporate or government bureaucracies and to live lives largely devoted to the uncritical support of American capitalism and its dominant values and institutions. Those of us from the FSM who participated in these critical educational discussions and debates concluded that it scarcely mattered what students majored in as undergraduates; corporations were interested only in whether B.A. earners could submit to years of institutional indoctrination so that they could adapt easily to their new hierarchical demands. We used the term "brainwashing" regularly and in retrospect, it was an accurate enough label for what passed as "higher education" in America.

Although many of us were profoundly political, the majority of our fellow students were primarily concerned with their own financial success and social status, especially acquiring future commercial contacts and developing intimate relationships. Their quest for good grades and academic honors rarely reflected a powerful commitment to intellectual inquiry or personal discovery. The structure and organization of the university, flowing from its bureaucratic rigidity, its retrograde curriculum, and its mission to train rather than to liberate human minds, made it merely one more entity in a complex socialization process designed to promote conformity and reduce dissent. It was remarkably successful in that objective—and it remains so in the early 21st century.

All of this eventually turned me into a university teacher with an interdisciplinary perspective that united with activist political concerns—a vision that has endured throughout my career. The Berkeley Free Speech Movement was the major incubator of my professional self.

The primary and overwhelming political issue, especially in Berkeley, was the escalation of the war in Vietnam. In his impromptu remarks following the student free speech victory on the Berkeley campus, Mario Savio told us that we had a war to stop. This was perfectly evident to me. After the Gulf of Tonkin incident in early August, 1964, as I awaited trial in San Diego, I immediately declared my opposition to American involvement in Vietnam to as many people who would listen. I mistrusted Lyndon Johnson from the start of his presidency and this only reinforced my suspicion. During the FSM, I voted in my first election against *both* Goldwater and Johnson, settling for Socialist Workers Party candidate Clifton DeBerry, an African American radical. Although I was no Trotskyite, I wanted to register my electoral discontent, which I did regularly in presidential elections. Indeed, the first time I voted for a winning presidential candidate was in 2008 for Barack Obama.

The Vietnam war began to supplant the civil rights movement as the chief focus of social protest in America, although the growing transformation of the nonviolent civil rights movement to the black power movement was increasingly evident, a development that I viewed sympathetically. Students at Berkeley, at least those with whom I associated, paid close attention to Vietnam. Outrage was intense in 1965 when President Johnson began bombing North Vietnam. That escalation enraged people throughout Berkeley, especially those who had voted for Johnson against the "pro-war" candidate Goldwater.

The University of Michigan was the first university campus to mobilize against Johnson's international aggression. In March, organizers in Ann Arbor conducted an anti-war "teach-in," which sponsored scholars and others to provide intellectual and rhetorical ammunition against the war. Berkeley followed suit on May 21, 1965. That event was monumental, lasting 36 hours. I stayed for almost the entire time, again neglecting my legal studies despite nearing the start of first year final examinations. It featured a veritable "who's who" of the political, literary, and entertainment left: Dr. Benjamin Spock; Norman Thomas; I. F. Stone; David Dellinger; Paul Jacobs; Bob Moses; Mario Savio; Norman Mailer; Paul Krassner; Paul Potter; Phil Ochs; and so many others. I recall listening to the taped message that Bertrand Russell sent to the gathering. I also remember Ken Kesey showing up, probably stoned, saying "Fuck it." I was a great admirer of his novel *One Flew Over the Cuckoo's Nest*, but I thought he acted like a schmuck that day. Supporters of the war were conspicuously absent, finding it difficult to counter such massive sentiment and to defend the indefensible.

This amazing event sparked a huge and durable Bay Area anti war movement, involving several organizations like the Vietnam Day Committee, Students for a Democratic Society, the DuBois clubs, and several others. The teach-in brought me into contact with many people, some of whom I have now known for more than 40 years. It also catalyzed my own anti-war efforts from then until the war ended in 1975. My activities were multifaceted, including substantial legal work after my law school graduation. I attended more anti-war rallies, marches, and demonstrations throughout the Bay Area, and elsewhere, than I can remember. Like my efforts in the civil rights movement, the sheer volume makes my memories blurry in levels of specificity and detail. Some, of course, were especially notable and memorable. For example, in October, 1965, the Vietnam Day Committee organized marches into Oakland. On one occasion, the Oakland police prevented us from entering the city. In the other, thugs from the Hell's Angels motorcycle gang attacked the marchers, and I was near the front of the march that day.

All of this activity was part of a growing national and international anti-war movement, of which I was merely one minor player, like millions of others, in a much larger struggle. Opposition to this war grew along with the body count of American military personnel and the horrific number of Vietnamese military and civilians. Several factors contributed to this anti-war resistance. A key event was Dr. Martin Luther King's courageous decision to join the protest in his majestic speech entitled "A Time to Break Silence" at the Riverside Church in New York on April 4, 1967. Despite some opposition from other civil rights leaders, Dr. King believed passionately that it was impossible to combat racism at home while remaining silent about the carnage in Vietnam. His speech reflected his usual rhetorical brilliance, calling attention to the moral foundation for opposing this unjust war. Above all, King revealed the striking contradiction of seeking social justice for African Americans at home while sending them to fight and die in Southeast Asia. The result was that much of the tremendous energy of the civil rights movement could be mobilized on behalf of anti-war efforts in the United States.

By 1968, opposition to the war generated massive political opposition to President Lyndon Baines Johnson. Minnesota Senator Eugene McCarthy mounted the key electoral challenge by opposing the President in the New Hampshire Democratic primary. Anti-war students and other activists enlisted in his campaign and McCarthy drew 42% of the New Hampshire vote. Although not a victory, it was sufficient to reveal the deep divisions in the Democratic Party. Senator Robert Kennedy also entered the fray, adding further anti-war momentum to the 1968 election. This cumulative pressure forced Lyndon Johnson to announce on March 31, 1968, that he would not seek reelection, making him a failed president whose legacy would forever be defined by the Vietnam War. Kennedy's subsequent assassination and the police riots in Chicago at the Democratic Convention in Chicago that nominated pro-war Vice President Hubert Humphrey for president led to the election of Richard Nixon in November.

Nixon escalated the war further, generating profound divisions in America, leading to increasingly larger street demonstrations, massive civil disobedience, and extensive draft resistance and military desertions. Large numbers of conscientious objection applications, well-publicized draft card burnings, and even raids on draft boards attracted widespread media attention throughout the nation and the world. Radical groups like the Weathermen engaged in violent actions, perceiving that the widespread opposition to the war had placed America on the brink of revolution, a view I had always found overly romanticized and delusional despite my own severe opposition to its fundamental policies and priorities.

Thousands of veterans returned from Vietnam, disillusioned from their experiences and determined to inform their fellow citizens that U.S. involvement was, at best, a colossal mistake. One of the most compelling documents came from Don Duncan, a former Special Forces sergeant in a piece from the leftist anti-war *Ramparts Magazine*. Entitled "The Whole Thing was a Lie," this essay exposed the fraud of American involvement in Vietnam. Duncan argued persuasively that our mission was not to preserve democracy, but to promote anti-communism. Many other prominent anti-war veterans, including Ron Kovic and John Kerry, added their voices to the resistance, making their voices and actions an integral feature of the anti-war movement generally.

These anti-Vietnam war protests intensified in 1970 when President Nixon ordered an incursion of American military forces into neighboring Cambodia. Demonstrations were greatest on American campuses and I took on a faculty leadership role at UC Berkeley. The shootings at Kent State University in Ohio and Jackson State College in Mississippi galvanized world attention, further increasing opposition to Nixon's war policies. Slogans like "one two, three four, we don't want your fucking war" and "hell no, we wont go" joined the earlier chants of "hey, hey, LBJ, how many kids did you kill today?" America had not been as divided since the Civil War, a reality that continued well past the time that President Gerald Ford finally ended the debacle by withdrawing the last of the troops in 1975.

Meanwhile, life in Berkeley generally was pleasant, a striking contrast to San Diego. I enjoyed the bookstores on Telegraph Avenue tremendously, loading up as much as possible, even at the expense of my law school studies. The "sacrifice" was well worth it. A common myth is that law students cannot read anything but law for three years. It's simply not true. I read plenty of good plays and novels, especially Camus and Sartre, and took liberal advantage of the vibrant film opportunities in the Bay Area. San Francisco was accessible and I enjoyed North Beach with its City Lights Book Store, run by Lawrence Ferlinghetti, with Allen Ginsberg and other luminaries hanging out there frequently. We could eat out inexpensively and drink cheap wine. Soon, after several trips to Napa Valley, I learned much more about wine and developed a much better, but not pretentious, appreciation for that lovely beverage.

At the University of California, I found a job in the library, working at the agriculture branch in my first year in law school. Once again, this was powerfully discouraged. Law students were not supposed to work. But I needed the money, and the people at the agricultural library were terrific, all politically progressive and willing to give me whatever schedule flexibility I needed. The subject matter was amusing to me: kumquat production, fertilizer chemistry, soybean technology, swine copulation, and other exciting topics that had previously evaded my intellectual curiosity. I studiously avoided the law school placement office and walked away from student discussions about law firm positions for the upcoming summer. I wanted nothing to do with that world.

At the end of the first year of law school, I worked full-time in the library for the summer. I watched the Watts riots in Los Angeles on television with fascination. None of this surprised me and I found myself sympathizing with the blacks on the streets. It was inevitable that economic and political frustrations and racial oppressions would give rise to violent responses. We managed to take a modest vacation. I think we drove up the coast and toured the pacific northwest. The physical beauty was spectacular and I appreciated this modest respite from my urban existence.

During the next academic year, I slogged through my law classes and worked more at the library. Little in the law school curriculum engaged me enormously, with some modest exceptions like constitutional law and labor law. As usual, I found my outside reading far more fulfilling and I continued reading methodically in several fields. My strategy of cramming intensely for law school exams near the end was marginally successful; it got me middling enough grades to pass, my primary concern. I also took as many writing classes as possible. This was easy for me and I could knock out a decent paper in a weekend or two, with an acceptable grade. Mostly, we enjoyed friends and the general intellectual and political ambience of the region.

But tensions were growing at home. Sherry was committed to our political activities, but we began having major differences about more private activities. She kept urging me to "loosen up," to smoke some grass, to join others in these social activities that were increasingly ubiquitous around Berkeley. Drug use made me nervous, although I had no particular objection to marijuana. I tried awkwardly to take a few hits at parties, but it had little appeal. I was, and am, a beer and wine guy.

The issues went much deeper. There was a growing divide between the political activists and the emerging "counter culture" in the Bay Area and elsewhere; it was a chasm that grew more intense in the next several years. Some political activists tried to bridge that gap. My friend Paul Krassner, for example, has done yeoman's work along those lines for decades. But my bottom line is simple. Despite my gregariousness, passion, and exuberance in politics and teaching, I have a lot of emotional repression, probably stemming from childhood, maybe even from the Holocaust. I value my inhibitions, and drug use threatens to liberate some of those that I want to keep right where they are, *very* far beneath the surface. "Letting it all hang out," "loving one another," and "groovy, man" all struck me as total horseshit, but I also found it deeply threatening and unnerving.

A travel experience in August and September 1966 set the stage for my subsequent research that would eventually characterize much of my scholarly reputation and identity. After another summer in the agriculture library, we managed to save enough money to travel by bus from Tijuana, Mexico to Guadalajara and Mexico City. (I think we needed permission from the court for this travel; I don't remember asking for it, but it's possible that I was paranoid enough to ask). The bus trip was an adventure, something like 50 hours from start to finish, broken up with a night in a dingy hotel room in Mazatlan. The best part of the bus trip itself was reading Joseph Heller's *Catch 22*.

This was my first major international experience and I was thrilled when I viewed the dramatic murals of Diego Rivera, José Clemente Orozco, and David Alfaro Siqueiros. Their fusion of artistic talent and critical political and historical commentary in visual form moved me powerfully. Looking at scores of these remarkable artworks, I saw how two of my most compelling interests, politics and art, could combine so engagingly and effectively. I had begun thinking, vaguely at first, about going into college teaching, somehow using a law degree as an entry point. I also thought seriously about getting immediately back into a Ph.D. program, especially because I would only be 24 when I finished law school, and the draft was looming larger and larger. I had no intention of serving in the military and looked to preserve my student deferment status.

I actually began thinking about how I could use such murals as a college-level teacher, notwithstanding that at the time I knew almost nothing about the vast literature on political art or about the theoretical and other controversies that such artworks generate. I was simply thrilled that these men could produce large-scale paintings with such provocative political content. What also impressed me was their public character. Anyone could just walk in and view these magnificent murals. No admission fees, no security guards, no hassles at all. Decades later, I still cite my Mexican vacation when I teach my courses on art, politics, and society.

127

Academic year 1966/1967 was another crucial time in my personal, educational, and political life. I remember walking up Bancroft Avenue to Boalt Hall to start my third and final year of law school. It felt extremely depressing. I dreaded another entire year of dull courses and uninspiring teaching. This is, to be sure, a common enough reaction among third-year law students, but I felt it intensely. Fortunately, I found a few classes that sparked some interest and, more important, plenty of political activity to occupy my time.

The 1966 elections were crucial. The Democratic contest for Congress was a grassroots campaign pitting Bob Scheer against the incumbent, Representative Jeffrey Cohelan, a supporter of Johnson's Vietnam War policies. Like many, or even most, Berkeley radicals, I had severe reservations about electoral politics. It seemed like capitulating to the system, with its inevitable compromises. It always meant working with the Democratic Party, the Party of Lyndon Johnson, Pat Brown, and several others we had come to despise. Emotionally, street agitation seemed so much more gratifying. But this was different. Scheer had established himself as an authentic radical, a man of immense courage, whose outspoken opposition to the war was inspiring. I had also read his cogent writings on Cuba and Vietnam. He impressed me enormously. I've known him slightly for many decades and have read his interviews, columns, and books for years. My initial judgment has intensified; he is one of the finest journalists we have had in my lifetime.

The campaign was fun. Scheer had vigorous support from civil rights and anti-war activists. I did a little scut work, handing out leaflets, knocked on a few doors in my shabby South Berkeley neighborhood, and urged people to register and vote for Scheer. In the end, he won in Berkeley but lost the election to the establishment Democrat. Years later, when we were both teaching at the University of California at Irvine, I mentioned that I had been active in his Congressional campaign. He nodded skeptically and said that everyone told him that. A few days later, I saw him again and produced one of the original "Scheer for Congress" buttons I had kept from 1966.

The other, more malevolent, election was the governor's race. The opponents were incumbent governor Pat Brown, seeking a third term, and Republican Ronald Reagan. The choice seemed especially repulsive, the worst example of lesser-evil electoral politics. I knew that Reagan was a reactionary. I despised his disgraceful activities during the "Red Scare" of the late 1940s, especially his supplying names to the FBI and the House Un-American Activities Committee of suspected communists in Hollywood. I remembered his speeches for Barry Goldwater. Above all, I was offended with his campaign for governor, when pledged to "clean-up the mess at

Berkeley." In essence, he ran against Berkeley activists. I took it personally, but I would not, could not in conscience, vote for Brown. Reagan's victory clearly used this strategy effectively, but I think too that many Californians had tired of Pat Brown after two terms in office.

In the late 1980s, a colleague at UCLA, a tired old liberal, angrily confronted me after hearing me defend the Free Speech Movement in particular and Berkeley student activism in general. He claimed that we were responsible for Reagan being in the White House, that it was all our fault. Apparently, we should all have shut up, become good Democrats, voted for Brown, and become solid liberal adherents of a structurally corrupt social order. I was polite in responding to my late colleague's charge, but I offered no apology. The Free Speech Movement in my view was one of the powerful moral highlights of the history of the University of California.

Shortly after Reagan took office, he arranged to have University of California President Clark Kerr fired. I think that Mario Savio's reaction reflected a great deal of sentiment among Berkeley students, especially FSM veterans: "good riddance to bad rubbish." I understood that as an emotional response and recognize that Clark Kerr had some redeeming qualities. His actions during the Free Speech Movement, however, were indefensible. Ronald Reagan's attack on him from the right only represented a more extreme version of political repression of activism, especially in the realm of civil rights. When I became a university teacher, I began developing a more systematic critique of Clark Kerr's vision of modern higher education, an inquiry I had begun in the immediate aftermath of the 1964 protests at Berkeley. I often assigned his book, *The Uses of the University*, as a course reading, and subjected it to a systematic critique, especially its implied advocacy of the university as an integral component of advanced capitalism.

By the end of the first semester of my final law school year, immediately after New Year I recall, my marriage finally fell apart for good. The personal divide mirrored the larger cultural divide. I was too political and Sherry really wanted to be a hippie, although that might be a bit harsh. It was entirely clear, however, that I could never embrace that alternative lifestyle. I was too political, too intellectual, but on some levels also much too conventional. I wanted a professional career, not the one I was being trained for, but one nevertheless. I was more rigid, more neurotic, and much less experimental in personal actions and behaviors. I could listen to the music of the time, even enjoy it, but it rarely moved me to new emotional levels. Not her. She left and I became temporarily depressed, but not morose. I recovered, as most of us do with break-ups. This is something I have explained patiently to hundreds of my students over the years, and with plenty of empathy.

129

I had authentically come to a critical view of the emerging counter culture by that time. My critique grew stronger a few years later, especially with the intense media visibility of San Francisco's Haight Ashbury district. I wrote and taught about hippie culture harshly, juxtaposing it with the political movements of that era. I have usually, especially in my classes, disclosed some of the emotional sources of my position. I have always been uncomfortable with an unfettered expression of personal emotion and I guard my inhibitions closely. Hallucinogenic drugs don't especially frighten me, but I strongly prefer personal sobriety. I don't oppose bizarre clothing and personal expressions of ecstasy in others, but it runs counter to my deeper need for stability and control. But above all, I regard the "counter culture" as dangerously apolitical—what Herbert Marcuse perceptively dismissed as harmless negation in *One-Dimensional Man*.

The one bright spot at Boalt Hall was a course in "Law and Morality" that I took with James Pike, the controversial Episcopal Bishop of California, who was originally trained as a lawyer. I knew of his unorthodox and progressive record, including his opposition to Senator Joseph McCarthy, his sustained commitment to African American civil rights, and his "correct" views on abortion, capital punishment, labor, women's rights, gay rights, anti-Semitism, and many other topics. His personal eccentricities were also well known, making him an engaging figure in the classroom. Accusations of heresy against him were also intriguing. There was no way I would miss that class.

I took assertive steps to know him, which I had not done with any of my other law school professors. He seemed to like my style and personality and we conversed several times outside class. He told me that he was going to fight the Episcopal Church heresy charges, mentioning that he would recruit some law students to assist his defense, even talking the matter into the civil courts. He asked me whether I would consider joining. I think that he was surprised but also intrigued with my reply. I argued that the Church could decide its own religious doctrines, however foolishly, and that the civil courts had no business, under the First Amendment establishment clause, getting involved in such matters.

Bishop Pike subsequently wrote me a recommendation for my first academic position at Berkeley. When he was a resident at the Center for the Study of Democratic Institutions at Santa Barbara in 1968, he invited me for the day to visit and meet the other fellows, including Robert Hutchins and Paul Jacobs, both of whom I had admired for very different reasons. His accidental death in the Israeli desert in 1969 saddened me, but it seemed curiously fitting for that strange and dynamic life.

Chapter 15
First Foray into Academia: Golden Gate College

The catalyst for my politicized, unique professional life as an academic occurred in late 1966, right before my marital break-up. During a visit to my parents' house in Berkeley, I conversed with their friend who was an administrator at Golden Gate College in San Francisco. He mentioned that he was looking for a part-time political science instructor in spring semester 1967. After discussing the job and the college for a few minutes, he asked whether I wanted to give it a try. He was also a leftist activist, so the match with his needs and values and my interests was especially congenial. I had told him that throughout law school, I used to imagine teaching, fantasizing about various classes, books, and teaching styles I might use. Fascinated, I eagerly agreed and he arranged for me to teach "Introduction to Political Science" in January.

I spent much of the winter break preparing the class and was both nervous and excited when I walked into the classroom of a dozen or so students as the teacher for the first time. Only a few minutes later, I felt perfectly at ease, and at the end of the initial class, at age 23, I knew that this is what I wanted to do for the rest of my working life. I enjoyed guiding the discussion and I especially liked interacting with students. One day into my first semester, I knew unambiguously that I would not be a practicing lawyer as a fulltime professional.

My course readings reflected both my political interest and my pedagogical vision, especially one that was thoroughly interdisciplinary. Having been excruciatingly bored with conventional political science and other textbooks, I decided on a radically different approach. I began the course with Ken Kesey's wildly popular novel, *One Flew Over the Cuckoo's Nest*. By focusing on the internal dynamics of power in a mental institution, I conveyed that politics goes far beyond the formal treatment of government and its institutions—the limited political science substance I had endured as an undergraduate. I wanted to show my students that politics was ubiquitous in human affairs. Above all, I focused on the role of the novel's protagonist, Randall Patrick McMurphy, especially as he challenged the authority of the hospital administration, particularly Nurse Ratched. This was, at bottom, the story of political resistance, perhaps the most enduring theme of my academic career.

I ended the class with a two-week unit on Vietnam, using *The Vietnam Reader* edited by Marcus Raskin and Bernard Fall. I explained my rationale to the students at the outset of the course. I told them that a political science course should, among other things, address contemporary political issues.

131

And in 1967, no issue was more important or controversial than the war in Vietnam. Accordingly, we discussed the war and its growing opposition in America and throughout the world. I made my own anti-war stance clear, but encouraged vigorous debate regardless of the views articulated. This has been my pedagogical stance for more than 40 years; I am clear, even passionate, about my own views and express them in order to encourage active student learning. I have never penalized students with opposing viewpoints, but I demand careful argumentation and effective expression of all views, including those that resemble my own.

I also managed to bring in my personal need for satire during class. I had been a longtime reader of Paul Krassner's *Realist* magazine, loving its unabashed irreverence. Sometime during the class, I gave an assignment using Krassner's bitingly satirical character he called the "Realist Nun" as an example. Krassner had taken a woman, a former hooker I recall, dressed her as a nun, and sent her into the streets of San Francisco to engage in decidedly unreligious activities, such as French kissing various men. I sent Krassner a copy of the assignment and he published it in the *Realist*. I don't include it in my professional vitae.

One social protest during my first semester of teaching had special emotional import for me. I told my students that I would participate, since I wanted to "do politics" as well as to teach it. On April 12, 1967, the State of California put convicted murderer Aaron Mitchell to death in San Quentin's gas chamber. Ever since the Chessman case seven years previously, I opposed the death penalty and this latest execution generated a large protest outside the prison grounds. I took a Dexedrine tablet and drove to San Quentin on the evening of April 11. There I joined the vigil all night long, sitting silently until Mitchell was put to death the following morning at ten. Throughout the long night, I kept a running dairy of the vigil events, which included a repulsive appearance by my old nemesis, Nazi George Lincoln Rockwell, whose murder a few months later was extremely gratifying. This document also recorded my personal feelings, and when I returned to Berkeley, I titled my writings as "Twelve Hours at San Quentin." I published it in an obscure radical newspaper later that month and also omit it from my vitae.

My personal gratification during this semester was huge. It turned out that teaching was also valuable in helping me heal from the rupture of my personal relationship. It was a valuable lesson: good work is no panacea, but it makes a big difference in the quality of one's life.

Golden Gate College was the start and I remember it fondly. My chairman was a man named Marcello Ramos, who was exceptionally kind. He encouraged me whenever he saw me, even though I was about as marginal as a faculty member could get. I took the bus from Berkeley, walked a few blocks to the college, taught the class, reversed the process, and went back to law school. One bus riding advantage soon presented itself. I recognized Eric Hoffer, the famous longshoreman/intellectual, sitting on the bus to Berkeley one day and went over and said, "I recognize you and I admire your book, *The True Believer*." I think he was pleased and he invited me to sit with him. We sat together five or six times and discussed his work. I was intrigued with his ideas about mass movements and mob psychology, and I'm sure that I told him about my Levittown experiences. Yet again, I found intellectual stimulation outside the academy.

Sometime during the semester, I also finally got off probation. Judge Hussey approved an early termination, acknowledging that I was a few weeks away from finishing law school, had written the papers consistent with the "rigorous" intellectual standards of the San Diego Municipal Court, and had broken no laws that he ever knew about. If he had any actual idea of my activities and my attitudes during the probation period, he would have had apoplexy. When I received the formal papers discharging me from the court's jurisdiction, I scribbled, "Paid in Full" over it and tacked it to the wall of my fleabag Berkeley apartment. *That* nightmare, at least, was over.

As much as I enjoyed the Golden Gate experience, I couldn't possibly anticipate in 1967 that for the next forty plus years, I would go on to build a highly successful, gratifying, frustrating, and thoroughly unorthodox academic career, almost entirely at the University of California. But that is what happened and that story will occupy much of the remainder of this memoir. But not all. I have also been fortunate to have a strong and durable marriage and family. My wife Ruth has been with me through the academic wars, as I faced the struggles that many radical academics have endured, but that few have survived. My extensive travels and my continuing political activism also occupy the rest of the story. Nevertheless, the academic focus is central to the narrative.

By accident and design, I have lived my professional life as an academic maverick, on the margin of institutional life, yet with increasing respect both at my home university, UCLA, and in the wider national and international scholarly communities. My interdisciplinary vision of the humanities and social sciences, rooted in my early years in college, has spanned a variety of traditional disciplines within these fields. My teaching and research have encompassed several traditional academic fields, including history, political science, sociology, philosophy, art history, film studies, and comparative literature, as well as newer areas of intellectual inquiry such as communication studies, African American studies, and women's studies. I resist identifying with any specific academic field or discipline, even though I

133

have earned widespread recognition as an art and cultural critic and historian. My "mantra" for many decades is that I believe in "discipline," but have no particular discipline. I have traveled a long way since law school.

But my early steps were extremely tentative. Because of my fundamental inexperience in both the academic job market and academic culture, I hardly knew how to proceed further. Unlike traditional Ph.D. students, I had no faculty mentors to help with personal contacts throughout the country. I also had no dissertation to show a protracted piece of scholarly research. All I had was a tiny amount of college teaching experience, a law degree from a prestigious school, strong verbal skills, and a lot of chutzpah. All I could think of doing was to type letters and send them out to various institutions. I still had little idea about institutional rankings and prestige; I merely wanted a job so that I could continue doing something that was personally enjoyable and intellectually satisfying. I started this process a few weeks before I graduated and continued through the summer.

My final law school exams finished, I graduated with my J.D. degree. I couldn't bother to attend the graduation ceremony because it meant so little to me and my alienation was so strong. I had to work that day and had no desire to sacrifice my hourly wages to see law professors and law students I would likely never see again. More immediately relevant, the day I finished law school, I had about $70 to my name and owed nothing; this is remarkable in today's context, where law school graduates typically have debts of well over $100,000. But I needed to make money fast. I arranged to work again in the agriculture library on campus and Golden Gate College offered me another political science class. I initiated a new course called "Politics and Literature," systematizing what would become my permanent teaching approach, using literature and other forms of artistic expression as valuable source material for social and political inquiry.

That prospect was truly exciting, because I could put together some major novels and make a coherent and engaging class. I recall using, among other literary sources, Franz Kafka's *The Trial*, and Alan Sillitoe's story "The Loneliness of the Long Distance Runner." My key reading was the play by Peter Weiss, *The Investigation*, concerning the prosecution of second and third level Nazi war criminals in 1965, long after the famous Nuremburg trials of the major Nazi figures. This was the beginning of a policy I have maintained rigorously my entire teaching career, addressing Holocaust issues somewhere during each academic year. It has been a personal pledge to myself, to my murdered family, and to the entire six million Jewish martyrs.

The course encouraged me to broaden my interdisciplinary focus. It went well; once again, I found substantial student satisfaction in my thematic approach and personal teaching style. During this time, I intensified my search for longer-term academic employment. I had several positive responses, but these mostly suggested subsequent inquiries and the submission of additional materials. As I recall, they were for all the following academic year, not the coming September.

One other responsibility hung over my life during this busy summer. I had initially decided to forego the California Bar Examination. I was so disenchanted with the law that I really wanted to leave it entirely behind. Enough people, however, convinced me that after putting in three intense years (they really weren't *that* intense), I should at least get a license to practice. Reluctantly, at the last minute, I registered for the exam, paying a late fee I could barely afford. Everyone advised me to quit my jobs and enroll in a preparation course, costing then around $400. That sum was far beyond my means and I adamantly refused to obtain a loan. My experiences with my parents made that psychologically untenable. Debt, even now, fills me with powerfully irrational fear. The result was obvious. I worked full-time and studied sporadically. I flunked the bar exam, but actually came fairly close to passing. The result next time, a year later, was different. I had more money, more time, and a better attitude.

On the academic job front, nothing concrete emerged until the middle of summer. Then I got a break. An exciting opportunity, I imagined, became available. I think that I saw an advertisement in an academic publication or a newspaper, but I could have spotted it in the general UC Berkeley placement office. I quickly responded with a strong cover letter.

Chapter 16
Cal Arts: A Forgettable, But Turbulent Year

Following a Los Angeles interview at the newly formed California Institute of the Arts, I was invited to join the Humanities faculty for the start of academic year 1967/68. I was fascinated by the merger of the Chouinard Art Institute and the Los Angeles Conservatory of Music and thought that a Humanities Department would be ideal given my increasing passion for the arts and for interdisciplinary teaching. Only 24, I had little experience in academic double-talk and institutional duplicity — lessons I would learn soon enough at Cal Arts and even more when I joined the UC Berkeley faculty a year later.

At Cal Arts, I believed my interviewers when they said that we could explore the range of the humanities and that we would have engaging, intellectually curious art and music students who would make our teaching lives a joy. Like many others, I discovered that promises and reality are sometimes polar opposites. The facilities were horrible; we taught, at first, in a dingy movie theater on Wilshire Boulevard, a mile or so from downtown. Then we moved to the Elks Building, perhaps the most bizarre setting for instruction I have ever experienced. Between "classrooms," we encountered old Elks (humans, not animals), coughing and hacking away. I watched them sadly, imagining various tumors growing rapidly in their decaying bodies.

My colleagues were mostly mediocre. One philosophy teacher, as far as I could tell, was a Christian who imagined himself a kind of spiritual guru. Another philosophy teacher, who held a B.A. degree alone, seemed to me to be a fascist. He went ballistic when I showed Alain Resnais's classic Holocaust documentary, "Night and Fog," to the student body. The science teacher taught Immanuel Velikovsky, the Russian Jewish crackpot uniformly rejected by respectable scientists throughout the world. The Department Chair and the school administration had no idea how to create an integrated humanities curriculum. The Chair told me that I was hired as "the new leftist." I knew that I wanted to get out by the end of the first week and began looking for another position almost immediately.

The art and music students, with a few exceptions, lacked serious intellectual curiosity. They were largely unresponsive to my questions and I quickly despaired, even questioning my own abilities as a teacher. A few students, fortunately, actually did the readings and revealed some interests beyond their own artistic work. But that was scarcely enough for me to find much satisfaction in this environment.

Almost immediately after arriving in Los Angeles, I confronted a challenge that millions of young men had faced during the Vietnam era. When I graduated from law school, I received a J.D. degree, and a few days later, a 1-A classification from the hated Selective Service System and its uniformly despised (in Berkeley, at least) director, General Lewis Hershey. I had decided that I would never participate in that war. I also determined that I would not leave the country for Canada or Sweden or anywhere else. I thought about conscientious objection, but I was not actually opposed to war in all forms, just to this one. I decided, reluctantly, that I would take a jail sentence if absolutely necessary. The draft was a constant, almost obsessive topic among young men in Berkeley. We had given thought to just about every option, including bizarre possibilities like personal mutilation or other bodily damage.

I had a legitimate medical out because I had suffered asthma attacks since childhood. In college, their severity lessened, but they have never disappeared. I still need an inhaler from time to time in my 60s. Anticipating this option, I sought medical attention both as an undergraduate and as a law student every time I so much as wheezed or had the slightest shortness of breath. In short, I had a substantial medical record, with a veritable mountain of medical documentation, by the time I reported for my pre-induction physical in Los Angeles in October, 1967.

The physical examination itself was predictably Kafkaesque. I decided to make myself look as emaciated as possible for this ordeal. For about 48 hours, I stopped eating and drank only black coffee, maybe as many as 50 or 60 cups during that time. Arriving at the armed forces building, the officer in charge looked at us all and remarked, "We've been waiting for you for 18 years." I said nothing, but thought, "Fuck you, Jack, you can wait another 18." We had the standardized intelligence test, which was insultingly stupid. And then came the interview with the doctor. Standing in my underpants, I clutched my medical records. When it was my turn, I disappeared behind a curtain and the doctor, who struck me as a mediocre graduate from a mail order medical school, looked at me for a second or two and said, "You look fine, follow the yellow line."

I didn't follow the yellow line. Instead, I ducked back into line and went to another doctor, behind another curtain. He looked at my medical papers for a few moments and rejected me from military service: a cherished 1-Y classification. I had a back-up plan as well. I had substantial documentation from a psychiatrist, over a two or three year period, attesting to my emotional inability to adapt to military service. Given my attitude towards authority, no truer statement could ever be expressed. I celebrated that night with two beers, one more than my usual limit.

About a month after the fall semester began, we had a major crisis at Cal Arts, one that I may have precipitated. Soon after the semester started we were called to an emergency humanities department meeting. The Chair announced that our classes had been cut back by half, therefore cutting our salaries in half from $8000 to $4000. The former sum was big money to me then, but I said immediately that I would resist the cuts. (Actually, I thought it would be a good excuse to go back to Berkeley, but I liked a fight). I immediately organized some faculty and many students, giving impassioned speeches and mobilizing parents. This went on for about two weeks and it was successful. The cuts were restored, but my visibility made me a target.

During the conflict, rumors about my political radicalism surfaced. Some parents told me that they had heard of my "communist" associations. On some levels, I was indifferent. I would get out of there by the end of the academic year no matter what. But I probed a little. The Disney Corporation dominated the Cal Arts Board. I regarded Walt Disney as a major political reactionary and anti-Semite and I later learned that one of the trustees was H. R. Haldeman, one of Richard Nixon's Watergate henchmen who served time in federal prison. It's satisfying to think that these people initiated the red baiting. I cannot prove it, but they were certainly capable of such action, as their records dramatically revealed. I decided to be especially provocative, sometimes wearing Mickey Mouse ears around campus in a gesture of contempt for the whole Disney empire.

Although the academic year experience was the most forgettable and frustrating of my life, I pursued other activities that fostered my subsequent teaching and research. I continued my political activism, participating in numerous anti-war and other activities in Los Angeles. I visited my former professor Jim Harmon several times. He was now teaching at the San Diego State satellite campus in Calexico. He plied me with more critical readings in political economy, but my intellectual interests were shifting powerfully.

Equally important, I took considerable advantage of the art scene in Southern California. I visited museums, galleries, and other artistic venues and talked extensively with several prominent local artists. I read voraciously, devouring as much art historical literature as I could. I took a methodical approach to these readings, with a special focus on the modern period from the 18th century to the mid 20th century, continuing my efforts as an art historical autodidact. By early spring, 1968, I was notified that I would not be rehired, both a forgone conclusion and emotionally irrelevant. I had commenced discussions with UC Berkeley, advanced in part because I then had a good friend on the speech department faculty there.

My saddest memory of that year was April 4, 1968, after hearing that Martin Luther King had been murdered in Memphis. Stunned, I walked aimlessly through my Fairfax neighborhood of Los Angeles for several hours. The emotional toll was gigantic, much more than anything I have ever felt, before or since, with the death of any public figure.

By the time I left Los Angeles, I had strong confidence that I would receive an offer at Berkeley. This confidence led me to travel to Europe for the first time. I had long paid close attention to European history and politics, especially in the post World War II period. My personal radicalism made me severely critical of the conservative governments of Western Europe, although I recognized that most of their social policies, like health care, were more progressive than those of the United States. My travel focus was on such traditional nations in Europe as England, France, Switzerland, Italy, Germany, and Holland as well as Soviet bloc nations like Czechoslovakia and East Germany. I specifically avoided Spain, where fascist dictator Francisco Franco still held virtually complete power, and Portugal, where reactionary Prime Minister Antonio Salazar had ruled for many decades.

I was eager to get some first-hand impressions about the "miraculous" new Europe. I assumed that the countries I visited would be remarkably similar to the United States, but with a deeper sense of history and probably greater physical beauty. That assumption was largely confirmed; capitalism seemed to be thriving and consumer values appeared to dominate popular consciousness. One conspicuous difference was the general absence of visible urban poverty that was so dramatic in most American cities. Still, I found it easy to identify distinct class differences in Europe while recognizing that racial and ethnic populations were far less diverse there than in the United States. I could well understand why working class men and women would challenge the existing order throughout Western Europe.

At the same time, I had always been suspicious of Soviet power and its repressive apparatus throughout Eastern Europe. I remembered the Hungarian Revolution in 1956 and the overwhelming brutality of the Soviet Union in squelching the rebellion. Though a committed socialist, I assumed that Soviet leaders and their surrogates throughout their satellite world were more interested in preserving their own power than in advancing the genuine interests of their populations. I had no illusions about their authentic desire to share political and economic power with the masses of people under their dominion. Although I rejected the mindless and relentless anti-communism I grew up with during the 1950s, I also understood that Communist power was totalitarian and often savage; a year later, in Czechoslovakia, I witnessed this terrifying reality firsthand.

I knew that the general political turbulence of the late 1960s (but especially in 1968) would increase my chances of participating politically in some of the dramatic continental conflicts. I followed the various uprisings against

139

conservative regimes in Western Europe and I anticipated similar rebellions against communist regimes in the East. I knew that I could be, at most, only an incidental player, not even a "minor" one. But I was determined to see as much of these events for myself as I could. That decision, like others in my life, had major implications for both my political and professional future.

As it happened, following a brief visit to London, I flew to Paris in the middle of the great worker-student rebellion of 1968. Paris was exhilarating; I had no interest in sightseeing when I could participate in political actions that could potentially bring down the government of President Charles de Gaulle. I joined demonstrations near the Sorbonne, where the student-occupied courtyard of that venerable institution had been transformed into a collective meeting place, replete with banners, posters, leaflets, and other documents. Most striking was the surprisingly conservative stance of the French Communist Party. Its newspaper, L'Humanite, seemed cautious, even hostile, to the student protestors. My minimal knowledge of French was only a marginal handicap. Several friendly radical students explained everything that was happening, sometimes minute by minute.

I saw egregious police brutality against student demonstrators and participated in numerous left bank marches and demonstrations. Those gendarmes meant business. They wielded their clubs brutally, much worse than the mild shoving I had usually experienced in the United States. The revolutionary posters excited me; like the Mexican murals I had seen two years earlier, they augmented my interests in political art. I collected a few of the originals and used them for years in various classes. I was also delighted to participate in the occupation of the Odeon, the national theater, a few blocks from the Sorbonne. Subsequently, many observers decried all of these actions as anarchistic and nihilistic. I saw it as an authentic expression of democracy, a highlight of late middle 20th century history, and, for me, a privilege to play a small part.

Later, I traveled to West Berlin, where I also joined various left-wing protests in the agitation then sweeping much of the world. Germany brought me complex emotions; Berlin was the city where the Gestapo arrested my father's family and transported them first to Theresienstadt and then to Auschwitz. I found it tough to look at anyone over middle age or so. What did they do during the war? Were they Nazis, even murderers themselves? Did they know everything but do nothing to stop the genocide? Were they still anti-Semitic? How would they respond if I told them that I was a Jew? Those feelings and questions have never left me in repeated research and pleasure trips to Germany.

My most moving experience, however, occurred during my brief visit to Prague, Czechoslovakia. On one level, the stultifying nature of communist orthodoxy was obvious. I went to the Museum of the Revolution and saw exhibitions that were veritable caricatures: heroic pictures of Lenin, ruddy and smiling peasants, cheerful workers with medals stating "Heroes of Socialist Labor." I have always been far too irreverent for such nonsense. Such displays always bring me back immediately to Jonathan Swift and George Grosz and any other savage satirists I know.

Prague, however, had a more promising reality. It was "Prague Spring," led by the reformist government of Alexander Dubcek. I sensed a new feeling of freedom in the air, confirmed in several conversations I had with young people during my brief visit to that hauntingly beautiful city. Dubcek, who had replaced the repressive regime of Communist Party hack Antonin Novotny, was liberating society, almost palpably. I witnessed freedom of expression never before seen in the communist world. Posters and graffiti abounded and Dubcek's slogan, "socialism with a human face," seemed pervasive. It made sense to me. But in August, Soviet leader Leonid Brezhnev ordered Soviet and satellite troops to invade Czechoslovakia, ending the Dubcek experiment and terminating the brief but exhilarating moment of "Prague Spring." Once again in Berkeley, I vowed to return.

Chapter 17
The Big Leagues: Teaching at Berkeley

A position as lecturer in the Berkeley Speech Department was formalized on my return from Europe. Delighted to join the University of California faculty, I had no real idea about the marginal status of non-ladder faculty members, especially in prestigious research institutions. Only later would I learn all too well the intricacies of the system of academic apartheid that uses and abuses men and women we now call "contingent faculty." Over the years, I have seen scores of talented teachers hired and fired cavalierly; many lost the opportunity for academic employment permanently. I am one of the very few long-term survivors.

I had one major task, however, before the academic year began. This time, I took the bar examination seriously. I enrolled in a prep course, read the materials meticulously, and studied 8-10 hours a day. I took the exam in San Francisco in August, making sure to leave the examination site during lunch break. I had no desire to see and mingle with thousands of anxious bar applicants any more than necessary. It was a painful three day ordeal and I had no idea about my chances when it was over. But I resolved that this was it and that I would live with whatever results occurred. In December, I learned that I had passed. I have never looked at legal issues so thoroughly since then. Interestingly, Judge Luther Hussey sent me a letter congratulating me on my membership in the State Bar, adding a line about his disappointment that I had chosen to go into teaching instead of full-time legal practice.

The bar exam did not keep me from closely watching the violence at the Democratic Party Convention in Chicago in August, 1968. Like millions of others, I watched Mayor Richard Daley's police thugs brutally assault thousands of anti-war protestors. Those actions, later officially declared a "police riot," marked a new, violent turn to the anti-war movement in the United States. I knew many of the demonstrators in Chicago, including a few who were injured, and sympathized with the new "Yippies." Above all, I was appalled by Vice President Hubert Humphrey's nomination for President and resolved never to vote for a candidate who would prolong this grotesque war. Naturally, I detested Richard Nixon, but once again, I refused to be drawn into an odious process of "lesser evil" politics.

The Chicago police riot helped to give birth to the Weather Underground, the extreme radical group that organized the "Days of Rage" on October 8, 1969, coinciding with the trial of the Chicago seven defendants arising out of the 1968 Convention disorders. The Weather Underground also commenced various bombings, targeting government buildings and banks. Its violent activities were a constant topic of discussion in Berkeley for several years. My view was clear. I thought these people were essentially mad. However monstrous its policies and priorities, America was not a revolutionary nation. I drew on my deeper skepticism about the human condition on this point, despite my fervent desire for structural political and economic change. To me, the Weather Underground was a sorry collection of romantic revolutionaries, doomed to failure and egregious self-deception.

The academic year 1968/69 at the University of California at Berkeley was momentous, marking the beginning of my "big-league" academic career. Early in the fall quarter, the Department changed its name to the Department of Rhetoric, seeking higher status and visibility within the Berkeley academic community and beyond. My first commitment was to make my teaching as effective as possible. I recall spending enormous time in preparation and thought about my instructional responsibilities. Above all, I sought to promote vigorous class discussions and sustained student writing—goals to which I have subscribed my entire career. Throughout the year, I used a variety of humanities-related materials, including literary works by Dostoevsky and Tolstoy and works in the Marxist tradition by Herbert Marcuse and others. Marcuse, in fact, was a frequent visitor to the Berkeley campus. I initiated a correspondence with him and met him a few times in Berkeley. I still regard his works as brilliant. His analysis of advanced capitalism remains perceptive well into the new century. I assumed, naively, that teaching excellence would be highly valued by my institutional superiors. At 25, I had much to learn about the realities of academic life.

This academic year at Berkeley was politically tumultuous and frequently violent. During fall quarter, a major controversy arose over whether Black Panther Party leader Eldridge Cleaver could be the instructor in a course called "Social Analysis 139X." That made perfect sense to me. Students should be exposed, I thought, to people deeply involved in the major political struggles of the times. Cleaver was a major Panther leader, had written a provocative book, *Soul on Ice*, and represented the militant wing of the black struggle. During the controversy, I met and spoke with him a few times and thought he had enough going for him to serve as a guest lecturer in that course. But I certainly knew that conservative forces in the administration would resist it fiercely.

Winter Quarter saw massive student demonstrations supporting the creation of black studies and other ethnic studies courses and programs. This struggle evoked even deeper personal passions because of my civil rights history. I joined this effort aggressively, often publicly with speeches from the steps of the administration building. Throughout the winter, I joined the almost daily demonstrations and witnessed several incidents of

143

police brutality on the Berkeley campus. I strongly believed that ethnic studies units were fundamental to the mission of the contemporary university. The history and culture of people of color had been systematically excluded from the curriculum. Black Studies, Chicano Studies, Asian American Studies, American Indian Studies—all these and more were exciting, offering marvelous opportunities for teaching and research. In 1969, I still had little idea about the deeper and more entrenched conservatism of most university faculty in traditional departments.

Equally important, as a new lawyer, I also served as legal counsel for many of the students and others arrested during these raucous demonstrations. I worked out of "Legal Central," and cooperated with the few lawyers I had come to respect over the years. I made numerous trips to various local jails, arranging release on bail, appearances in court to enter "not guilty" pleas, and participating in plea bargains so that my political clients could avoid jail time and any other serious consequences. I developed a good reputation as a local political lawyer even while focusing primarily on my academic responsibilities. All this activity was fairly visible, with substantial press coverage. It did not go unnoticed in my department.

Spring quarter involved the People's Park controversy, even while anti-war activity heated up in the Bay Area and throughout the nation. Because of the violence on campus, many of my classes this academic year were held in nearby churches and other community settings. I got used to teaching all over the periphery of campus and developed some gratifying relationships with Berkeley clergy and church staff, all of whom seemed in total sympathy with the student movements. I have continued to have enormous respect for socially progressive religious people, especially from Christian and Jewish communities, despite my own absence of religious belief.

The dramatic events in May, 1969, however, exceeded anything we had experienced ever in Berkeley. I knew about People's Park because I often walked there during my frequent forays to Telegraph Avenue bookstores south of campus. The plot of land, owned formally by the University, had been appropriated by various students and others who planted trees, flowers, and shrubs and generally turned it into a pleasant enough oasis. I was not especially engaged with the effort. It smacked too much of counter-cultural activity, with overlays of nature romanticism and probably drug use. But I had no objection to its fundamental challenge to University property rights.

Everything changed the morning of May 15, 1969. Governor Ronald Reagan directed a large force of California Highway patrol officers to clear and block off the park, securing it with a chain-link fence. Students responded with a large noon rally, which included several student leaders,

144

calling on students to retake the park. This precipitated a massive conflict, erupting into unprecedented violence that afternoon.

Student protestors encountered massive police force, specifically members of the Alameda Sheriff's Department, labeled "Blue Meanies," for good reason. One protestor was killed and many others were injured, some seriously. Reagan declared a state of emergency, ordering a curfew in Berkeley and dispatching a large contingent of National Guard troops. This was my first experience of a military occupation and it was unnerving. Reagan's field commander was Ed Meese, later the reactionary Attorney General during his presidency.

The police and military brutality angered and mobilized me, transcending my indifference about the original People's Park issues. I witnessed plenty of outrageous conduct. In one case, I saw Alameda Sherriff's deputies driving by an unrelated motorcycle accident near Telegraph Avenue. Their patrol car slowed down, stopped, and the officer lobbed a tear gas grenade at the injured cyclist. I was too far away to get any identification.

More troublesome was Meese's conduct on the Berkeley campus. He ordered National Guard helicopters to drop CS gas on a large crowd near Sproul Hall Plaza. I was trapped there with many hundreds of others. It was my first tear gassing and the first bombing of an American campus. I vomited intermittently for several hours after the attack.

During the curfew, lawyers with clients were exempted. Once, when I went after curfew to the Berkeley City Jail to inquire about clients who had been arrested, a guardsman stopped me at bayonet point. I angrily produced my California State Bar card and eventually he backed down, after a superior officer intervened. I sharply told both of them that Ronald Reagan had no authority to suspend the Constitution.

There was also one mass arrest on Shattuck Avenue in downtown Berkeley, which included demonstrators as well as citizens fortuitously caught there. These people were taken approximately 30 miles away to the Alameda County Jail in Santa Rita, a place I came to know well. I was one of the first lawyers on the scene and I witnessed some flagrant brutality, including deputies using blackjacks on prisoners. I worked feverishly to get personal information to get back to court and have these people released as soon as possible. Deputies at Santa Rita often tried to obstruct the lawyers' efforts. Once, when I asked to use the restroom, a guard refused. Apparently, the constitutional right to counsel failed to include the right of the attorney to pee. Fortunately, I again found a superior officer with a more rational perspective. I think I was there for over 12 hours. When I returned, I went to court and got many of these prisoners released without bail. But it was a genuine nightmare.

145

Despite (or because of) my political involvements, I compiled an exemplary teaching record in 1968/69. My student evaluations were high and I had a strong sense of my academic accomplishments. At the end of the academic year I met with the head of the rhetoric department to discuss my efforts. The conversation was mostly *pro forma* and he commented favorably on my teaching. Then, in a statement I have never forgotten, he told me that this was Berkeley, where faculty members have to publish. His final comment was chilling: "We don't give a shit about teaching." Shaken, I said nothing in return but I seethed inside. I also resolved mentally never to capitulate to a scheme that was detrimental to serious education.

I returned to Europe that summer with the specific intention of participating in the mass demonstrations that I knew would occur in Prague commemorating the first anniversary of the Soviet invasion of 1968. I had corresponded with several people I met there and had information that several protest activities would occur. Before entering Czechoslovakia, I spent several days in Vienna, mostly to check it out and because it was close to Bratislava, where I thought I would enter Czechoslovakia a few days later. Vienna was abuzz with rumors about what might happen in Prague. I don't recall the circumstances of our meeting, but I found a Viennese journalist who had been denied an entry visa to cover the impending protests. When I showed him my own Czech tourist visa, he asked me to phone him daily from Prague with my observations.

I met students both in Bratislava and in Pilzen who were planning commemorative protests. But the big actions were in Prague. I arrived several days in advance of the anniversary. I found some of the people to whom I had written and joined them in the demonstrations that began several days before the first anniversary of the Soviet invasion of 1968. Language was not a serious barrier. My contacts spoke English and my knowledge of German was useful generally in the country. The big protest was scheduled for August 21, when a general strike was scheduled; people were to stay home from work, avoid public transportation, and assemble at Wenceslas Square for a huge rally. Each night I placed the call to the reporter in Vienna, giving a detailed report of my observations.

I reserved one day, however, for an intensely personal pilgrimage. I decided to take a short bus ride to the Bohemian town of Terezin, the site of a Nazi concentration camp called Theresienstadt, the fraudulent "paradise ghetto" that the Germans claimed was the finest example of their humane policy towards the relocated Jews. I had read all about this deception before my visit. But my emotions ran deeper. This is where my grandparents had been sent, before their murder in Auschwitz. I needed to see it. When I arrived, I spoke to the front office bureaucrats in charge, who gave me the standard Stalinist line: communist heroes were imprisoned there and they fought heroically in the resistance. Enough of that, I thought. I asked to speak to the Director and explained that my grandparents had been inmates there. My story moved him, obviously deeply. His grace and hospitality were amazing. He opened the camp to me and said I could see whatever I wanted. He showed me the pictures that children had drawn. I wondered; could one of those drawings have come from my Uncle Rolf? He invited me to examine whatever documents I wanted to see. I was there for most of a day. It was emotionally exhausting. I returned to Prague ready to fight.

The anniversary date of the Soviet invasion was equally moving, but in a very different sense. I joined the immense crowd in Wenceslas Square. At noon, everyone sat down and sang the Czech national anthem. It was another of those transcendent political moments for me, one that will stay etched in my mind until my death. I've tried to explain it often to my students as an eternal yearning for freedom. But it must really be experienced in person to grasp its full emotional impact.

The official repression began almost immediately. I saw Czech police officers force people onto streetcars at gunpoint, and then photograph them in order to show that the boycott failed. Soon the attacks escalated. Both police and the army went on a rampage on the streets of Prague, beating and jailing large numbers of demonstrators with impunity. I fled down side streets with hundreds of others, as armed officers were in close pursuit, shooting tear gas constantly. Then, almost magically on one narrow street, doors opened and residents pulled us inside to safety—another unforgettable moment.

That day or perhaps the next, as street protests in Prague continued, I witnessed something for the first and only time in my lifetime of political confrontation. I saw someone shot to death. This is how it happened. A group of demonstrators were confronting the police, taunting them and perhaps even lobbing stones and other projectiles. I was forty or fifty yards away, far enough to avoid immediate personal danger. Then a policeman took out a revolver and shot a man on a low hanging balcony. The victim tumbled over, apparently dead. I read later that five people were killed that August. I dutifully reported everything I observed to my Vienna contact.

Later that evening, my Prague friends advised me to get out of the country as soon as possible. They knew that the authorities were blaming "westerners" and "imperialists" for the troubles on the streets. They were anxious to find agitators from Western Europe to blame (Americans would also be fair game). They had a point. I had been stopped a few times walking by myself on the streets and asked for my passport. Once, an army contingent stopped me. I played the dumb tourist, saying in English that I

147

didn't understand. A German speaking officer asked me what I was doing in Prague. I told him that I was just visiting and knew nothing about politics. I just wanted to go back to my hotel and then go home. Suitably convinced, he let me pass.

I wanted to stay and continue. But they persuaded me to leave and I reluctantly purchased a ticket to Berlin. The train ride was routine for about two hours. Then the train stopped at a small station. I sat there, not even remotely concerned. Suddenly, everything changed dramatically. Several uniformed men entered the car and made their way to my seat. They motioned me to get up and accompany them. I followed them outside the train and into the station.

In a few minutes, after confiscating my inexpensive camera, one of the officers began questioning me, in Czech. I repeated in English that I couldn't understand. He brought a German speaking official, who actually seemed sympathetic. Why had I been in Prague? I was evasive. I will never forget my initial answer. I told him that I was a tourist and that I had come to Prague to visit Franz Kafka's house. He asked a few more questions and was a little taken aback when I asked where I was. I specifically asked for the name of the town—in German, the "Dorf." He said it wasn't a town, but a city—in German, "eine Stadt."

A few minutes later, I was escorted under guard to the town (or city) jail, placed in a cell, and made to wait. I knew nobody and had not registered with the U.S. Embassy in Prague. Soon to follow was more questioning, in German and in broken English. Essentially, I told my interrogators that I did nothing wrong, but that if I did, I was truly sorry.

At about 8 p.m. or so, I said I was hungry. Then the most bizarre experience of my political life occurred. An armed guard took me from the station to a restaurant a block or so away. He told me to order dinner. I asked the waiter for a plate of Czech goulash and a glass of Pilsner Urquell beer. As I sat, I motioned to the waiter and said another beer for my friend, the guard, please. The guard accepted the offering. Czechs love their beer. I had enough Czech currency to pay the tab.

Then I was marched back to the station, where the officer in charge informed me that I would be deported from Czechoslovakia and placed on a train to Berlin shortly after midnight. I waited in the cell and then finally boarded the train, pleased to get out of this Stalinist lunatic asylum. A few hours later, I would encounter another moronic communist bureaucracy, this time in the German Democratic Republic.

I arrived in East Berlin in the early morning at Friedrichstrasse Station. It was still dark outside and I was determined to get to West Berlin immediately. I knew the geography from a previous trip and began walking

148

towards Checkpoint Charlie, perhaps a kilometer or so away. I walked into the East German checkpoint, showed my U.S. passport, and assumed that I would be allowed to cross over. No deal. The guard explained that the East German visa I purchased on the train to East Berlin did not authorize me to go by foot. I only had a "transit visa," permitting me only to go by underground subway. There followed a brief and absurd discussion about what constituted being "in transit." I tried an acting gesture by walking a few steps, moving my feet up and down, saying "Transit." The guard replied, "Nein!" This whole discussion was almost Talmudic, worthy of the kind of rabbinical commentaries on commentaries on commentaries.

The border guards held their linguistic and philosophical ground and would not permit me to cross into West Berlin, a few hundred yards away. But this was not the Gulag. They sent for a limo, a large black Russian-made sedan, invited me to sit in the back seat, and drove me back to Friedrichstrasse Station. Then an official, efficiently, escorted me through the immigration procedures. In typical German fashion, there were lots of papers to be stamped. We went to the platform and waited for the S-Bahn, a subway that went under the Berlin Wall, which would take me to West Berlin. But during the wait, I witnessed an unforgettable incident. An East German man tried to get to the platform, apparently to escape to the West. Communist guards jumped on him, beat him severely, and took him away. Still a passionate socialist, I had seen the true face of Stalinist brutality. I have never been a Soviet apologist. These experiences also persuaded me that American communists, whom I still generally liked and appreciated, had a tragic blind spot when it came to the Soviet Union and its Eastern European lackeys.

Finally, I arrived in West Berlin as day broke. I have never been so pleased to see capitalist decadence in my entire life. I got a hotel room and slept the rest of the day, ate, drank, and went to see close friends in Amsterdam. My feelings were similar to those during the civil rights movement in the south. I could go home, but the people in Prague had to stay and endure the oppressive consequences of the invasion. I well understood my own privileged position.

I returned for my second academic year at UC Berkeley. I continued to work on my teaching and began to think about embarking on a research program. I published a few pieces, but nothing that really addressed my sustained interest on art, politics, and society that would emerge a few years later. My classes dealt significantly with the pressing issues of the era: Vietnam, the draft, race, class, and even gender.

Then my personal life was permanently changed. My increasing political visibility gave me reasonable contact with women, but I was no Lothario, unlike many males I knew. I often explain to my students that life is a series of fortuitous events. One of these many events happened to me, putting me indirectly in contact with Ruth Chervin, then a Berkeley graduate student in botany, who later obtained a Ph.D. from the newly created interdisciplinary Graduate Group in Science and Mathematics Education, and now my wife of almost 40 years.

Here is what happened. I was on a teaching assistant selection committee in the rhetoric department. We had gone through a list of applicants and I was anxious to go home, because I had a serious headache. We had been debating an applicant from another department and there was some disagreement about his merits. Finally, I told everyone that I would take him, and if it proved to be a mistake, I would bear the consequences. That satisfied everyone. We hired him and I went home and treated my headache.

It *was* a modest academic mistake, but a splendid stroke of personal fortune. The applicant was disappointing; he revealed a troublesome irresponsibility as my TA, as I recall in grading papers on time and in his arrogance in dealing with my lower division students. But mostly he was a schmuck in his personal dealings with women, joining some thousands of other men around Berkeley. The ambience of sexual liberation at the time generally meant that men were free to hop from bed to bed; they merely had to be "honest" about their carnal proclivities. I never liked this feature of 60s culture all that much. It also brought out the more conventional, even conservative part of my psyche. These men seemed incapable of any kind of commitment, engaging in the kind of serial infidelity that has become a familiar and legitimate complaint for many decades. Ruth was one of his victims. I had known her slightly some months before when we had double-dated in San Francisco, with me paired with her roommate. I had later remarked to my parents that I would have preferred being with her.

It was a visceral and mutual attraction. She was vivacious, intellectually engaging, had taught in a historically black college, appeared politically compatible, and was Jewish. Above all else, I felt a powerful emotional connection to her, more than I had ever felt in my life. Her overall attractiveness made me realize that I wanted to spend my time with her, probably the rest of my adult life.

When Ruth broke up with him, she phoned me, ostensibly to ask about him. Both of us understood the real agenda. She was available and I took quick advantage of her availability. We stared seeing each other almost immediately thereafter. Our first "date" was to see Robert Altman's satirical movie "MASH," a huge hit in Berkeley. Things went well from there, and eventually we moved in together late in 1970 when her lease expired. When

150

my students ask for advice about finding intimate partners, I instruct them to gain membership on teaching assistant selection committees.

The campus, like much of the country, exploded in spring quarter, 1970, following President Richard Nixon's military incursion into Cambodia. Many teachers, including myself and Ruth, a teaching assistant in biology, "reconstituted" their classes in order to focus on the war's dramatic escalation. At that point, I had become an experienced public speaker, giving anti-war presentations on campus and in the wider community. I addressed professional groups and laypersons alike, doing whatever I could to mobilize anti-war opposition. The events of the day were catastrophic, including the killings at Kent State University and Jackson State University. My speeches incorporated all these items, but my most sustained focus was on the war itself.

I also continued to serve as legal counsel for demonstrators arrested and charged with various offenses. I became skilled in emergency criminal law, developing decent contacts with jail personnel in Berkeley and Santa Rita in order to expedite my clients' release from custody. I also developed some rapport with local judges. They came to trust my representations about defendants' contacts with the community. It was easy for me to get my political clients, especially students, released from jail on low or even no bail. I enjoyed these court appearances and kept a sports coat and tie in my campus office in case I had to hustle down to the local Municipal Court several blocks away.

I also augmented my *pro bono* practice with anti-draft and military legal work. Through my own personal experience and the many cases I handled, I had become extremely knowledgeable about the Selective Service System and the multitude of laws and regulations about this highly specialized area of practice. In short, I could keep young men out of military service at almost any stage in the process. I think I handled about twenty cases without a single loss. I established an especially strong record of successful conscientious objector applications. I also developed strong and reliable contacts in the anti-draft community and knew many doctors and clergy who were willing to supply strong and persuasive documentation supporting my clients' claims for deferments. I got referrals constantly, not really counting the students whom I counseled informally.

Some elaboration about the conscientious objector claims is worth noting. My clients *were* sincere in their objection to all wars. They met the legal standards, especially as defined in a landmark 1965 Supreme Court decision *United States v. Seeger*. There the Court held that exemption from military service as a conscientious objector would be available to men whose views about war were derived from a "sincere and meaningful belief which

151

occupies in the life of its possessor a place parallel to that filled by the God of those" in traditional pacifist religions like the Quakers, Mennonites, and Brethren. This meant that I could successfully claim CO status for draft registrants without conventional religious backgrounds. I assisted them with their claims, often writing substantial portions of the CO applications myself. I enlisted clergy even from mainline religions. I consulted with Protestant ministers, Catholic priests, and Jewish rabbis, finding theological doctrine to support my clients' appeals. But I never lied and never went beyond the law. Later, Selective Service System officials and some U.S. attorneys complimented me for my zeal and for my honesty. I did most of this work without fee, but in a few cases, I accepted nominal payments, usually at the insistence of grateful clients.

I got considerable satisfaction from this work, but I still never considered doing it as a full-time professional. This was political work and I had some special skills. Perhaps I should have thanked Judge Luther Hussey for his sentence in 1964, but my animosity toward him would never permit any favorable comment, even when his actions had unexpectedly desirable consequences, then or since. All of this was still an adjunct to my academic and scholarly efforts that occupied my major personal attention.

This external political and legal work naturally influenced my teaching at Berkeley, which continued throughout the next two academic years. I had published slightly, but without a consistent thematic focus. I was still feeling out the intellectual terrain and a few years away from the focus that would gain me some major scholarly visibility. Everything seemed fine from my daily contacts with departmental authorities. When the department head decided that he wanted an upper division course to attract more students, he turned to me and I developed a new class I called "Advanced Writing: Argument and Discourse." He gave me freedom to put together an interdisciplinary mix of readings drawn from literature and social analysis. I enjoyed this process of curricular development and it has been a central feature of my academic life throughout my career. Students responded especially well to this new course offering, pleasing me enormously.

I had little inkling that my popularity with students had an inverse effect on the rhetoric department senior faculty. My students liked my approach and teaching style. My formal course evaluations were outstanding, both quantitatively and qualitatively. A private student guide to teachers, the Slate Supplement, which arose out of FSM and post FSM student protests, rated me highly, advising undergraduates to enroll in my courses.

But my naiveté about the realities of academic life was astonishing. Eventually, I came to realize that in major research universities, popularity with undergraduates was dangerous. It often signified that a faculty member was a mere entertainer, a panderer to student fashion, a dispenser of easy grades, a person incapable of serious research, a superficial dilettante — in short, not a member of the club. I also came to realize that these reactions also concealed, not very effectively, some of the senior faculty members' own profound inadequacies as teachers and educators, perhaps even as human beings — what Nietzsche perceptively labeled *ressentiment*.

My personal life was going especially well. I made one short final trip by myself to Europe in summer 1970. I had no dramatic political clashes, but I wanted to return to Prague to check on friends I had met during the protests the summer before. I also made my first trip to Israel that summer. I was curious, but it was not a journey to solidify my Jewish identity as much as it was to get a glimpse of the Jewish state. I had been supportive of Israel during the 6-day war in 1967. I thought (and still think in theory) that a Jewish Israel is important in a world full of anti-Jewish sentiment and action. Over the next 40 years, like other leftists, I have become fiercely critical of Israeli politics and of Israel's racist and unconscionable actions against an occupied Palestinian population.

But in 1970, I needed to see Yad Vashem, the Israeli memorial to the Holocaust. It was powerfully emotional and that experience inevitably reinforced the central feature of my Jewish identity. Israel on the whole was interesting, including the unified Jerusalem, an astoundingly beautiful city. I went to the Wailing Wall; my atheism precluded any spiritual impact, but I could well appreciate its historical significance. I also found the ultra-orthodox Jews in Mea Shearim and elsewhere bizarre. I had one amusing incident in the Tel Aviv bus station, while waiting for a bus to Jerusalem. A young Hassid approached me and inquired whether I was a Jew. I replied yes. Then he proceeded to place tefillin on my arm. I had no idea what this was all about, perhaps some kind of strange Jewish "s & m" ritual. I am none too proud of my ignorance, but that was my honest reaction at the time.

Headed back to Prague, I heard that Czech officials were closing the border, to prevent western "agitators" from fomenting trouble. I managed to gain admission anyway, sneaking in with a group of Slovakian tourists in Vienna. I got on their bus and somehow passed through the border with no problem. But in Prague, I found only a few of the people I had met earlier. Their mood was despairing. Repression had set in and the new government under Gustav Husak was little more than a stooge regime for its Soviet masters. Saddened, I left and returned to London.

In England, I had another adventure. Ruth's former roommate had given me the name of someone she had met in England. She told me his name, Harvey Matusow, and said that I would find him fascinating. She had no idea about his past history. I did find him fascinating, but for other reasons.

In London, I telephoned him and immediately asked, "Are you *the* Harvey Matusow?" Momentarily stunned, he invited me to his home, an hour train ride from London.

When I arrived at his cottage, I immediately provided a narrative of his life history, astounding him. He had been a McCarthy era informer, a Communist Party member who turned against his former leftist colleagues and associates. He worked for McCarthy and the odious Roy Cohn. His testimony was responsible for sending labor leader Clinton Jencks to prison. To the left, he was anathema (including my father, who was horrified when he learned that I had met Matusow). Then Harvey Matusow recanted, publishing his book, *False Witness*, in 1955, in which he claimed that he was lying the whole time, encouraged by McCarthy and Cohn—surely a plausible scenario. For that, he was convicted of perjury, serving a three year sentence in federal prison.

I had read the book and knew the entire story, which I recounted to Matusow. He was intrigued if somewhat disconcerted. But he was an engaging rascal, a consummate Jewish hustler, known in his young CP days as "Kid Nickels." I concluded that he was never seriously political. He *was* seriously opportunistic. In England, he had become a music promoter and general impresario. Seemingly, he knew everybody. We got along well. Mostly, he told fantastic stories. He told me he met Wilhelm Reich in prison. He gave me fascinating personal accounts of the 50s hysteria, including tales of Cohn and others I despised.

Later, when he returned to the United States, he would drop in on Ruth and me, unannounced, almost out of nowhere. In 1972 or so, he was my passenger when an uninsured junkie slammed into the rear of my car in Berkeley. My back was badly hurt. He was so fat (Orson Wells fat) that he was entirely uninjured. My father visited me in the hospital and deliberately snubbed him. Then Matusow disappeared until I heard of his death in 2002.

One of Matusow's contacts was the American literary and cultural critic Seymour Krim. He introduced us and we met a few times for drinks and dinner in London. This was also a splendid opportunity to learn firsthand about the New York literary and intellectual scene. His observations about the "Beat" scene were especially valuable to me. Some of the people he knew personally had written essays, books, and poems that I had found influential. Krim had been in the middle of everything and his essays were perceptive and enjoyable to read. His comments about hustling a living as a freelancer were also revealing. He also talked about photographer Diane Arbus, whom he claimed as a lover. I had been fascinated with her work and published a small essay about her strange but compelling images. As usual, I found this

154

kind of conversation a valuable complement to my continuing intellectual quest.

On March 23, 1971, Ruth and I were married, between winter and spring quarters, at her cousin's house in Watsonville, California. The simple ceremony was performed by Rabbi Edgar Siskin of Glencoe, Illinois, the father of two of my Berkeley undergraduates. He and his wife had driven out to officiate for the wedding. It was a Jewish wedding, but with minimal religious content in light of both our identities as nonobservant Jews. Friends and family members were present, including Ruth's parents. I have never had much of a relationship with either of them. We really had nothing in common to talk about; neither had any intellectual interests and her father cared little about sports, my usual fallback conversational tactic. They never disliked me, but rather found me odd. I was hardly their ideal choice for a son-in-law. My politics (was I a communist?), my intensity, my irreverence, and my high-strung personality are strikingly different from their lower middle class, conservative, tight-knit Worcester, Massachusetts background. But I married Ruth, not her parents or her seemingly endless supply of cousins, a few of whom I actually came to enjoy.

After the academic year ended, we returned to Europe on a delayed honeymoon. This was Ruth's first trip there and this time, it was purely for sightseeing and to visit my friends in Holland, who have remained close friends all these years. No politics at all: I had no demonstrations to attend and even in Prague, I hardly saw anyone I had known during the turmoil and violence of 1969. It was enjoyable to revisit the scenes of the Parisian barricades of '68 and to investigate more seriously some of the political artworks that I would soon write about more methodically. In Paris especially, I looked carefully at the works of Daumier in major museums and galleries. Moreover, we bought original Daumier lithographs inexpensively, sometimes in the bookstalls by the River Seine. Those days are finished.

By academic year 1971/72, I naively assumed that my excellent teaching record would keep me employed year to year indefinitely. I was still unaware of the University of California "8-year rule," which prohibited lecturers from continuing full-time after eight years of faculty service — a rule that would dog me for decades to come and one that I had a hand in finally abolishing much later in my career.

155

Chapter 18
The First Battle: Berkeley, 1972

Winter quarter, 1972 marked the beginning of my protracted battles with University of California authorities at several levels. Returning from class, I found a terse letter from the department chair informing me that my contract would not be renewed after June 30 — in essence, I was fired. I was shocked, although not altogether surprised, having noticed a diminution of conversational banter and friendliness from my administrative superiors for several months. I never got a straight answer about why I was not renewed. The official rhetoric of "changing directions" and "new departmental approaches" rang hollow; I believed, then and now, that my political activism, my visibility, and my popularity with students were the true reasons for my dismissal. I had plenty of experience with such linguistic doubletalk. Academics, perhaps better than any professional group, are skillful in twisting language to conceal rather than illuminate reality. As a lecturer, I had no formal responsibility to do research and publish, though this was not mentioned during the ensuing conflict.

I resolved immediately to fight this action. My long political organizing record informed my strategic battle plans. I had no idea, at the time, that much (not all, by any means) of my political activism would be confined to struggles within and against the University of California. Almost at once, I decided on the historically successful route of 60s style student activism. I informed both present and former students, members of the student government, and campus political activists about my firing. I generated substantial support, because these students agreed that politics played a huge role in the dismissal. A key feature of the battle was publicity; reporters from the campus newspaper, the *Daily Californian*, were prominent supporters. They ran stories about the struggle, making a simple departmental personnel issue into a major campus controversy.

At the same time, students began making appointments with top campus officials, arguing that if the University were truly interested in excellent teaching, it should retain and reward faculty who implemented that ideal. The timing was good; in the post-FSM period, the University of California and other similar universities realized that undergraduate education was severely deficient. They recognized, but rarely acknowledged publicly, that the research and publication focus of academic life dominated their institutional priorities. University officials felt compelled to proclaim the importance of teaching, mostly rhetorically but occasionally with token measures to appease student activists. Clearly, some UC officials wanted no more public embarrassments. A few even appeared to take the issue seriously, notably Vice Chancellor Mark Christensen and Humanities Dean Thomas Rosenmeyer. Throughout campus, my fight for retention at Berkeley became known as the "children's crusade," an extension of the recent tradition of student political activism on campus.

Following a huge *Daily Cal* story, the administration acted, albeit with a face saving compromise for the rhetoric department. I had personally met with key administrators, including the chancellor. In June, they offered an attractive deal: I would be given a position as lecturer in the newly established division of interdisciplinary and general studies (DIGS), under the direction of Professor Alain Renoir of the English department. Scion of a famous family heritage, Renoir had a strong educational vision and was impressed with my own educational views as well as my strong four year teaching record at Berkeley. He welcomed me to the new program and gave me considerable latitude in generating new interdisciplinary courses under the general rubric of the social science major. He indicated his hope that DIGS faculty would soon be given regular faculty status with traditional mechanisms for promotion and tenure. Subsequent events would contradict his optimism and further transform my maverick and marginal academic life.

The rhetoric department chair, understandably, was none too happy with this development. He wanted me gone, period. He wrote to the Academic Senate Committee on Privilege and Tenure, complaining that I had violated academic protocol when I revealed the content of his original non-renewal letter to the *Daily Cal*. It was, he maintained, "confidential." The committee chair, a constitutional law expert, wrote me, requesting a response. I cannot now locate my letter, but it was extremely short. I replied that the letter was my property and that in any case, I had a First Amendment right to publish it whenever and wherever I wanted. I never heard from the committee again.

This fight was emotionally exhausting, more so than most of my external political struggles because I was at the center and the personal stakes were so huge. Every day seemed like a siege, a constant whirl of organizing, strategizing, and contending with the highs and lows of each move and counter move. Ruth's support was invaluable. These affairs require extensive and sustained emotional sustenance and I was fortunate to have it at a crucial time in my life.

DIGS Chair Renoir told me when I started that if I wanted a durable academic career, I had to increase my scholarly record—the sooner the better. When he mentioned that I should write a book, I replied that I wanted to write about the connection of art and politics, especially the tradition of visual art with strong social and political commentary and criticism. I had begun ruminating about this topic anyway and this was the perfect

157

opportunity to move from thought to concrete action. He gave me *carte blanche* to proceed, even suggesting that I use a new course in the program to formulate my ideas. The idea of writing a book was initially overwhelming. I soon discovered that it is a huge challenge, but actually quite doable. It helps to have a decently compulsive personality, a trait I have regularly exhibited in life.

In winter quarter, 1973, I initiated a class entitled "Art and Social Content," meeting for three hours a week in the evening in my Berkeley home. I choose a select student audience for this seminar. Each week I spent enormous time in selecting and making slides of the major and minor figures of visual social commentary. I spent equal time in reading historical and art historical works to provide a strong historical context for my class—a focus that would soon be the hallmark of all my research and publication. In my entire academic career, I have never devoted so much time preparing for one class—easily 30 hours each week the first term. The class was extremely successful—so much so that I got permission to extend it for another quarter. Early on, I wrote my preparation notes as potential book chapters, a method that I would follow in developing all my art history books for more than 30 years.

In the early stage, I teamed up with several colleagues for an introductory course in the program. The coordinator of that course, to put it charitably, was not well organized or efficient. We covered intriguing intellectual material, including subject matter from the ancient world, one of Alain Renoir's key personal interests. Several students resisted this focus, but I found it a splendid opportunity to expand my own intellectual horizons. I had never read Thucydides, Herodotus, Cicero, Qunitilian, and other ancient figures. They intrigued me and over the years I have modestly incorporated some of their works into my own classes. The real problem, however, was team teaching. In principle, I believe that it is a fine idea. It encourages students to experience multiple faculty perspectives, even specific clashes and arguments. My strong personality and style as a teacher, however, make me a mediocre practitioner in this arena. That is regrettable, but my major narcissism, substantial inflexibility, and loud mouth are poor ingredients for effective team teaching.

My teaching in DIGS soon became entirely individual. It remained highly political in content and tone and I began exploring deeper issues of intellectual, political, and moral resistance, using writers like Nietzsche, Camus, Sartre, and others. I also developed course units on critical approaches to higher education, reflecting my personal experience and commitments to postsecondary educational reform and interdisciplinary approaches. I finally used Clark Kerr's book, *The Uses of the University*, and provided students with a strong critique of his famous "multiversity" notion. I began publishing on the topic even while conducting my major research on political art. And I continued my external political involvements, especially against the Vietnam War, this time with no apparent hostility from my academic unit.

The following year, my sixth year at Berkeley, Chairman Renoir asked me to serve as the Vice Chair and head of the social science major. This position gave me some influence in hiring and curriculum development, both of which reflected my views on both education and politics. My classes went well and I increased my strong reputation with my students. At the end of the academic year, Chairman Renoir nominated me for an academic senate Distinguished Teaching Award, which I received in June 1974. It was, however, both revealing and disconcerting that some senior faculty friends and colleagues urged me to withdraw from the competition, noting that such awards could be tantamount to a "kiss of death." This confirmed my view that teaching was severely undervalued at Berkeley and that high teaching visibility was actually dangerous.

My friends were correct. By the start of my seventh year at Berkeley, I had begun paying closer attention to the apparent administrative hostility to innovative programs like DIGS. The new dean of the College of Letters and Science spearheaded the drive to eliminate the program. Institutional assaults on DIGS took the form of various review committees, which ironically concluded that the program met its educational objectives effectively. The dean finally appointed a committee that shared his own biases and DIGS was eventually slated for elimination.

At the heart of this educational conservatism was (and remains) my deep-seated commitment to the disciplinary structure of higher education. This commitment is akin to a matter of religious faith. Questioning disciplinary hegemony among conventional academics (including many who purport to be politically radical) is similar to denying the divinity of Jesus Christ to devout fundamentalist Christians. Defenders of the rigidity of traditional academic departments were themselves trained in that tradition during graduate school. They learned that scholarship in history, political science, economics, art history, or English or any other single academic field was *the* exclusive route to success and professional recognition. Their beliefs in the sanctity of this scheme of narrow specialization were reinforced throughout their academic lives. In due course, this effective socialization paid off handsomely and they in turn became the guardians of the same system that rewarded them.

This arrangement is also the foundation of the internal political structure of American higher education. Higher level administrators are generally selected from faculty members who have achieved recognition within traditional disciplinary units. Typically, they have served as departmental chairpersons and have decided to pursue administrative roles mid-career, seeking increased power, status, and higher salaries. Like their disciplinary colleagues, they have a vested interest in maintaining disciplinary domination, especially in large research universities. Their resource allocation decisions usually reflect their biases, and dominant departments generally wind up winners, especially in tough fiscal times. The system becomes effectively self-perpetuating, supported by academic rationalizations like "excellence," one of the most overused and dubious expressions in higher education.

The division of the university into discrete academic disciplines is a rational enough way to organize a large institution administratively. I had (and still have) no problem with teaching and scholarship confined to specific disciplines, as long as those activities are not the exclusive focus of academic life. An early 20th century organizational scheme has decreasing epistemological and practical value in a dramatically changing late 20th and early 21st century world. Problems of poverty, race, class, and gender inequities, global environmental degradation, and scores of others demand interdisciplinary and multidisciplinary investigation. Ironically, the modern university remains a deeply conservative institution, structurally resistant to internal change. Its academic rigidity often ill equips it to respond urgently to local, national, and international problems. Its departmental ossification poorly serves its students as they prepare to confront the daunting challenges of the new century. For me, it severely hindered my academic career because I sought to work in an exclusive interdisciplinary program at Berkeley and I was openly hostile to disciplinary hegemony. Later, at UCLA, I encountered precisely the same barriers while teaching in various interdisciplinary programs and fighting for my academic survival.

All of this deepened my understanding of the underlying realities of life in prestigious research universities. It became increasingly clear that most faculty members in traditional departments, no matter how progressive they purport to be about the external world, are at bottom deeply conservative about the internal operations of their own institutions. They are sophisticated protectors of the university status quo, especially of their own derivative class and financial privileges. They are suspicious of all academic innovations and they resent any transfer of resources from their traditional units to anything new and different. They rarely say this expressly. Open venality would be unseemly. Instead, they use the rhetoric of "standards" and "quality" to preserve their hegemony. They find committees to do their dirty work, thus providing a collective academic cover for the more sordid objectives they really have. Ironically, many academics may not even be cognizant of this process. They are often astoundingly incapable of self-reflection and introspection. Top university administrators, however, generally know the score. Their internal cynicism about power and resources is perfectly obvious, especially to those on the losing side of institutional battles.

Simultaneously, whether coincidental or not, another institutional battle at the University of California was taking place hundreds of miles south of Berkeley. A popular program at UCLA was undergoing the same despicable process of review and termination. The speech department was disbanded and attempted to reinvent itself as a communication studies program. After considerable political jockeying, the program managed to survive, eventually bringing high quality undergraduate education to thousands of UCLA students. I had no clue that nine years later, I would join that academic program and continue working in the academic margins in my unorthodox academic career.

The Berkeley Administration's hostility towards DIGS also reflected a suspicion about educational reforms brought on by the recent student activism. I believe that it reflected a deeper anxiety about more radical educational programs, especially those that brought critical thinking about history, politics, and society directly into the classroom. Many people, including faculty, at Berkeley had never recovered from the tumultuous activity of the Free Speech Movement and its activist progeny. They were troubled by the presence of former campus radicals, including me and some of my DIGS colleagues, now teaching on "their" campus. Liberals have a hard time with those whose critique goes far deeper. They seem content to vote for the Democratic Party, give a few dollars to liberal but entirely safe charities, express cautious indignation about repressive national conservative policies in faculty halls and offices, and continue to enjoy the benefits of class privilege. I had seen this phenomenon elsewhere and it appeared to me to be a replay of the past in a different political setting.

This Berkeley faculty liberalism, in microcosm, reflected a deeper phenomenon in American politics. My view for several years had been that conventional liberalism, both in its rhetoric and its action, sought to weaken political radicalism. This was usually if not always intentional, but it was inevitably the consequence. My experiences revealed that most liberals were, at bottom, relatively content to maintain the status quo at all levels, save for minor tinkering that would at worst only marginally affect their status, wealth, and power. This principle applied to politics, economics, law, race, education, and every other field I had studied or in which I had been active.

Berkeley faculty liberals reminded me of those southerners who simultaneously proclaimed their belief in racial equality while urging militants to abandon their sit-ins and mass demonstrations. They were like Democratic legislators who fought for incremental minimum wage increases and higher safety standards in the workplace while ignoring the structural inequities of wealth and power. They were similar to judges who imposed somewhat more modest sentences while refraining from criticism of the deeper racial and class biases of the criminal justice system. In short, they were content to live with a "softer" capitalism and its progeny, a corporate "multiversity" with a fraudulent but publicly appealing commitment to genuine undergraduate education. I shared the widespread radical disdain for liberalism at the time and it remains a view I have never abandoned.

By academic year 1975/76, the familiar academic battles again dominated my personal and professional existence. In addition to the fight to retain the program, I formally encountered the 8-year rule, which limited non-tenure track faculty to no more than eight years of full-time faculty employment. The dean informed me that at the end of the academic year, I could work no more than 50% as a UC Berkeley faculty member; this rule prevailed independent of the quality of my teaching, research, and service. With a new chair, I still had decent support, but nothing like the commitment of Alain Renoir. When my first book, *The Art of Social Conscience*, appeared in 1976, my joy was tempered with the realization that I had to find other academic employment or engage in yet another exhausting institutional struggle.

I put my full energy into that book. I wrote in on my own time, furiously during vacations and summers. Lecturers were ineligible for sabbaticals or any other time off and I continued my full teaching responsibilities. I wrote in longhand at the kitchen table, sometimes from 6 a.m. until late evening. I often had the televised Watergate hearings on, enjoying the process of watching Richard Nixon go down. I even mentioned Senator San Ervin and his colleagues in the book acknowledgements for stimulating my adrenalin.

This book marked my emergence as a socially oriented art/cultural historian and began the process of gaining a reputation beyond the Berkeley campus. I wrote about such iconic political artists as Goya, Daumier, Kollwitz, Rivera, Orozco, Siqueiros, Shahn, Lange, Bourke-White, and many others. Deliberately, I added a chapter on concentration camp art, reflecting my compelling need to bring this tragic visual tradition into public awareness. I discussed the artists' efforts within the historical contexts in which they worked. I made it clear to my readers that I sympathized with their critical perspectives and their political views. The book was a major rejection of formalist criticism and established me as a controversial figure in the field, all the more so because the work had nothing to do with my formal

162

academic training. Above all, it established my research agenda that still thrives more than 30 years later.

Well before I started writing the book, I had read systematically in the field, transforming myself into an art historian without formal training in the discipline. My readings were broad and deep, especially in modern and contemporary art. I augmented this process with hundreds of visits to museums and galleries in the United States and Europe. Much of my interest centered on visual artists outside the specific tradition of political and social commentary that has concerned me throughout my teaching and scholarly career over the decades. I like and admire many of the classic examples of visual modernism even though they are not a part of my academic focus. As I have often told my students, I go out of my way to see their exhibitions. Even now, I make strenuous efforts to catch shows on American abstract expressionism and European and other nonfigurative artists whose works capture my imagination and provide me immense visual pleasure.

The liberation of painters and sculptors from conventional academic art particularly intrigued me during my intellectual apprenticeship in the field. I found that liberation to be a progressive development in art, enabling thousands of artists to expand their creativity and to bring engaging visual works to larger, more appreciative audiences. It was scarcely necessary for me to cover this ground again. That story had been told and retold so often that any comments from me would have been entirely superfluous.

My goal was to liberate artistic *criticism* and art historical *scholarship* from its narrow and conventional academic focus. Above all, I wanted to bring politics into these arenas, showing my readers that visual artists were fully capable of offering perceptive critiques about dominant issues of political and social life. I had read plenty of art historical material about such artistic luminaries like Goya and Daumier and several others that hardly addressed their incisive political commentary and instead analyzed the formal structure of the paintings, prints, and sculptures. My major focus, on the contrary, was on the social content of their work and I was candid in noting that the artists' ideas were the overriding perspective in my book. I found that an overemphasis on formal analysis, however rigorous and precise, fundamentally avoided more controversial issues that would compel art historians and critics to leave their comfort zones. And I also found purely formal artistic analysis dull and pedantic. Critical ideas were far more exciting and I have pursued this vision throughout my career, in all my books, articles, and teaching, with plenty of peer support and plenty of peer disdain, but less of the latter over the years.

The book was generally well received. One Marxist reviewer despised and trashed it, pointedly noting that I was a (mere) lawyer. I have never been Marxist enough for some; this is fine with me. One distinguished UCLA art historian, I later learned, remarked to one of his graduate students that "Von Blum was out to destroy art history." Fortunately, he had retired by the time I had arrived there and I can report that his fear about the fate of his discipline was overblown. I remain thoroughly eclectic and the book itself gave plenty of emphasis to visual satire, reflecting my more pessimistic view of human nature generally. Over the decades, *The Art of Social Conscience* has been acknowledged as a key work in fostering and legitimizing the field of political art as well as stimulating others to investigate artistic work during the Holocaust.

Like many radical academics, I view my research and publication as an integral feature of my politics: fighting with a pen (now with a computer) as well as on the streets. I disputed the post-war notion of "objective" scholarship. I thought that C. Wright Mills and others in his tradition were absolutely correct in arguing that this "non-ideological" work, especially in the social "sciences" and the humanities, was little more than ideological justification for the existing power relations of modern capitalist society. I saw my own research and publication as part of a longer tradition of scholarship that openly expresses and promotes the authors' ideological positions. This has been the case with my art historical books and my numerous articles in several fields, including educational and legal topics. That has been my vision in all of my art-related, and other publication, since 1976.

On campus, I helped lead the fight to preserve DIGS as an academic unit while also trying to preserve my own position. This time, I helped organize students and their parents to place as much pressure on UC Berkeley administrators as possible. The addition of parents made a difference; they were taxpayers, not merely transient undergraduates. I also took the controversial step of contacting sympathetic politicians in the State Assembly and elsewhere. This meant that the ultimate funders of the University of California were involved. Among many others, we obtained the support of Assemblyman John Vasconcellos, a leading critic of higher education, and Lt. Governor Mervin Dymally. UC officials were clearly not happy with such intervention, but my years of political organizing persuaded me to find allies wherever they were available. My students and I testified before legislative committees in Sacramento and did everything possible to keep the controversy in the public eye. These efforts also attracted some favorable press attention, generating further wrath from various high-ranking university officials who wanted to get rid of our academic program.

By the end of my eighth and ostensibly final year on campus, the Administration offered yet another arrangement that kept me in the

164

classroom. Consistent with the 8-year rule, I was reduced to a half time lecturer position. For the other half, I was given the title of "Academic Coordinator," an administrative designation that also permitted teaching. It was essentially a bureaucratic ruse and I continued teaching the same classes as before, never abandoning the critical political material in my courses and never letting up on the broader struggle to maintain the program. I had earned the "troublemaker" label that I knew marked me on the Berkeley campus. That label is long lasting and universal. It applies to all institutions, including manufacturing companies, banks, tobacco producers, real estate conglomerates, government bureaucracies, pre-schools, and colleges and universities.

When the end of this academic year arrived, I was informed that the "coordinator" arrangement had expired. The administration proposed a new deal: I would continue as a half time lecturer and would now move from my DIGS office to another office on campus, where I would be a halftime "pre-law advisor." Although I had given plenty of law school advice to hundreds of students since 1967, I had no interest whatsoever in diluting my academic work in this fashion. I declined the latest deal unambiguously. After intense meetings with the vice chancellor and others, I reiterated my position.

My strong standing with students mobilized the UC Berkeley student government into action. The Associated Students voted to fund me for the other half of my position, designating this as payment for my advising functions. I informed the new DIGS chair (a historian who disapproved of my political efforts and who found me threatening and contentious) that I would continue to teach all but one of my classes and would continue to advise my many students in the major and elsewhere. I viewed the arrangement as a powerful vote of confidence from the main constituency I have had throughout my long career: my undergraduate students.

Throughout the tenth year at Berkeley, I worked assiduously to maintain DIGS. The dean of letters and science demanded that I relinquish my advisees and distribute them to other faculty. The chair accordingly ordered me to comply. I refused, in a deliberate act of insubordination, and invited him to institute disciplinary action. I would be dishonest here if I failed to indicate my visceral contempt for the new chair of the division of interdisciplinary and general studies. In my view, he was not evil, but disgracefully cowardly. I believed that he was installed precisely to facilitate the dismantling of the educational program; I was well past the point of concealing my feelings during our increasingly infrequent contact. Generally, I prefer courtesy in professional relationships, even adversarial ones, and mostly I have adhered to this standard. Here, that position was emotionally impossible.

He then distributed my advisees to others on his own authority. Throughout the year, very few students accepted their reassignment and continued to see me for academic advice and approval of their quarterly study lists. As it happened, I faced no charges for my insubordination, which I regarded as a morally required act of civil disobedience.

The Berkeley administration then changed the name of the Division of Interdisciplinary and General Studies to the Division of Special Programs, a linguistic and political dilution. A few other programs were added to the unit, making it more of an umbrella structure for alternative educational operations — or, as many suspected, a mechanism to ghettoize nontraditional and politically critical academics and their courses. Most students and faculty ignored the change, continuing to refer to the program as DIGS. Still, the name change constituted a tacit admission that the program would not disappear. As of 2010, it still exists.

Chapter 19
A D. C. Interlude

By June, 1978, I had grown exhausted with the constant struggles at Berkeley. I knew that I would never have a permanent position in DIGS (now DSP) and my situation was becoming increasingly precarious. In September, Ruth, who had provided invaluable moral support in the struggles, took a position as a program officer in science education at the National Science Foundation in Washington, D.C. After becoming only the fifth person to earn the Ph.D. in 1972, she had joined the faculty of the Group in Science and Mathematics Education, she was invited to join the faculty as a lecturer. She also conducted research at the Lawrence Hall of Science on campus. But this too was marginal and we both needed to think about the longer term, personally and professionally.

I informed UC officials that I would leave shortly, but that I wished to take a formal leave of absence rather than resigning. They granted the request; my assumption was that they were anxious to be rid of me and understood that I was unlikely to return. Throughout the entire fall quarter, we lived apart, she in D.C. and I in Berkeley, teaching a half-time load. This was essentially an unpleasant arrangement, however temporary. A serious marriage requires togetherness and I decided I would go to Washington whether I found a suitable position or not.

After several trips to Washington, I found a position as a "humanist administrator" at the National Endowment for the Humanities, commencing in January 1979. I wanted to continue teaching, but this was not possible, at least in the short term. The NEH position was funded under the Intergovernmental Personnel Act, which meant that while I was paid by the federal government, the money was actually provided to the University of California. I continued, formally, to be a UC employee while working at NEH and each month I received a regular University of California paycheck.

I enjoyed my brief service in NEH. My colleagues were friendly and my record at Berkeley gave me decent status in an agency where academic pedigrees and credentials were crucial. I had responsibilities in the Fellowships Division, where I helped make grants to scholars addressing issues of legal and medical ethics. I had little political opportunity in my work, but I managed to increase the number of women and minority scholars serving on NEH review panels. My division superiors also took advantage of my teaching record by sending me to oversee various National Endowment seminars throughout the country. That feature of the work was exciting. I sat in on many sessions in several major universities, met some intriguing people, and presented, I think, intelligent feedback about the educational strengths and weakness of the programs I observed. I also managed one minor internal triumph. These trips were limited to "senior staff" (including me for the first time in my life). I pushed hard to take a junior colleague, an intelligent young African American woman, with me on a trip to Syracuse and Cornell universities. Her work was exemplary and I helped to break down, at least modestly, the entrenched hierarchical culture of the agency.

Once a week, I offered informal tours of local museums and art galleries to NEH staff during lunch breaks. But for all the gratification I had, especially the absence of university crises, I desperately missed the classroom and extensive contact with students. I knew that NEH was an interim arrangement for me. I began looking for teaching positions throughout the country.

Some features of the National Endowment work were both revealing and troubling. The usual governmental bureaucratic procedures were sometimes irritating, with more memoranda and useless meetings than necessary, but these were tolerable enough. In my position, I had access to thousands of recommendation letters that grant applicants had requested from colleagues, often from their dissertation advisors from front rank, prestigious institutions. Many were informative and strong. But many others were useless, *pro forma* recitations of superlatives that offered little insight into the actual proposals we were evaluating. But some—more than a few—were malevolent, ranging from damning with extremely faint praise to outright verbal brutality. I saw examples of the latter from scholars with international reputations, men (always) of supposedly impeccable character and reputation. It taught me a valuable lesson. In my own professional life, my policy is simple; if I cannot write a decent recommendation, I inform the student or colleague directly. When I write one, whether it is confidential or not, I always send a copy to the person for whom I have written it. I have become extremely suspicions of academic confidentiality. It may indeed promote candor, but it can also promote slander (more accurately, defamation).

The personal features of life in Washington were outstanding. Most exciting, Ruth was pregnant and she found excellent prenatal care. We had delayed starting a family because of the uncertainty and daily aggravation of these protracted academic battles at Berkeley. At this point, it was almost now or never; Ruth was 35 and I was 36, not ready for the geriatric ward, but "getting on" for this feature of married life. Earlier, in London, she had had a miscarriage, an emotionally traumatic experience that landed her twice in the hospital. British health care, in that instance, was far from stellar.

168

We also took powerful advantage of the cultural life available in the Washington area. We lived off Wisconsin Avenue, a few minutes away by foot from Ruth's NSF office across the Maryland state line and extremely close to several movie theaters. The museums were incomparable, especially the Smithsonian institutions. We discovered the magnificent artistic resources in D.C., visiting several institutions frequently. I augmented my personal knowledge of social and political art during our time there and I have often returned to conduct research in those venues. We had easy car and train access to New York and to other locations throughout the East Coast. In short, except for the generally lousy weather, we loved being there.

I had several promising academic employment leads, but the most intriguing appeared to be at the University of Southern California in Los Angeles. On the threshold of parenthood, both my wife and I were eager to return to California. I accepted the position of Associate Director of the University of Southern California Center for the Humanities in Los Angeles. In August 1979, I formally resigned from NEH, but in legal terms, from the University of California. We prepared to move back to California and made specific arrangements for our baby daughter to be born in early October at a Kaiser-Permanente Hospital.

Meanwhile, we had begun childbirth classes in Washington in preparation for the birth. I reverted back to my mediocre student days, barely paying attention to the teacher. My excuse was that as we got much closer to the birth, I would do what I had often done successfully: cram at the last minute. Biology intervened dramatically. In late August, Ruth knew that the baby was imminent and we rushed to George Washington Hospital. It was a week of extraordinary anxiety. Doctors performed several tests and determined that the baby's lungs were immature. The birth had to be delayed. Finally, after several days of bed rest, the doctors decided to induce labor and on August 26, 1979, our daughter, Elizabeth Sarah Von Blum, was born, five weeks premature. That was her message to us, that *she* would now be in charge. During her 30 years, she has demonstrated this principle regularly, bringing us incredible joy and a few years of despair.

I had to conclude my NEH duties and arrange the logistics to get to Los Angeles. Elizabeth remained in neo-natal intensive care while Ruth needed to stay in town to remain with her. I decided to drive across the country with a friend from NEH. The trip was pleasant enough, and I saw a few friends along the way. We also stopped to see some excellent smaller art museums that would ordinarily be off the usual East Coast/Chicago cultural circuit. The "highlight" was a visit to the compound of Gerald L. K. Smith as we passed through Eureka Springs, Arkansas. I had known of Smith's reputation as one of America's most notorious anti-Semites and was eager to see his "legacy."

His religious theme park was a veritable cornucopia of right-wing Christian kitsch. My Jewish colleague and I had a perversely enjoyable time looking at the Bible Museum, the area where "The Great Passion Play" was performed, and the library, which contained such classics as Henry Ford's *The International Jew*, the infamous *Protocols of the Elders of Zion*, and a stunning array of other fascist material. A guide reverently showed us the graves of Smith and his wife, remarking about his wonderful life and his magnificent Christian contributions to the region. I had to suppress my inclination to giggle.

Chapter 20
A Temporary Trojan and Rebirth at UCLA

At USC, I had hoped for vigorous involvement in an interdisciplinary humanities program that would also encourage public outreach. The match seemed ideal. But like many jobs in academia and elsewhere, promise and reality diverged dramatically. The day I arrived, I was told of a major embezzlement that had occurred at the center. The alleged perpetrator had been a center staff member. I have long since repressed the details, but the amount was huge and it also involved a major criminal investigation by the District Attorney's office. My responsibility was to "handle it." With neither experience nor interest in accounting and budgetary minutia, I felt swamped with details beyond my competence.

Ruth and Elizabeth had just arrived by plane from D.C. and we had settled into a spacious apartment in a nondescript neighborhood in West Los Angeles. The transition was extremely difficult. Ruth suffered from serious postpartum depression, which went unrecognized in its early stages. Unseasonable heat and severe smog compounded our distress. My unhappiness at USC exacerbated everything and I began immediately thinking about finding another position, even getting out of Southern California.

Alienated from the outset, I despaired about my professional prospects generally. Only a few weeks into this job, I began applying elsewhere, hopeful to leave an arrangement that left me emotionally debilitated. The daily work at the humanities center was profoundly unfulfilling, especially the highly detailed administrative trivia the director threw at me regularly. Only on rare occasions could I participate in genuine intellectual work, and even then my efforts were largely in a supportive role. But the experience was instructive; it helped me realize that climbing some administrative ladder, in academia or anywhere else, was entirely incompatible with my inclinations and temperament. I met some colleagues in other academic units on campus and found them intellectually impressive and personally engaging. My general unhappiness there, however, made it take me some years before I could properly appreciate the University of Southern California for its authentic institutional and educational quality.

By December 1979, I had made contact with UCLA, activating contacts from my Berkeley years and through my work at NEH. Soon after, I commenced negotiations with UCLA and in early spring, I had accepted a package that cobbled together a variety of responsibilities, including teaching and administering an interdisciplinary program. I resigned from USC with great relief in May, shortly before the director would have fired me.

Understandably under the circumstances: I made my unhappiness clear, offering my negative observations to whomever would listen. One example stands out. I took advantage of USC's excellent dental school during my service there. I needed major bridgework, which required several visits of three or four hours each. I used sick leave time for this procedure, returning to the center and telling subordinate staff members that drilling and novocain injections were preferable to my professional responsibilities. I knew and didn't care that this comment would reach my administrative superiors. Immature, of course — but emotionally necessary. Dissatisfied workers find resistance opportunities whenever they can, especially when they know they are leaving the job soon.

I figured that working at UCLA would be a new start, for me and for my family. Ruth, meanwhile, found a grant-funded position in the physics department at the University of California at Irvine, doing science education development work in computer-assisted instruction that drew effectively on her training and experiences. We found good child care and began to establish a new family routine. Los Angeles was still an adjustment, but with new friends and with a new house that we bought in Venice, our prospects were looking promising.

As I soon discovered, my UCLA academic arrangement was fragile and provided even less job security than I had had at Berkeley. My formal job title was "Senior Administrative Analyst" and I was to be in charge of the Freshman/Sophomore Professional School Seminar Program. This program brought faculty from UCLA's 11 professional schools to teach undergraduate seminars, and I would be a participant with an adjunct faculty appointment in psychiatry in the medical school. I was also scheduled to teach in the Medicine, Law, and Human Values Program, an interdisciplinary effort devoted to medical ethics and related social policy issues; for me, this was an excellent opportunity to broaden my interdisciplinary humanities and social sciences interests. The senior administrative analyst title was a ruse to cover my educational activities and everyone knew it.

I enjoyed the first year at UCLA immensely. My courses offered a critical focus on the professions, especially law and medicine, and I augmented my use of literary sources, including works from Franz Kafka, Arthur Koestler, George Bernard Shaw, Alexander Solzhenitsyn, and others. I created another course where I explored race, gender, and class issues in American health care. My student evaluations were high, rivaling those I had received at Berkeley. I made several valuable contacts throughout the campus and had hopes of achieving some decent measure of employment stability. I became involved in other campus activities, including the College Honors Program and the Academic Advancement Program, which provided support and

172

additional services to minorities and other historically underrepresented groups. I have continued both these involvements for thirty years.

Rumblings of discontent appeared during my second year at UCLA. I was informed that I was becoming become "too visible," and that as a non-ladder faculty member, I should remain quiet and anonymous. Technically, I was a "mere" staff member with an adjunct faculty title, a double marginality. One incident in particular generated this response. At the suggestions of several exceptionally bright undergraduates, a film crew requested a few minutes to film my discussions in class. The clip, a few seconds in duration, was used for UCLA promotion purposes, including at least one nationally broadcast UCLA football game. Apparently, it was seen by "regular" faculty who resented my presence.

Despite the ostensible soundness of this advice to remain invisible, I am not emotionally constituted for that role. My classes have always been vigorous and students invariably respond enthusiastically to my efforts. I also reacted to the deeper message of that advice: lecturers and others not in regular faculty ranks should be grateful to be employed and, like non-whites in apartheid South Africa, know and remain in their "place." And like African Americans during the civil rights days in the South, only a shuffling, obsequious acceptance of second-class status would satisfy their political superiors. I rejected this notion at Berkeley, and had absolutely no inclination to capitulate at UCLA.

In my third academic year, I accepted an invitation from the honors division dean to initiate a special course on the social and political commentary in the arts. This was a major extension of the earlier course I initiated at Berkeley, which gave rise to my first book on the history of political art. In 1983, my new book, *The Critical Vision: A History of Social and Political Art in the U.S.*, had just been published by a leftist publisher, South End Press. This work continued my research into artistic political commentary, focusing on specifically American examples and increased my visibility in socially oriented cultural history circles. I named my honors course after the book title and continued to introduce UCLA students to an artistic tradition that has been fundamental to my professional life. I persuaded the Berkeley art history slide collection curators to borrow the thousands of slides I had made there and I had them duplicated for use at UCLA. The course was spectacularly successful; once again, I received stellar student evaluations for my instructional efforts.

This book brought me into contact with a person who became a close friend and one of the most extraordinary intellectual influences anyone could ever have. One of the stellar figures in the UCLA art history department was Professor Albert Boime, perhaps the foremost social art historian in the world. Amazingly prolific, Al Boime was also a rarity in American higher education: a dedicated teacher and a warm human being. I had known of his work long before I arrived at UCLA and I was eager to meet him personally. He vigorously approved of my political approach to art history. Like him, I was committed to explaining visual imagery fully within its historical context. I agreed with him that any other approach made little sense.

From then on, I consulted with Al about all my projects and he regularly reciprocated. I gave several guest lectures over the years in his classes. We had many students in common, including several M.A. and Ph.D. students. He, his wife Myra, Ruth, and I all became close personal friends, eating together and often seeing films and other cultural events. I often drove him to and from the UCLA campus. Our discussions naturally dealt with a social vision of art history, but we regularly discussed pedagogy and radical politics. We exchanged views about our mutual Jewish identities. He was more observant, but fully tolerant of my secular Jewish vision. During his final illness, I tried to provide as much transportation and other logistic help as I could. I taught his final class at UCLA, telling students, hopefully but erroneously, that Professor Boime would return the following week. When he died in October, 2008, I was one of the speakers at the Jewish memorial service in Los Angeles. We will not see another like him in the academy.

The publication of *The Critical Vision* reinforced my scholarly reputation nationally even if it did little or nothing for me at UCLA, one of the continuing ironies of my unique academic career for more than 40 years. Equally significant, it also propelled me into a new arena of political activism. Since relocating to Los Angeles, I made contact with numerous artists and community art organizations sharing my basic vision of linking art with a broader commitment to social criticism and change. I worked with the key mural organization, the Social and Public Art Resource Center in Venice (SPARC), the California African American Museum, and several other entities. I became a visible advocate for community and public art and assisted several individual political artists in gaining grants and exhibition venues. This continued my longer term advocacy for underrepresented artists and was a key extension of my political research and publication. That focus has remained a strong element of my political life in Los Angeles, most recently involving extensive efforts with the African American artistic community.

The honors course proved to be one of my final, but temporary, educational triumphs at UCLA. On June 1, 1983, the administrator in charge of my "senior administrative analyst" position summoned me and announced my termination at the end of the month. Her ostensible rationale was budgetary, noting that UCLA made various organizational changes that,

174

among other things, necessitated my position's elimination. I believed nothing she said; her comments revealed her disappointment with my public visibility, noting that I had essentially replicated my Berkeley troublemaking reputation at UCLA.

Yet again, I felt compelled to struggle. I had substantial student support, but nothing like the wide protests I had catalyzed at Berkeley. Still, these political efforts met some success. Professor Paul Rosenthal, Chair of the Communication Studies Program (the same unit that fought off termination during the 1970s, with hostile review committees and substantial administrative disdain) offered me a part-time position teaching "Introduction to Oral Communication" for the following academic year as well as two courses for the coming summer session. In so doing, he defied the objections of the Provost of Letters and Science and other campus officials determined to see me disappear forever from UCLA.

The provost, in particular, revealed more personal animus than I had ever previously encountered in my career. For whatever reasons, my continued presence at UCLA was a source of special irritation to him. Throughout my turbulent career, however, I have always been fortunate to find allies and supporters among tenured faculty, committed to undergraduate teaching excellence, with the courage to resist administrative pressure. They are a small minority of academics, but their presence is vital to genuine institutional vision. Few, however, have had the sustained moral courage of Paul Rosenthal.

Chapter 21
Joining the Ranks of Contingent Faculty

For the next 12 years, I joined the burgeoning ranks of American contingent (nonpermanent, often *very* temporary) faculty, succeeding in that role albeit with huge personal insecurity and major emotional fallout. Always concerned with external political developments, I continued to be outspoken about such issues as American support of reactionary regimes in Central America, the growing indifference of the Reagan and Bush administrations to the poor, racial and ethnic minorities, and other marginalized populations, and similar national and international problems. I also maintained a robust publication agenda, despite the pressures of job hustling. Still, my preoccupation with employment involved cobbling together a living in the expensive region of Southern California. The experiences were both gratifying and bitter. They have made me remain an outspoken advocate for the thousands of insecure, yet talented faculty who still perform the academic equivalent of piecework.

Limited to 50% academic employment at the University of California under the 8-year rule, I continued to teach at UCLA while finding temporary teaching assignments in various local colleges and universities, writing and educational evaluation jobs, and public speaking engagements. In academic year 1983/84 at UCLA, the student government, in a modified reprise of what happened some years previously at Berkeley, paid me to organize various educational programs for undergraduates. I also continued teaching my "Medical Ethics and Public Policy" course, focusing on such topics as the Tuskegee Syphilis Experiment, the mistreatment of women patients throughout history, and the growing problem of occupational health and safety in America.

As always, the teaching itself went well. In the introductory speech class, I introduced major innovations, including substantive readings on topics of major intellectual importance, many with a critical vision of politics, society, and history. Among other things, I brought students on field trips to the Los Angeles County Jail, where they could see in person the growing use of incarceration to deal with African Americans, Latinos, and other "superfluous" populations—what Angela Davis has accurately called the "prison-industrial complex." Since I began teaching in 1967, a critical view of dominant institutions and policies, combined with discussion-based classes, has remained central to my pedagogy.

Ruth had used her own skills in obtaining grants to make a fascinating shift at UCLA. She received funds from the Exxon Education Foundation to

176

conceive and create a computerized writers-aid software program for English composition. She worked with several talented people on campus, unfortunately not including the principal investigators who were required to be ladder faculty members at UCLA. These men provided little intellectual guidance throughout the project, but were considered equal partners when sharing the profits when the program was sold to a major publisher. Most egregiously, when Ruth wrote an article about the work, one of her superiors demanded that she include his name on the publication, although he had contributed nothing to the piece. She adamantly refused and I examined the prospects of sanctions and legal actions if that became necessary. He backed down, but again, we saw the morally flabby underbelly of an institution that presents a far more positive face in its public relations material. But most insiders know that universities are little different from any other large organization, including multinational corporations and government bureaus.

Our daughter Elizabeth appeared to be happily enrolled in preschool in the UCLA Childcare Center. Sensitive personnel whom we admired and trusted totally staffed the Center and she seemed to respond well to the daily activities. School troubles, however, would soon appear on the horizon. In public school kindergarten, she ran into the kind of unimaginative teacher that I had had throughout most of my own school experiences. Once, when I came to pick her up, her teacher solemnly informed me that my daughter was having some difficulty. I asked for specifics. She replied that Elizabeth was not keeping her letters within the lines, and then added ominously, "and she seems to be doing it on purpose."

I had heard all of this before and I sympathized with my daughter. Actually, she demonstrated a remarkable artistic ability from a very early age and was very creative about "going outside the lines." But neither Ruth nor I had any inkling, for a very long time, that she also had some serious learning disabilities that fundamentally interfered with her progress throughout school. In the early 1980s, few parents were aware of the parameters of such disabilities.

My personal zeal to create new courses, originating during my Berkeley faculty service, served me well from 1983 throughout my period of contingent academic labor until approximately 1995. Contingent faculty members need a keen sense of entrepreneurial imagination. I taught in several UCLA departments and programs across the humanities, social sciences, and professional schools. I probably hold some record for having taught in more academic departments and programs than anyone in the history of the University of California or anywhere else (14 departments and other instructional units on five UC campuses). I refined my political art class, adding works from more women and artists of color. That refinement

177

eventually lead to two more substantial art historical books, one in the 1990s and one in the early years of the new century.

I also resurrected a communication studies course called "Agitational Communication," which lay dormant for many years. Still one of my staples, this course is a comprehensive history of American social protest movements, with a major emphasis on the labor movement, the civil rights movement, student movements including the Berkeley Free Speech Movement, anti-war movements from Vietnam to Iraq, feminism, environmentalism, gay and lesbian rights, and others. This class enables me to link my personal activism to its deeper historical roots. It has remained unusually popular for an elective course at UCLA, now typically drawing over 300 students. Above all, it allows me to provide historical perspective and real personal experiences on the honorable tradition of dissent to students who typically receive little more than the standard treatments that romanticize white men, glorify capitalism, praise American military adventures, and downplay or eliminate those courageous women and men who challenged oppressive authority. "Agitational Communication," in short, represents the epitome of my politically influenced teaching career.

In January 1986, the University of California at San Diego sociology department offered me fulltime academic employment for winter and spring quarters. Although not thrilled to make the Los Angeles to San Diego commute, I welcomed even this short term stability. Once again, however, I ran across the 8-year rule. What ensued was the most disheartening moment of my entire academic career. I wanted to teach both at UC San Diego and at UCLA to maximize my income. The administration refused, demanding that I choose either UCSD or UCLA—and not more than half time for *any* academic quarter. By then, I had become active in the Union, the American Federation of Teachers local at UCLA, and I appealed for assistance. The Union attorney filed an emergency appeal for a temporary restraining order in the Los Angeles Superior Court, asking to block the University action in forcing me to choose between both campuses.

The UCLA Vice Chancellor for Faculty Relations appeared personally at the hearing, presided by a judge who had actually been the Vice Chancellor's former student. The proceeding itself, from my perspective, was another Kafkaesque legal process. After exchanging pleasantries with his former professor, the Judge ruled against me and the union. With 20 years of excellent teaching in my record, I found it bizarre, even grotesque, to have a senior university official come to court to keep me out of the classroom. The Judge himself was no Luther Hussey. More intelligent and urbane, he held the hearing in his chambers, where I immediately noticed his copy of *The Nation* on his desk. He was another good liberal, whose official actions

178

nevertheless reflected his deeper adherence to the established patterns of institutional power. Thousands like him serve in the judiciary.

Discouraged but still resilient, I chose to teach half-time at UC San Diego. I drove the 2 ½ to 3 hours down to San Diego early in the morning, held office hours, taught in the late afternoon, and drove back to Los Angeles. Sometimes, I stayed with friends for the night to reduce the exhaustion of this schedule. I organized a new course on "Film and Society," using another form of expressive culture to address issues like genocide, including the Holocaust, the military coup in Chile in 1973, the civil war in El Salvador, women's rights, and other politically contentious topics. As previously, I earned high praise and strong evaluations from my students during my brief time on campus. Sociology department authorities scarcely noticed.

My past political record in San Diego gave me many ambivalent feelings there. I made no contact with previous civil rights colleagues and largely kept to myself. I still regarded the city as an intellectual wasteland and did little more than explore the UCSD library and a radical bookstore located in the center of the sprawling campus. I made a few preliminary inquiries about more durable faculty employment, but my reputation as a troublemaker, and my even longer appellation as a lecturer, made this fruitless. In any case, my heart was not really in it because I had no desire to return to San Diego ever again. My most enjoyable times during the two terms I taught were going to a shell shop in La Jolla and purchasing "sea treasures" for Elizabeth each week.

I also remained active in research during this period, continuing to publish articles on political art and artists, often using the pages of leftwing *Z Magazine* for my efforts. I had originally conceived of writing a comprehensive book on current American developments in socially conscious art. I imagined this as a major and extensive successor to my previous books on political art. Quickly, I determined that such a project would be too massive, even for a lifetime, and that I would have to narrow my focus into smaller, more focused publications. That decision eventually led to two more book length treatments of visual art and its close linkages to history and politics.

My major publication of 1986, however, was my book, *Stillborn Education: A Critique of the American Research University.* I had begun this following my travails at UCLA. The book focused on the misplaced priorities of research institutions, which especially in the post-war era devalued teaching and elevated research, often including prosaic and trivial efforts that advanced personal careers far more than human knowledge. Obviously reflecting my troubled experience since 1968, it also allowed me to systematize the critique of Clark Kerr's model of the multiversity that I had started thinking about in the wake of the Free Speech Movement at Berkeley more than twenty years previously. This book followed a long line of critical works on American higher education, starting from such early iconic figures as Thorstein Veblen and Upton Sinclair and later figures like Robert Hutchins, Paul Goodman, and others.

One of the chief ironies of my maverick career is my personal commitment to research and publication. I have always agreed with University of California and comparable officials who proclaim that research productivity can lead to better classroom teaching because it brings to students front-line discoveries and new interpretations. It also keeps teachers intellectually alive and vibrant. My objection, throughout my career and expressed in detail in *Stillborn Education*, is that research priorities often overwhelm teaching and contribute to a culture of contempt for undergraduate education, which I believe is a continuing reality at major research institutions. Over the years, I have made this critique a central feature of my more comprehensive political consciousness and activism.

The supreme irony of 1986 occurred when I received word, while still teaching sociology at UC San Diego, that I had received a UCLA Academic Senate Distinguished Teaching Award. Unlike other nominees (including my earlier award at Berkeley), no department or other academic unit advanced my candidacy. Instead, a group of UCLA undergraduate and graduate students compiled a large dossier of evaluations and support letters from students and faculty. I flew from San Diego to Los Angeles to attend the award ceremony, listening to UCLA administrators offer flowery rhetoric about excellence in teaching. Both the official who had fired me in 1983 and the Vice Chancellor who had appeared in court earlier that year were in attendance at the ceremony.

I returned to UCLA and continued finding other teaching and related work throughout Southern California. My most significant political activity reflected my personal struggles as a maverick academic. I increased my activity in the teachers union on campus, viewing such collective action as beneficial to me and to thousands of other contingent faculty members. I did some recruiting and contributed to the campaign to make the AFT the official bargaining unity of lecturers, librarians, and other academic personnel at the University of California. I helped organizing efforts by speaking at UC campuses at Santa Barbara, San Diego, and Riverside. Not surprisingly, university officials vigorously opposed this campaign, arguing that there was no need for collective bargaining because the university was a collegial institution fully capable of resolving conflicts and promoting faculty fairness. Like other academic union activists, I found this reasoning specious and absurd.

180

My personal visibility and troublemaker reputation increased when in 1986 I became the plaintiff in a lawsuit sponsored by the union against the Regents of the University of California. I alleged in substance that my years of service entitled me to *de facto* tenure, a position supported in various documents from the American Association of University Professors. The deeper strategic consideration of the litigation, far beyond my specific personal faculty status, was to support the organizing efforts of the union. One of the chief targets was the 8-year rule, which was eventually repealed after the union won its organizing campaign. But suing the university placed me in even greater jeopardy. I know from reliable internal sources that high level administrators viewed litigation as the quintessential act of disloyalty. During a deposition, a hostile UCLA administrator took issue with the union attorney who had noted my record of teaching excellence. Asserting that I was "merely popular," he maintained that that I had a great capacity to "entertain" my students—a rap I had also encountered at Berkeley.

My continuing perspective is that legal action is—and should be—politics in another form and that universities, no less than other institutions, are appropriate targets when they act oppressively. The lawsuit eventually failed, but its larger strategic objectives prevailed. I continue active participation in a union that has finally provided others and myself with a least modest, contractually enforceable job security and that provides a vital counter force to institutional power and misconduct.

All of this, moreover, revealed yet again the extreme difficulty of the fight for equal rights for non-tenured faculty, especially those ineligible for tenure no matter how talented or accomplished they are. A personal incident made that painfully obvious. During my period of hustling for courses in the 1980s, I managed to snare a course in the UCLA Art History Department on the history of mural art, focusing on the Mexican mural tradition, the American tradition during the Works Progress Administration during the Depression, and the more recent manifestation of ethnic community murals in the wake of 1960s social and political agitation. This subject matter reflected my research interests and I was perfectly suited to teach this course. The course went well and students expressed great satisfaction with the material and with my teaching. Naturally, I sought to repeat the class. This time, however, I ran into opposition. One extremely prominent senior faculty member in art history objected. A friend in that department later told me that he remarked, "We're not here to do welfare."

That specific "welfare" comment, on its face, was absurd and insulting. I applied to the department to teach a class and to teach it with a high level of excellence. I hardly sought a handout; I intended to work hard for my salary, preparing the material carefully and delivering it engagingly. In a nutshell, his attitude reflects the pervasive contempt of many regular faculty for their less fortunate academic peers. His stupid and boorish remark bespoke the widespread arrogance of many professors whose privileged positions, all too frequently, emerge from mere luck and little else. They often see it differently, ascribing their positions to superior intellectual attainment alone. Closer scrutiny, however, reveals a somewhat less idealized reality.

Many "regular" professors, including those with perfectly legitimate scholarly accomplishments, seemingly suffer from significant but unrecognized personal insecurities that impel them to attack and otherwise disrespect the legions of American faculty members who do the bulk of post-secondary teaching. This Mandarin class consciously and unconsciously creates and reinforces a discriminatory academic system based on severe exploitation of an underclass of underpaid and overworked personnel. Its members especially disdain lecturers, which is a title that in rarefied academic circles is not especially different from the racist label "nigger." This is a harsh and distasteful analogy, but perceptive academic insiders know all too well that non-tenured contingent faculty toil in a system of academic apartheid.

I have routinely experienced the specific consequences of this apartheid scheme during my 41 years of University of California faculty service. One feature is especially revealing. Throughout that time, I have rarely had the right to vote despite my service on innumerable campus and departmental committees. As a lecturer (even as a senior lecturer), I have had no formal voice in departmental affairs and am excluded from departmental meetings that decide curricular and personnel actions that intimately affect my professional life. In one especially egregious case, I spent well over 60 hours on a departmental search committee, only to be informed that I was ineligible to vote on the final selection. This is an unjust arrangement and I can reluctantly report that only a few courageous regular faculty members, in my experience, have undertaken the moral leadership to condemn it.

At worst, contingent faculty members float from campus to campus, juggling several classes to earn a barely livable income. Often lacking health and other benefits, they sometimes go without offices and mailboxes or are forced to share minimal space with several other marginal academic transients. Their privileged colleagues, meanwhile, often ignore them, occasionally feeling quite comfortable in replacing them with favored graduate students or cronies as circumstances dictate. The consequences are severe: horrible morale, a growing, perhaps insurmountable divide among elite and marginal faculty members, and weakened educational prospects and opportunities for students as transient instructors dilute their educational activities owing to the sheer necessity of finding other work.

182

No easy solutions to this denial of rights to non-tenure track faculty exist. It is naïve to think that the elite faculty will come to their senses and correct the injustices of the present system. My view is that stronger faculty unions, in conjunction with legislative action in public university settings, will be necessary. American professors love to proclaim their commitment to "shared governance," but the truth is that they are often profoundly incapable of governing their affairs effectively and humanely. Legislatures will have to direct universities to treat *all* faculty members decently, providing them with acceptable compensation, benefits, and job security commensurate with their efforts.

At home, Elizabeth was articulate, insightful, imaginative, and extremely personable. In school, she was silent and fearful. Naively, I ascribed it to the same alienation I had experienced at that age. But her problems were very different. Her major learning disabilities, especially in math, continued to go unrecognized. Public school was unsatisfactory, so we settled on an exclusive private elementary school that turned out to be extremely inappropriate. The teachers there had no patience with her and a few weeks into third grade they told us that she had to leave. That was an act of cruelty; it devastated Elizabeth and us. Years later, I still cringe when I pass that school. It took us weeks to find another, a Summerhill-like school called Play Mountain Place, where the curriculum and activities largely followed the children's lead. There, teachers had much greater emotional sensitivity, but unfortunately, while she mastered reading and wrote well, Liz (as she demanded to be called) never received a solid foundation in math.

Another specter from the past returned to complicate my life. For several years, my parents managed to survive reasonably well in Berkeley. I maintained extremely good relationships with them, seeing them frequently during trips to the Bay Area. My mother was especially good with Liz, who enjoyed her enormously. None of the Quaker remnants remained and both parents now fully identified as Jews, which pleased me enormously. My father, ever hesitantly, spoke a little of his background and of the Nazi persecution of his family. Each of my younger siblings had done reasonably well and had left home. One sister, Carey, had settled in the Los Angeles area and we saw her and her family occasionally.

But finances were again a huge problem. My parents had entered the travel industry as travel agents. Initially, that went well. My mother and father took enormous advantage of travel opportunities and went on numerous ship cruises. They loved the bourgeois lifestyle and saw much of the world. They even wrote a Fodor's travel book on cruising, on which I helped to negotiate the publication terms. But then my father's congenitally poor business sense manifested itself again. The agency fell into severe debt and in due course, he lost the enterprise. We had to lend them money and when they lost their house, we stepped in by renting them the upstairs apartment of the duplex we had owned in Berkeley since 1971 at a rate they could afford. They refused to accept it rent-free. My parents never recovered from their final economic catastrophe, but they could at least live their final years with some dignity.

My continuing search for courses to teach at UCLA yielded good results, especially in 1988 when the African American Studies Center accepted my proposal to teach a new course entitled "Paul Robeson: An American Life." This development marked a huge turning point both in my career and my personal intellectual focus. My proposal reflected my long involvement in struggles for racial justice originating in my teenage years. I had long cherished the memory of Paul Robeson and had highlighted his stunning artistic and political accomplishments in many of my classes over the years. All of this originated in my family's political engagements going back as far as the Progressive Party campaign in 1948. Since that time, I had read assiduously about Paul Robeson's life and work. I had seen most of his films, had read most of his writings, had listened to almost all of his records, and had spoken to many people who had known him personally. I was a Robeson "buff" and now aspired to go far beyond that perspective.

I had often fantasized about an entire course about him and his life, especially because it would offer profound and disconcerting observations about 20th century American history. As I have noted in several publications and presentations, Robeson had become a forgotten figure, a victim of both McCarthyism and selective and distorted historical presentations at all educational levels. I spent significant time in developing a course that I regard as my most important single educational achievement.

Political activities in the late 1980s at UCLA helped catalyze my interest in teaching a Robeson course. I took part in the campaign to divest University of California funds from the racist apartheid regime in South Africa. I had closely followed the anti-apartheid struggle for many decades. Even earlier, in Berkeley, Ruth and I had youthful activists from South Africa stay temporarily with us after they were forced to flee their country in the final but protracted campaign to end apartheid. As usual, I gave speeches and worked organizationally; much of this activity reflected the same emotions that earlier civil rights struggles provided. Racism: it has always had a visceral linkage to my deepest political and moral passions. Knowing that Robeson himself opposed apartheid and was deeply involved in African issues fostered my enthusiasm for the course.

It turned out to be remarkably successful; more important than the course alone, it brought me into the growing interdisciplinary field of African

American Studies, which even now remains my home academic unit. I had been a vigorous participant at Berkeley in the frequently violent struggle to create ethnic studies. Now, I was part of what I helped create, and no longer a mere supportive presence from the sidelines. Paul Robeson, my enduring intellectual, artistic, and political hero, brought me into a program that has increasingly defined much of my personal academic identity for over twenty years.

Through developing this course, moreover, I have published several essays and articles about Robeson. Even more important, I have become a serious player in the community of Robeson scholars and have regularly made presentations about Paul Robeson at academic conferences and in public forums. I know that I enjoy strong respect in that community, even when I criticize Paul Robeson, as I do regularly, for his blind spot when it came to Stalin and the monumental crimes of the Soviet Union, including the anti-Semitism that Robeson fought so courageously throughout his magnificent life. Once again, my curricular interests have given rise to deeper levels of intellectual expression.

But administrative hostility at UCLA remained. I still had to hustle for courses to make a living and I continued to accept part-time positions and freelance writing opportunities elsewhere, including serving as a writing consultant at Loyola Law School in Los Angeles. That has proved to be the best moonlighting arrangement I have ever had, one that has lasted for over 20 years. It reconnects me, minimally, to my training and marginal practice as a lawyer. I work with students individually on their legal writing assignment projects, one afternoon a week. Many of the law students need extensive tutoring because their writing skills are severely deficient. Sometimes they lack even elementary knowledge of grammar, punctuation, and syntax. This is not surprising. Many have graduated from prestigious universities, including UCLA, where they have earned excellent grades but have received little or no critical feedback on their papers. As a longtime critic of university priorities, I am never surprised.

The individual tutoring has added a dimension to my overall teaching record, which includes lower division, upper division, and many M.A. and Ph.D. committees. But the real satisfaction is that many law students committed to public interest careers seek me out and I find special satisfaction in helping them along. Most important, I have substantial faculty and administrative respect at Loyola. My elite law degree and my extensive publication list have served me well there over the years.

As a freelance writer, I co-authored two high school level supplementary history texts in conjunction with the Constitutional Rights Foundation in Los Angeles. In both cases, I added my own perspective, especially about the

185

historic civil rights struggles, including material on the Chicano Movement, a topic of special relevance to young audiences in Southern California. These efforts enabled me to extend my educational vision to audiences far beyond the university. To complement this writing, I have also made guest appearances in local high schools, including schools in juvenile "correctional" facilities. My youthful audiences always appreciated my vigor and enthusiasm. None of this work counts at all as part of University of California faculty service efforts. On the rare occasions that I even mention that I have spoken at a high school, UCLA faculty colleagues usually give me puzzled looks. It makes no difference to me; I know the resulting educational value and personal satisfaction well.

Then, in 1990, I applied for a position as a Student Recommended Faculty Member at the University of California at Irvine. This was a unique innovation that allowed students to hire faculty to meet articulated student interests. My strong teaching record and my demonstrated rapport with undergraduates made me an attractive candidate and I was pleased to accept the full-time position. My focus would be on media and politics. I negotiated with Irvine officials to allow me to teach the Robeson course at UCLA, which I was extremely reluctant to relinquish.

Chapter 22
Orange County Exile

In Fall Quarter, 1990, I embarked on my self-imposed Orange County exile by joining the UCI Department of Politics and Society. I was happy to be away from UCLA, save for my efforts in African American Studies. It was initially enjoyable to teach political science, bringing me back to my undergraduate major and my first college teaching experience. Once again, student response was enthusiastic and favorable.

I taught my usual way: vigorous, discussion-based, provocative, and controversial—in short, the antithesis of the usual university fare. I had spent a professional lifetime developing an effective teaching strategy and a coherent pedagogy. I was acutely aware that this approach always generated opposition in time. If it is not always true that people never change, it is true that I rarely do.

I met a few graduate students with whom I developed long term friendships and found congenial colleagues in various departments throughout campus. At the end of the year, the political science chair invited me to return in a part time role. Because I had about a half-time arrangement at UCLA, I agreed and thus embarked on divided responsibilities at two relative nearby University of California campuses. Summer teaching, which I had done for many years (and which was exempt from the 8-year rule), enabled me to craft the equivalent of a decent faculty salary.

My second year at Irvine was uneventful. I resumed some external political work, especially in the wake of the Los Angeles urban rebellion following the outrageous acquittal of the police officers who had savagely beaten Rodney King. As a UCLA faculty member in African American Studies, I was repeatedly interviewed in the media. I know that some of the radio and television interviewers considered me an "exotic," a white man teaching in a field that was supposed to be reserved for blacks. I took advantage of this opportunity to discuss broader issues of police brutality and racist elements inherent in the judicial process.

I had become media savvy, delivering critical content quickly within tight time and space constraints. This was part of a personal vision of public intellectualism, encouraged among others by the record of African American activists like W.E. B. DuBois, Paul Robeson, Martin Luther King, and many others. That vision has been crucial to my broader intellectual identity. In 1987, I had read Russell Jacoby's brilliant book, *The Last Intellectuals*, which decried the growing paucity of intellectuals like Lewis Mumford, Philip Rahv, Paul Goodman, Susan Sontag, and others who were always engaged in the arena of public discourse. Jacoby also acknowledged academics like C. Wright Mills, John Kenneth Galbraith, and Noam Chomsky who also went far beyond the academy to articulate their ideas to broader public audiences.

Fully recognizing that I could hardly play in that exalted league, I still sought to communicate widely outside my university home by talking to community groups and making regular media appearances. Most of my university colleagues, including several identifying themselves as progressive or Marxist, seemed perfectly content to confine themselves to narrow academic debates filled with esoteric jargon and minuscule professional audiences. Some, of course, were not effective speakers or comfortable with modern electronic media. More troublesome, but hardly surprising, some dismissed public intellectuals as "mere" journalists. I recognized these labels as the usual code words that reinforce hierarchy in the academy. In fact, I have always thought that intelligent journalism had much better insights about politics and society to offer than most social science scholarship. That is why it has remained one of the staples of my personal reading.

My courses went well and in June, I was awarded honors as Outstanding Social Sciences Professor by the Irvine student government. Unfortunately, teaching prizes, as I had already found at Berkeley and UCLA, are problematic and offer recipients little more than collegial contempt. Friends on campus, including senior faculty members, told me that there was discontent that a part-time UCLA "interloper," a lecturer no less, had garnered the teaching award and had developed such a high visibility at UCI.

One colleague, who sincerely appreciated the quality of my teaching efforts, told me that in order to reclaim my reputation, I should lower student grades in all my classes, to demonstrate my academic "rigor." No one with my record and political consciousness could conceivably agree to such a preposterous request. I reflected on the deeper significance of the view that classes with a mediocre (or even lower) distribution of student grades automatically means that the teacher has high intellectual standards and displays serious instructional rigor. That struck me as a transparent rationalization for ineffective and indifferent teaching. Teachers who claim that "no one can get better than a 'C' in my class" are not rigorous; bluntly, they are fools. In daily conversation, I prefer far more colorful language to describe them.

Doubtless, any class, especially large classes, will have a natural distribution of student talent, personal motivation, and academic performance. But the point of effective teaching is to elevate everyone's performance as much as possible. I know that some university teachers artificially inflate grades in order to garner better evaluations and student favor. But in a quarter century of teaching, if this had been my strategy, I deserved an academy award rather than a teaching award. Many conventional academics don't want to hear it, but excellent teachers *should* elevate students' academic work and their grades *should* reflect their improvement.

As I entered my third academic year at UC Irvine, while still teaching part-time at UCLA, I discerned a growing coldness, even though I participated in numerous campus functions, sponsored political science honors theses and independent studies, and helped to modernize the undergraduate major in social science. The dean of social sciences had initially responded favorably to my inquiry about a longer term, more stable faculty arrangement. Ultimately, I found empty rhetoric rather than concrete action. UC Irvine appeared willing to keep me as a marginal, low paid lecturer (Irvine salaries were *up to* $4000 per course to contingent faculty, unlike UCLA, where each course was calculated as a percentage of my full-time equivalent annual salary), but to offer no more.

More significant, I became more personally and permanently disillusioned with the discipline of political science. My classes were, as always, concerned with real political issues, especially issues of race that had been matters of intense public attention since the Los Angeles "riots" of 1992. I had recently published my third art historical book, *Other Visions, Other Voices: Women Political Artists in Los Angeles* and dealt at length with sexism and gender issues in various classes. On my own initiative, I joint-listed my Political Science course on "Arts, Politics, and Society" with the UC Irvine Women's Studies Program, focusing on feminist literature, film, and visual art in class. I heard, and believed, rumors that senior political science faculty members in political science were dismayed—or worse—with this focus. Above all, I heard that they viewed such teaching and research as far beyond the scope of the discipline.

Oddly, they were correct. The same empiricists and grand theorists that C. Wright Mills had perceptively critiqued years before, in *The Sociological Imagination,* dominated the discipline. The dogma of "rational choice" prevailed, a vision that in my view provided intellectual cover for existing power relations in America. My position, to be sure, was similar to that of many other critical academics throughout the United States and elsewhere. I still found it bizarre that actual political issues found almost no place or collegial approval in political science. Indeed, the field seemed to be desperate to show its empirical reliability and its genuine scientific status, a focus I had found problematic even as an undergraduate many decades previously. At bottom, I took severe issue with this view. I had never

189

thought that political science was actually scientific and in retrospect, I think that I was unable to conceal my view (and probably my contempt) during my Irvine service. To complicate my situation, I was honored with yet another Outstanding Teaching Award, this time in conjunction with the UCI Alumni Association. Although I never solicited this honor, I could not, and would not, decline it.

Other Visions, Other Voices reflected my artistic political activism. I realized when I began working in the field that women were historically excluded from the canon. In the Los Angeles area, I found many vibrant female artists of different backgrounds and ethnicities whose work deserved extensive critical recognition. One, Beth Bachenheimer, had been my student in 1967 at Cal Arts. Her personal experiences as a second generation Holocaust survivor were reflected in several of her artworks, which also resonated with my personal emotions. Many of these talented artists had a difficult time breaking through the "boy's club" art world atmosphere. In some cases, I used my growing scholarly reputation to help them in their careers by supporting their faculty applications and promotions and in facilitating opportunities for individual and group exhibitions. As usual, I saw my publication as part of a deeper lifetime political identity.

The most dramatic example of my political activism in the arts, however, occurred in 1994 and 1995, just as my feminist art book was coming out. I had participated in several mural selection panels in Los Angeles during a time when the city had an active public mural program. My selection on these panels reflected my own academic expertise, which included substantial knowledge of the public mural tradition throughout the United States. I enjoyed this community service because it enabled me to promote my own vision of political and public art. As an active panel member, I was relatively persuasive and many of my personal favorites were eventually funded and became powerful additions to the Los Angeles mural scene.

On February 4, 1994, our panel, meeting at the Social and Public Art Resource Center, enthusiastically selected a young, talented African American woman, Noni Olabisi, to produce a mural entitled "To Protect and Serve," on the side of a hair styling salon in a predominantly African American neighborhood. We elected this mural on the basis of its strong design and its passionate community support. The design chronicled the positive impact of the Black Panther Party, including its leaders and its social programs as well as its food and clothing distribution and its medical care efforts. More controversially, the mural design also revealed images of police brutality and a corrupt judicial system, with a bound and gagged Bobby Seale evoking memories of the "Chicago Eight" trial. Even more provocatively, the design showed a strong black male holding a rifle reflecting his commitment to self-defense.

The panel suspected that the Los Angeles Cultural Affairs Commission, appointed by Republican Mayor Richard Riordan, might find the mural objectionable. We were right. When we appeared with the artist, some commissioners voiced negative comments: "The Panthers were bad people, they killed police"; "the guns are so violent"; and "it doesn't show police in a positive light." The Commission rejected the mural, the first major censorship of a public mural since the city covered up David Alfaro Siqueiros's famous "America Tropical" in 1933.

We organized a massive petition drive in support of the mural and I played a strong role in the broader struggle to get the mural painted. I enlisted various community leaders to speak before the commission and support the project. I also helped obtain legal assistance from the ACLU and I testified personally before the commission, noting the long tradition of critical political content in African American mural art. In the middle of my presentation, the Commission Chair abruptly cut me off, saying that he "didn't want a lecture on art history." He said he only wanted to hear from our lawyers. I glared back, replying, "you're hearing from one" and then launched into a legal defense. Eventually, the Commission relented in the face of successful political pressure.

Noni Olabisi began painting her radical mural in 1995. The Los Angeles Police Department sometimes stationed a patrol car nearby, photographing her and her visitors. Not intimidated, I often walked up to the police and invited them to photograph me. Since the mural's completion, I have given more than 50 tours of the site, discussing both its controversial history and its provocative political imagery and implications.

At Irvine, everything came to a head at the beginning of Fall Quarter, 1994. The political science chair called me to his office and made allegations about my lack of academic standards and my role as a classroom entertainer. His diatribe—no other word truly captures his ethos—reminded me of all the reprimands I had received in school as a child and adolescent. It revealed yet again how deeply these experiences remain embedded in my mind. At 51, I was in no mood to play the admonished child. His allegations of entertainment especially annoyed me. I replied calmly that he himself was obviously not an entertainer, referring obliquely at least to his well deserved reputation as a classroom dullard.

Disturbed and angry for the rest of the day, I returned to my Los Angeles home to determine my response; by then, I had had no stomach for a fight to remain at a university I wanted to leave. In 48 hours of frenetic activity, I made arrangements for full time faculty work at UCLA starting the next quarter. I returned to the Irvine campus and resigned, adding that I would honor my teaching commitment for the rest of the academic term. Overall, it proved a wise decision. I regarded many of my administrative superiors at Irvine as minor league Machiavellians, resorting to rumor and innuendo and conducting academic programs that clashed with both my political and pedagogical visions. When I turned in my grades to the registrar in December and left campus for the final time, I felt a huge sense of relief.

My time in Irvine coincided with some difficult personal developments. In February, 1992, my mother died of a heart attack at 71. Like many women in America, she succumbed to a silent killer, another reminder of the woefully inadequate standard of health care in this nation. The loss of a parent is always difficult. Less political than my father, she was nevertheless much warmer, much more personally enjoyable. It hit my father hard after a marriage of more than 50 years. He insisted on reciting Kaddish in an orthodox setting, perhaps drawing on the Jewish childhood he had repressed for so long. I also think the loss affected my daughter powerfully. My mother was clearly her favorite grandparent and now, as an emerging teenager, she had another huge set of problems to confront.

Those problems were not trivial. School remained problematic and she began acting out more seriously. Ruth and I thought that her choice of friends was especially immature, although we realized that such a parental reaction was certainly common. In the end, we were correct about her friends. School continued to be troublesome for her. A succession of private schools appeared to make little difference. One exceptionally positive thing emerged. Elizabeth began to reveal striking artistic talent, especially as a painter. I was positioned to confirm the judgment of her art teachers because of my own professional work as an art historian and critic.

Chapter 23
Rebirth: Stability at UCLA

Driving north to Los Angeles, after clearing out my Irvine office, I felt a rare sense of optimism about my academic future. My union had negotiated a contract that provided lecturers with excellent teaching records renewable three-year contracts, a standard I was confident I could meet easily. The 8-year rule no longer impeded my academic work. And I had solid arrangements with three academic units at UCLA, guaranteeing me substantial work, including summer teaching if necessary to augment my salary. Shortly after my return to UCLA, a new set of collective bargaining converted these three-year appointments into "continuing appointment" status, including seniority and due process provisions.

From 1995 to the present, I have remained fully employed, distributing my classes among the African American studies program, the department of communication studies, and the division of honors, which bestowed on me another major distinguished teaching award in spring, 2008. I designated African American Studies as my "home" unit, a decision showing both a political choice reflecting my anti-racist personal history and the convenience of dealing with friendly colleagues and staff in the Ralph J. Bunche Center for African American Studies on campus. For a few years, I still had to hustle for additional courses to complete a fulltime load. Richly experienced in this form of academic entrepreneurship, I also taught a course on world literature in the comparative literature department and on feminist art in the women's studies program. Each of these presented marvelous opportunities to link the arts with deeper political, social, and ethical concerns and to interact with students eager to understand and act upon these connections.

The world literature class was especially enjoyable because I could combine multiple themes that appealed to me and my students from different time periods and different cultures. I started with Jonathan Swift's "A Modest Proposal," which allowed me to express my darker vision of human nature. I also dealt again with the Nazi Holocaust. I ended with literary examples from post-apartheid South Africa. As usual, students rated my teaching highly and several enrolled in other of my UCLA courses. But I had gained four graduate students assigned to me as teaching assistants; I had nothing to do with their selection. I have never permitted this again. I always hire my own teaching assistants. No exceptions. They seemed bewildered throughout the term. Once, they collectively approached me and inquired when I was going to start teaching "literature," apparently instead of merely discussing the central ideas of the stories, plays, and novels on my reading list. This was another striking reminder of the difference between academic work and intellectual work, which have never been identical and sometimes seem to be polar opposites.

The women's studies course, not surprisingly, attracted mostly women students. It was never an issue that I was a male teaching this subject, just as it has never been an issue with my teaching African American studies. I used many powerful examples from female artists that addressed issues of patriarchy and that provided a strongly feminist perspective on other social and political themes. The students responded outstandingly to the course material and to my style of teaching, again evidenced in extremely high student evaluations. Consistent with my pedagogical approach (when I have smaller classes), I allowed small groups of students to organize art exhibitions on campus, with a serious catalogue containing critical essays. This project is in lieu of writing a major research paper and is actually more difficult, although students sometimes think otherwise until they get immersed in their projects. The result was some powerful feminist art shows that constituted a splendid cultural contribution to the UCLA campus community.

On December 24, 1995, my father died of a burst aneurism while flying to visit my sister Aimee in Albuquerque. He had been in ill health for a long time and my mother's death clearly exacerbated his emotional and physical ailments. Fortunately, he had a woman companion, Eleanor Goldman, who lived with him in his final years. Although some of my siblings seemed troubled by this relationship, I thought it was fine. I think that my father left an admirable legacy with his children and his political and moral vision, as I have indicated throughout this memoir, was crucial in my own development. His relentless anti-racism was a touchstone in my life. So too was his intellectual perspective, despite his lack of formal education. Overall, I cannot avoid the conclusion that he lived a largely unhappy life. I think that emotionally, he never escaped the horrific circumstances of the rupture of his family life. Unfortunately, Hitler's legacy was also his, and to some extent, my own.

My relative stability at UCLA also encouraged some additional personal travel for Ruth and me. We had always enjoyed travel, spending the majority of this time in Europe and Mexico. Both locales encouraged me to add to my knowledge of socially conscious art and after each trip I could augment my courses through my most recent discoveries. Moreover, through our close friends in Holland, Hans van Marle and Antje de Wilde, I had several opportunities to make classroom presentations and formal lectures at the Rietveld Art Academy in Amsterdam. I had lectured in other institutions throughout my career, mostly throughout the United States. The

Rietveld students were far from spectacular, but they often knew more about American history and current events than many of my UCLA undergraduates.

In the mid 1990s, we began visiting the Caribbean regularly. I was anxious to add West Indian culture to my storehouse of knowledge, especially its vibrant tradition of visual art. Over the years, we have visited numerous countries and territories, including Jamaica, the Bahamas, the Dominican Republic, Turks and Caicos, and Puerto Rico. Artistic examples from all these lands have been fruitful additions to my teaching and research. In many places, I enjoyed visiting neighborhoods far beyond the tourist centers, where ordinary people conducted their daily lives. In some instances, I had warnings to stay away because of possible crime and danger. That was an increased incentive for me to visit. My experience has always been that expressions of personal respect and authentic interest generate a reciprocal response from people everywhere I have gone, even in parts of Los Angeles I have been told to avoid. Nothing has happened: no robberies, no assaults, not even very many strange looks.

The Caribbean travel has also given us a close-up view of what passes as American tourism, especially the curious phenomenon of cruise ship travel. I could never understand my parents' attraction for this perverse phenomenon, except that perhaps it gave them a few days of opulence that they never had in their regular lives. In the Caribbean, we watched American tourists, vulgar caricatures of themselves, rolling off the ships after a dozen high calorie meals a day, parade into overpriced stores and shopping centers, and purchase gaudy items and bottles of liquor and Cuban cigars. Then they returned to their floating luxury hotels and repeated the process in another port. Our most perversely enjoyable incident: walking in Ocho Rios, Jamaica, we overheard an American couple remark that there were so many black people there!

Two times we have defied American regulations (which I regard as unconstitutional and unconscionable) and traveled to Cuba. Those have been remarkable experiences. I went with the idea of seeking a positive impression of the country and its people. Mostly, I left with that viewpoint. I have no illusions, of course, about the human rights abuses under Fidel Castro during his half-century rule in Cuba. Previously in this text, I have expressed disdain for communist tyranny in the old, unlamented Soviet Union and in Eastern Europe. Castro's treatment of political dissidents and homosexuals has often been disgraceful. I have no interest in serving as an apologist for his regime or for anyone's human rights abuses.

On both visits, we saw extensive poverty, but it was shared poverty without the horrific disparities of wealth and power in most of the rest of the

195

world. I fully understood that American sanctions exacerbated Cuban economic hardship. In conversations with ordinary Cubans on the street, we saw no strong evidence of despair and no eagerness to return to the rapacious capitalism of the past. In Santiago de Cuba, it was emotionally exhilarating to ride through a neighborhood that had been full of mansions for the wealthiest Cubans before the Revolution. These formerly opulent residences were now child care and educational institutions, serving populations that Castro's regime, for all its imperfections, has favored since its inception.

An experience in Havana was especially moving. We found a guide, a former schoolteacher, who at our request took us in a 50s American sedan to a Jewish cemetery on the outskirts of the capital city. The graves had remains of many German Jews who had made their way during the War to Cuba. Some gravestones were etched in German, Spanish, and Hebrew, a reminder of the Jewish Diaspora that has so often reflected historic patterns of persecution, a reality I have lived with consciously for more than 60 years. It also reminded me of "the voyage of the damned," when Cuban officials in 1939 turned away 800 Jews (including Ruth's Ph.D. dissertation director, Frederick Reif) on the ill-fated German ship St. Louis, dooming most of its passengers to death on their return to Europe.

On our first clandestine trip to Cuba, Ruth and I flew from Montego Bay, Jamaica to Santiago de Cuba on an old Soviet cargo plane that Cubana Airlines had converted to a passenger plane. This plane was probably a half-century old. Its Russian language signs were poorly covered with Spanish language paste-on labels. The seats were rickety and the flight attendants served the most unappealing sandwiches I had ever seen. But it got us to the airport where we were greeted with a large image of Che Guevara. Cuban immigration officials were solicitous and agreed to refrain from stamping our passports, so that we would have no problems in returning to the United States. When we flew back to Jamaica on the same aircraft, the Cuban pilots invited passengers to come to the cockpit. Despite Ruth's admonition of danger (her father was a pilot), I accepted the offer. I stood behind the pilots throughout the short flight, even accepting a swig or two of their bottle of rum. I remained standing, however foolishly, until we landed in Montego Bay. It was a glorious view, surely worth the personal recklessness. Ruth disagreed.

The other profound change in our travel agenda occurred in 1998, when we made the first of several trips to South Africa. It was a magical experience. I found the new South African democracy exciting and the people's hope seemed palpable on the streets. Over the years, this has changed, because some of the problems of economic inequality and poverty seem horrifically intractable, regardless of political change at the top and the creation of black majority rule. The crisis of the AIDS epidemic in Africa has exacerbated the suffering of millions of black South Africans. Still, to visit a land where everyone's projections a few decades previously, including my own, was that only violent revolution could dislodge the Nazi-like white racist regime was remarkable.

As I earlier noted, I had played a minor role in the divestment struggle at UCLA during the 1980s and my wife and I had known several South African exiles who had been forced to flee the oppressive apartheid regime. I started reading extensively about the South African liberation struggle as an undergraduate. It was a natural complement to my intellectual interests and civil rights activism in America. I remember vividly when Nelson Mandela was captured, tried, and sentenced to the long imprisonment that eventually turned him into one of the most iconic figures of contemporary times. I identified completely with the resistance, the moral equivalent of opposing any fascist regime in the world, but especially one with such monstrous racist practices as the illegitimate white minority South African government.

I steeped myself in the history of South Africa, a topic that rarely received much attention in any of my classes and only superficial coverage in the mainstream American media. I read extensively about the African National Congress, the chief but not the only resistance organization that struggled for decades against white minority rule. I followed its development from its founding in 1912 through its period of peaceful opposition to apartheid, to its more militant years of underground activity, especially its armed struggle, under the leadership of Mandela, Oliver Tambo, Walter Sisulu, and many others, including the heroic women who rarely received recognition for their courageous and risky political activities. I knew of its close alliance with the South African Communist Party, always a key force in the protracted struggle against apartheid. I was struck by the number of prominent anti-apartheid Jews like Joe Slovo, his wife Ruth First (who was murdered by a bomb mailed to her by apartheid police while she worked in exile in Mozambique), Rusty and Hilda Bernstein, Albie Sachs, among many others.

My investigations led me further into the fascinating history of this struggle. The Pan African Congress, under the charismatic leadership of Robert Sobukwe, also played a powerful role in mobilizing massive opposition to oppressive white rule. The PAC had organized a campaign against the hated pass laws, which were designed to restrict the movement of the non-white populations in the country. These laws were also deeply humiliating and reinforced the system of racial inferiority at the heart of the apartheid system. The resistance against the pass laws resulted in the infamous Sharpeville Massacre on March 21, 1960, resulting in the murder of

69 people and scores of injuries to peaceful apartheid protestors. I remembered my anger at the time even as a high school senior, with no sense that decades later this event and the broader liberation struggle would be a staple of my teaching and research.

Years later, as a university teacher, I identified closely with the final stages of the South African liberation struggle. The Soweto Rebellion in 1976 galvanized world attention. The heroic actions of young students protesting the imposition of Afrikaans as the language of instruction in schools heralded the beginning of the end of apartheid. The emergence of the Black Consciousness Movement, with its courageous young leader Steve Biko, similarly evoked international attention and outrage. His brutal murder while in police detention in 1977 accelerated the demise of white supremacy. Although white police power still prevailed, the authorities never completely controlled the majority population. Equally important, oppressed peoples throughout the country began to believe that the rebellion would eventually succeed and that a new, multiracial democracy would replace the racist order. Still, state sanctioned repression continued and even intensified during the 1980s and reports of murder and torture were ubiquitous.

Throughout the 1980s, growing opposition throughout the world began to impact the white rulers in South Africa. Economic and athletic boycotts isolated the nation, making it an international pariah. Only the United States under President Ronald Reagan failed to contribute to this isolation. His policy of "constructive engagement" was fraudulent, a convenient way to continue to support the regime without appearing to endorse apartheid itself. Eventually, new South African President F. W. de Klerk, recognizing that the old system could not endure, released Nelson Mandela from prison. The sight of Mandela walking free on February 11, 1990 mesmerized me along with hundreds of millions of other global television viewers.

The legalization of the African National Congress and other anti-apartheid groups led swiftly and inevitably to Mandela's election as President of a new, democratic, and multiracial South Africa. Watching black and "colored" South Africans stand for hours in long lines to cast their first votes was exhilarating. This historical context set the tone for our visit and it was especially gratifying that our arrival at the Johannesburg International Airport occurred during the presidential administration of Nelson Mandela.

Our first trip brought us both to urban and rural South Africa. I loved both Johannesburg and Cape Town, two vastly different cities. As usual, the most enduringly gratifying feature of the trip was to talk to South Africans themselves. These discussions included artists and intellectuals as well as others with more prosaic positions. I had the opportunity to make presentations to college groups in Johannesburg and in Soweto, the historic black township where young students in 1976 ignited the revolts that eventually toppled the brutal apartheid system. At the small black Funda College in Soweto, I gave a presentation on African American art, using some especially sharp and poignant images. One young black woman art student responded with strong emotion, telling me that she would devote her own art to serving her people for the rest of her career. Experiences like this, much more than seeing the Cape Town's Table Mountain or even Nelson Mandela's Soweto house, represent the essence of serious travel.

One of the most lasting consequences of the first South African visit was to see the extraordinary visual art, especially examples that reflected the powerful and courageous resistance for many decades. Every medium was represented: paintings, prints, sculpture, and photography, among others. I met several visual artists and began researching this tradition systematically. I knew that I wanted to incorporate these works into my classes and into my writing. In 1998, I had little idea that this focus would become a major extension of my work in the field of socially engaged art. I was especially intrigued with the photography of Peter Magubane, the key resistance photojournalist against apartheid for almost half a century. I saw many of his images in Soweto and purchased several of his books during our first visit. I resolved to learn more about him and his life, a promise I fulfilled more than I could have imagined at the time.

In 1997, Liz graduated from private Newbridge High School, her second private secondary school, which she had selected herself when her earlier high school refused to let her graduate unless she took Algebra 2. She managed to do well at Newbridge. Her artwork was outstanding and her final project was an art exhibition that she presented to the entire school. This effort was remarkable. It had numerous works, mostly watercolors that revealed tremendous talent and extremely high imagination. Her work was strong, enough for her to gain admission to the California Institute of the Arts, now located in Valencia, California. This was a prestigious admission, and I hoped that Cal Arts was very different from the Cal Arts that I despised so much more than 30 years before.

Everything went downhill after that. She was plainly not ready for any college experience. Our high expectations for her, with all their attendant pressures, took a huge toll. She just made it through the first semester and merely completed one course in the second, albeit with some distinction because of the quality of her artistic work. Mostly, this result reflected her personal anxieties about being in school at a time when she was unprepared for such independent responsibilities.

She went through two very rough years but she pulled her life together. She eventually found full-time work. In 2008, she realized that low paying jobs were a dead end and she returned to full-time college studies, focusing again on her exemplary artistic skills. So far, she has done extremely well in this return to school. Ruth and I, of course, are extremely pleased.

In the early state of this crisis, I finally sought therapy for myself, especially after years of wrestling with job insecurities. One catalyst occurred when I thought I might be having a heart attack. Although this was unlikely, given my low blood pressure, daily running regimen, and healthy diet, I was in my late fifties and my mother had died of heart disease. At Kaiser-Permanente hospital, doctors found that I had a stress induced panic attack.

I was hesitant about psychotherapy, recalling the forced experiences from my school days. Earlier short term voluntary therapy experiences were unsatisfactory. Basically, I had little respect for the therapists, finding them unremarkable in their psychological insights and deficient in their understanding of the deeper roots of my anxieties.

This experience, fortunately, was different. Through my longtime friend Bob Ehrlich in Berkeley, himself an academic and psychoanalyst, I contacted Dr. Jimmy Fisher in Los Angeles. Fisher was a trained intellectual historian as well as a psychoanalyst. A political leftist, he shared that vital component of my entire life story. I had no plans for extensive psychoanalysis. I have read Freud and others in that tradition for years and respect psychoanalytic theory, but even now I remain skeptical about that therapeutic process. Anyway, I hardly wanted to expend the time and the money for that protracted process.

Beyond Liz's immediate problems and their impact on my relationship with her and Ruth, Jimmy Fisher understood the roots of my Jewish angst, including the Holocaust on my parents, especially my father. His enormous empathy—the key feature of any therapeutic relationship—gave me insights into my continuing anxieties about money and economic insecurity. Perhaps above all, he understood and gave me solid concrete advice about my academic travails. He had had his own earlier bouts of academic marginality, so he well understood my frustration and my rage. The experience has given me a more favorable view of psychotherapy, but it still requires the delicate match of therapist and patient, not always an easy combination.

In the midst of this family drama, I tried to maintain an active political life. In fact, it provided a valuable emotional interlude from my daughter's problems. On rare occasions, Liz even accompanied me to political meetings. Whatever her personal struggles, she shares the family tradition of progressive politics. Her moral vision is powerful and acute, and she is impressively articulate about it, which is also profoundly gratifying.

The key political events occupying my attention during that time occurred in Los Angeles in the summer of 2000 during the Democratic National Convention. I participated for an entire week in the massive demonstrations outside the Democratic Party Convention in Los Angeles, when Vice President Al Gore and Senator Joe Lieberman gained the nominations for president and vice president in the November election. Throughout this week, I served as a volunteer attorney for the National Lawyers Guild, trying to protect the constitutional rights of thousands of protestors. I witnessed numerous instances of police misconduct and joined my Lawyers Guild colleagues in gathering data that eventually culminated in a settlement with the city authorities.

Hundreds of officers, many attired in full riot gear with batons, rifles, and other weaponry, dominated the streets. Marching and jogging in military formation, these men and women intimidated protestors, delegates, visitors, and residents alike. They shadowed the demonstrators from start to finish, often waving their batons menacingly. Screeching drives through the area in patrol cars and motorcycles, scores of police on horseback and ubiquitous helicopters flying overhead intensified the entire surreal spectacle. I was appalled at the intermittent brutality and pervasive harassment throughout the protest week.

The most dramatic was the egregious overreaction at the Rage Against The Machine concert on the evening of August 14, where hundreds of concert goers, demonstrators, media representatives and innocent bystanders were trapped and shot with rubber bullets. Less publicized, various LAPD officers shoved and clubbed protestors throughout the week. I personally observed several incidents; in one especially savage case, I saw an LAPD officer use his baton to strike a young man on the back of his leg. The young man had done nothing to provoke anyone. Although I was only a few feet away, I could not identify the officer as he jogged quickly from the scene.

I had a modest personal taste of this police abuse. An officer tried to prevent me from observing a nonviolent act of civil disobedience. When I explained that I was a lawyer trying to ensure a peaceful disposition, the officer shoved me twice in the stomach with the end of his baton, remarking that I was "violating his personal space." New age rhetoric had apparently merged with the old police brutality.

One other personal example stood out. I represented a group of older demonstrators protesting outside a gathering of wealthy Democratic Party fundraisers. Calling themselves the "Dot-Commies," they raised enough ire that the police arrived. I informed them that the demonstration was fully protected under the First Amendment. They had no choice but to concur. The lead officer asked me if the group members were communists. I replied that they were not, but that they were Dadaists. He asked me to spell the word and I gladly complied.

Los Angeles Police Department personnel also destroyed marchers' puppets, picket signs, and other physical signs and symbols of political resistance. All too often, officers prevented people from joining various marches and closed off streets to disrupt protestors' unity and communication. More ominous, police isolated people outside the main marches and engaged in many unlawful searches. Young people dressed in black—allegedly dangerous "anarchists"—were frequently stopped and searched, especially in metro stations and on side streets. Being young, wearing political t-shirts or face masks, and looking "scruffy" hardly constituted probable cause for anything other than police paranoia. Legal observers and others who questioned these tactics were themselves threatened with arrest. Many reports of questionable jaywalking and traffic citations have also surfaced. I personally witnessed several instances of demonstrators receiving such citations in circumstances that can only be regarded as selective and discriminatory law enforcement.

I had *never* seen such a systematic display of police firepower and personnel in all my past experience, from the early civil rights movement to that time. The closest parallels were the worker/student rebellion in Paris in 1968 and the first anniversary demonstrations against the Soviet invasion in Prague in 1969. Throughout the week, many police officers routinely ignored the Bill of Rights. Violations of the First, Fourth, Sixth, and Fourteenth Amendments were legion. I documented these violations in an op-ed piece I published shortly after the events. Later, I published a more extensive scholarly law review article about my experiences and reflections. I also used my media experience to provide interviews to print and electronic journalists during the turmoil itself.

Candor also compels a recognition that I observed several LAPD officers who acted admirably and decently. I was gratified to find many reasonable police officers with whom I could negotiate a fair accommodation for both public safety and demonstrators' First Amendment rights of free expression. Some, in fact, were especially effective in this domain. Since that time, I have continued my work as a legal observer for the Lawyers Guild, often using my negotiating skills during mass protests against George W. Bush's outrageous war in Iraq.

Increased stability at UCLA encouraged me to focus on my courses with renewed vigor. In African American Studies, I added more offerings, including "Race, Racism, and the Law," "African American Art," and "African American Film," each one of which is inextricably linked to broader political and historical issues. My "African American Art" course has also become a staple of my UCLA teaching, typically drawing well over 100 students each year. The focus is necessarily on the substantial tradition of African American art dealing with slavery, racism, and related themes. Institutionally, the course is concurrently offered with the Art History Department, allowing me a modest relationship with the field to which I have devoted much of my teaching and research energies throughout my career.

I have likewise developed several new courses in Communication Studies, again with strong linkages to my political background and identity. I resurrected a course called "Criticism and the Public Arts," allowing me to offer the themes of literature, film, and visual art and their connection to politics and society to well over 200 students each time I taught the class. I have also created two entirely new courses, one on "Visual Communication and Social Advocacy" and the other on "Films of Persuasion." The former examines public (and highly political) art forms like cartoons and comic strips, posters, documentary photography, and community murals to generate deeper student discussion both about the strengths and limitations of art as a means of social criticism and about the substantive social and political issues themselves. The latter uses politically oriented films to achieve the same educational objectives; the extensive availability of socially conscious films, especially in the rich UCLA film library, ensures a strong future for this particular upper division offering. Each of these courses in both academic units, moreover, encourages me to include artists of color and women, in itself an important expression of my anti-racist and anti-sexist political vision.

During Liz's crisis period, I initiated one of the most intriguing curricular innovations of my long academic career. Not without some institutional difficulty, I persuaded the history department to allow me to teach a class exploring the long and convoluted history of African Americans and Jews. Entitled "Mutual Reflections: A History of African American/Jewish Conflict, Cooperation, and Coexistence," the course attracted a sizable number of both Jewish and African American students as well as a few others who usually took any course I offered.

The topic was both intellectually and personally compelling. I had spent much of my life in both communities. When my father arrived in America, he almost immediately noticed the pervasive racism against blacks. This precipitated his, and in turn, my own, enduring fight against racism in all forms, including anti-Semitism. The civil rights struggles included a disproportionate number of Jewish volunteers. In recent years, unfortunately, schisms developed between the communities as Jews in America increasingly became more conservative. At their worst, some also

203

exhibited racist attitudes and behaviors. Some African Americans also sometimes exhibited anti-Jewish attitudes, and not only Louis Farrakhan of the Nation of Islam.

I thought it was time to explore these issues in a university class. I identified myself as Jewish at the outset of the course; this is not my usual practice, although I never hide my identity. I thought that with this particular subject matter, this kind of personal candor was appropriate. I used both scholarly and popular readings and explored numerous themes throughout the term. I tried to puncture as many myths and misconceptions as possible. Jews were *not* major players in the slave trade. Blacks and Jews had *very* different histories, especially in America. Political alliances between the two groups were matters of expediency, *not* deep feelings of inseparable brotherhood. Affirmative action was *not* a conspiracy directed primarily against Jews. Above all, I sought to demolish the all too common game of "who has suffered the most."

Mostly, students responded extremely thoughtfully. There were moments of passion and heated debate. Emotion belongs in the classroom and the teacher's job is delicate: to allow it and even to foster it, but also to keep it in check to accomplish the deeper intellectual objectives of any course. My impression was that many of the Jewish students were more defensive than their African American counterparts. Affirmative action issues were particularly touchy, especially for Jewish students seeking admission to prestigious law schools and other professional programs. Many complained that they were being frozen out, almost as if it was a birthright of their social class privilege. The topic of Israel also made some Jewish students nervous, mirroring a deeper problem with a widespread lack of American Jewish criticism of foolish and immoral Israeli actions over the years. I found myself, mostly, siding with the African American students, although I was never reluctant to criticize African American leaders and others when I saw them slipping into anti-Semitic rhetoric or worse.

This has been a regular refrain in these pages, but my course reviews were as superb as ever. The experiences enabled me to deepen my own knowledge and feelings about the complexities of the relationships between African Americans and Jews. A few years later, I pursued the topic further by writing a paper, which I presented at a Conference on Jewish arts at the University of Wisconsin at Madison, on Jewish artists who sympathetically treated black themes in their art and African American artists who treated Jewish themes sympathetically in their art. There is much more for me to explore, to teach, and to write in this domain.

After our first trip to South Africa, I discovered that the California African American Museum was planning to present a major retrospective exhibition on the photographic work of Peter Magubane. The originator of the idea was Roland Charles, the Director of the Black Photographers of California, one of the groups I had researched for the book I was writing on the history of African American art in greater Los Angeles. The group invited me to participate in the planning sessions, knowing of my interest in South Africa generally, and Peter Magubane particularly. I played an active role and decided to get first hand knowledge by returning to South Africa to meet and interview Magubane personally.

Ever since our first trip, Ruth and I were anxious to return to that fascinating land. After our arrival, I arranged to meet Magubane at his Johannesburg home, in the fashionable suburb of Melville, a neighborhood that we soon came to know and enjoy enormously. I explored his life and work as thoroughly as possible, recording some of our conversations for future use. I also spoke with many people who knew Magubane and his work, and several people who had been deeply involved in the long resistance against apartheid.

Peter's story was both remarkable and inspiring. I concurred with other scholars that his stature compared favorably with that of the finest socially conscious photographers of all time. He combined remarkable technical expertise with chilling but compelling subject matter. From his clandestine photographs of apartheid police and military brutality to his recent documentation of South Africa's indigenous cultures, Magubane created a powerful body of work that will endure for generations.

He recounted his life to me in meticulous detail. Like millions of other blacks, he witnessed and experienced the daily realities of racism. He recalled signs marked "No Dogs and Natives Allowed" and other signifiers of white supremacy. He had a deep personal foundation for his future resistance activities in the struggle for racial equality and human dignity. This reminded me of the conversations I had had years before in Alabama, Georgia, and Louisiana during the civil rights era.

We also discussed his early training in photography and his later conflicts with apartheid authorities. He was regularly arrested and jailed, enduring harsh treatment and even torture while incarcerated. Mostly, we discussed the iconic and wrenching images that helped generate worldwide knowledge of the brutality of South African apartheid. Like so many of the artists I have interviewed in my career, Peter Magubane linked his life and his work. He repeatedly told me that his work was inseparable from his lifelong commitment to South African freedom and justice. He was a partisan in the struggle, a view that mirrors my own self-perception.

In South Africa, Ruth and I reconnected with people we had earlier met and spent some time just exploring the country. A highlight was to drive along the "garden route" from Port Elizabeth to Cape Town. The nature is amazingly beautiful and even someone as hopelessly urban as I am can appreciate its grandeur. In Cape Town itself, we visited the Robben Island prison where Nelson Mandela was incarcerated for so many years. Former political prisoners there conduct the prison tours. Our particular guide was impressed by my substantial knowledge of the history of the anti-apartheid struggle and we met him later over drinks in Cape Town. As always, these travel experiences proved most fruitful and enduring.

The interviews with Peter Magubane helped pave the way for the planned Los Angeles exhibition of his work. Then, suddenly, Roland Charles died, leaving a serious void. The Visual Arts curator of the California African American Museum, John Riddle, stepped in and undertook responsibilities for the show. He was an extraordinarily accomplished African American artist with a long record of socially critical themes dealing with the black experience. I admired his artwork but treasured his friendship even more. We often discussed art, politics, and life in general and I continued in an increased advisory role for the Magubane exhibition. John's plans for the show were visionary and promised to bring knowledge of South African art and history to a wide public audience in the Los Angeles area.

Then, in 2002, John Riddle succumbed to a heart attack. Now the exhibition was in severe jeopardy and it appeared that these years of meticulous planning would be in vain. With some prodding, I decided to step in, becoming the curator of the exhibition. I had some modest experience with other art exhibitions, usually as an academic advisor, but I had never undertaken something of this magnitude. I had extremely fine support from the Museum staff and others and I added this enterprise to my broader work in the arts.

I returned to South Africa again to do even more preliminary work for the show. I was able to arrange another feature of Peter Magubane's presence in Southern California. I persuaded UCLA to invite him as a special Regent's Lecturer for two weeks. This is a special honor reserved for distinguished people outside academia. The honoree typically makes several class appearances and gives a formal lecture or two. This third trip to South Africa also helped me with details for Peter's forthcoming campus visit.

We also took an auto trip with Peter to one of the indigenous villages he knew well, a key site of the Ndebele population north of Pretoria. The women of this community are known for their colorful clothing and for their beautiful abstract murals. I had known of their work from one previous visit and from my own research, but this was a unique opportunity to speak to the artists themselves. The murals were spectacular, reflecting a skill passed for generations from mother to daughter. Peter introduced us to his friend,

Esther Mahlangu, the Ndebele artist who had received the most critical recognition throughout the world. The visit was wonderful. She was a gracious host who answered all our questions. We purchased one of her paintings, adding to our growing collection of South African art.

Once again, Ruth and I took advantage of our contacts there and explored the land as thoroughly as possible, including some trips to see some of the wild animals. I also enjoyed that part of the visit, but I mostly wanted to return to see more artists and their work. So while Ruth and a friend went off to Kruger National Park, I returned to Soweto, alone, violating numerous warnings about such trips and the dangers I would face. It was fine. I met a young artist and her family and thoroughly enjoyed myself, as usual emerging without any personal harm.

Most memorably, we met one of the most intriguing persons in South Africa or anywhere else. One of my former students had a family connection to Constitutional Court Justice Albie Sachs. That court is the equivalent to our Supreme Court and President Nelson Mandela appointed Sachs to the post by after his election in 1994. I phoned him at the court and he invited us to his chambers. He had been a young Jewish lawyer, defending people charged with various apartheid era offenses and had himself been jailed during those repressive times. He left the country in exile, eventually landing in Maputo, Mozambique to teach law. The South African security forces placed a bomb in his car. When it exploded, he lost an eye and his right arm, spending months in the hospital recovering. I had earlier read his poignant yet upbeat account of his experiences in his *Soft Vengeance of a Freedom Fighter*.

After he recovered and the African National Congress was permitted to operate again, he returned to South Africa, where he worked on the new Constitution. It is a remarkable document, encompassing a progressive vision of human rights, better and more comprehensive, I think, than our own Bill of Rights. Albie Sachs also helped select the magnificent art collection in the new Constitutional Court building, at the site of a notorious former prison in Johannesburg.

He was a gracious host, serving Ruth and me lunch and introducing us to another former dissident couple. He gave us a personal tour of the grounds, paying particular attention to the artworks after I told him of my own interests in both law and art. We have seen him again in a subsequent visit to the court. His life is a splendid reminder of how people can overcome unspeakable adversity and do such remarkable good in the course of their lives.

Peter Magubane had a successful stay during his two weeks at UCLA. My students found his presentations especially illuminating and his public presentations went equally well. I also arranged a mini-exhibition at the California African American Museum in conjunction with the South African Consulate. The big event came a year later with the full exhibition "Deconstructing Apartheid: The Photography of Peter Magubane." It showcased 84 photographs and artifacts documenting the egregious practices of apartheid and the stirring resistance that eventually led to a nonracial democracy in 1994.

Thousands of Southern California residents and visitors viewed the exhibition during its eight month run. Several events augmented the educational objectives of the exhibition itself. At the opening, Magubane spoke about his life and works to a large audience. South African dancers, poets, and others added additional artistic dimensions that appealed especially to young visitors, including children from many area public schools. Shortly before the exhibition closed, an academic symposium with the curator and local African scholars reviewed the current prospects for South African democracy and indicated the political, economic, social, and healthcare challenges that its residents face in the early years of the new century. I participated in organizing all these activities. They were a valuable public extension of the intellectual work that had defined my professional life.

My work on this show related closely to the scholarly efforts that had brought me the most satisfying personal connections throughout my academic career. In 2004, The UCLA Ralph J. Bunche Center for African American Studies published my fourth art historical book, *Resistance, Dignity, and Pride: African American Artists in Los Angeles*, which provided the first comprehensive treatment of African American visual art in the Los Angeles region. This book, however, was the culmination of many years of work in this field. As long ago as my faculty service in Berkeley, I began seeing the central value of African American art in the larger arena of art history, despite its egregious neglect in most of the discipline's major journals and texts. I ascribed that neglect to the deeper, usually unrecognized institutional racism that pervaded so much of academic life generally.

In 1977, I published an article in the field in *Black Art*, the premier journal in an emerging field. The journal editor then was Dr. Samella Lewis, one of the legendary African American art historians of the 20th and 21st centuries. I contacted her because of my interest in learning more about the visual works of black artists. I had read most of her publications and I knew that she had strong record of political activism throughout her career. Her background fit nicely with my civil rights activism and my interests in socially conscious art.

I have maintained close contact with her since my initial contact. Happily, she lives in Los Angeles and remains active both as a scholar and as a practicing painter and printmaker well into her 80s. I devoted an entire chapter to her work in *Resistance, Dignity, and Pride*. More important, she has been an art historical mentor like my late UCLA colleague Al Boime. Although I have muscled my way into recognition through sheer persistence and voluminous publication, Samella has always provided personal encouragement without any concern about my unorthodox credentials and my role as a non-African American teaching and writing about the tradition of African American art and visual culture.

Even before I published my book on the topic, I wrote numerous articles on individual black artists, primarily but not exclusively, in Southern California. That work has generated some of the most enduring and extraordinary personal relationships that Ruth and I have had since our move thirty-one years ago to Los Angeles. In a few cases, these creative artists have become close friends. I visit them in their homes and they frequently reciprocate. I usually attend their exhibition openings and other events and they, in turn, often come to my speeches and gallery presentations. We often run into each other at bookstores, street festivals, and various community events. My work in the field has made me, I know, a familiar figure in black Los Angeles, which is profoundly gratifying to me personally and professionally.

Frequently, I invite African American artists to my classes because I want my students to talk to working artists as an integral part of their art historical education. I also take students to their studios, adding that valuable dimension to the curriculum. My friendships with the artists make those visits especially effective. The artists explain both their techniques and the meaning and implications of their artistic themes. I used to be astounded when my students mentioned that they had never previously seen artists in their work spaces. The large separation of the university from life no longer surprises, but it still disappoints me.

Some of the artists whom I originally contacted many years ago, simply because I wanted to learn about their lives and work and publish my findings, became extremely close personal friends. My memoir would be incomplete without some mention of their role in my life, especially in my teaching. One, Bill Pajaud, has remained active into his mid-80s. One of America's finest watercolorists, he and I (and our wives) have enjoyed each other's company for many years. A magnificent raconteur, he is an endless source of stories that I have turned into effective teaching material in my own university classes.

One chilling example: when Bill came to Los Angeles as a young man in the 1950s, he was one of the first black students at the Chinouard Art Institute. Mrs. Chinouard, the owner/director, told him that he could not bring his "little pickinninies" to campus and that he should not stand at the bottom of the step and "look up under the white girls' dresses."

Another good friend was Ernie Barnes, whose unusual trajectory from former National Football League player to nationally known figurative artist caught my attention early in my research in this field. Beyond writing several articles on his work as well as a chapter on him in my book, I spent considerable time in personal conversation with him. Our topics ranged across the spectrum, but focused extensively on the failure of so much of American education and the tragedy of imprisonment for thousands of African Americans. These were always exquisitely enjoyable times.

Ernie also gave me a valuable supply of stories I could use in my classes. The best one occurred when he was a freshman at historically black North Carolina Central University. After a field trip to a local museum, he asked the middle aged white woman who conducted the tour about artworks by "Negro artists." Her reply: "I'm sorry son, but your people don't express themselves in that way." I have often begun my African American Art course with that story. When Ernie died of cancer in April, 2009, I interrupted my regular thematic progression by offering a two-hour tribute to his life. I thought that I could do this with minimal emotion after almost 42 years of teaching. I was wrong.

Not surprisingly, African American artists have fewer commercial galleries to exhibit and sell their works than their white counterparts. In the Los Angeles area, there is only one gallery devoted exclusively to this market. For over 20 years, the key area art gallery devoted exclusively to African American art has been the M. Hanks Gallery in Santa Monica. Founder and proprietor Eric Hanks has positioned this institution to occupy a central role in regional African American cultural life. Its multifaceted program of exhibitions and educational programs incubates and encourages this culture of collection, both among experienced and novice private collectors alike. I have worked closely with Eric by speaking regularly at the gallery, by writing essays for his catalogues, by supplying student interns to work there for an academic term, and by taking students to see specific exhibitions and some of his permanent collection. All of this reflects my commitment to strengthening the institutional infrastructure of African American visual art in this region. I see it as a broader feature of my academic and political identity.

My relative job security since 1995 has also generated a deeper and more extensive personal commitment to external political issues, enriching my role as teacher and writer. While I always participated in progressive politics, my career narrative reveals that for many years, much of my political energy necessarily had to be directed to internal struggles within the University of

210

California. The personal, to be sure, *is* political and my long quest for academic stability and legitimacy has been inextricably linked to my critique of university priorities, especially the mediocre commitment to undergraduate education, the scandalous treatment of contingent faculty, and the continuing presence of second class academic personnel, even now properly viewed as a system of academic apartheid. All of these are continuing problems and will unfortunately persist long after I have left the scene.

Among many other issues, I have renewed my family heritage and my personal energy to tackle the vexatious problems of racism. In Los Angeles, race has always been at the forefront of public concern, especially since the traumatic violence of 1992. In 1996, California voters passed proposition 209, amending the California Constitution to prohibit public entities from discriminating on the basis of race, ethnicity, or gender. This racist measure, deceptively called a civil rights initiative by its proponent, African American former University of California Regent Ward Connerly, had destructive effects on minority group enrollment throughout California's public universities. Its effect was especially dramatic and disheartening at UCLA. I made numerous public and media appearances defending affirmative action, mostly using my skills as a public speaker and my experience in radio and television interviews.

Once again, a prominent political controversy had significant implications for my work as a faculty member. I neither need nor want all black students in my African American Studies courses. I maintain at the start of each class that African American Studies classes are for *everyone*, both to learn and to teach. But I also need a critical mass of black students in these classes; their experiences and perspectives are vital to my subject matter and their voices are especially important in the broader educational development of non-African American students. Although I have earned great credibility in examining African American history and culture among students and colleagues, I need the vigorous discussion of African American students to augment my own perspectives. The struggle for affirmative action is a struggle for the soul of a nation with a tragic and continuing legacy of racism. It would be inconceivable for me, with my personal history, to avoid deep involvement in this issue.

Since the terrorist attacks of September 11, 2001, I have spoken out against the egregious violations of civil liberties that the George W. Bush administration fostered, the odious facility in Guantanamo, Cuba, the increasing use of torture as an instrument of national policy, and the repressive implications of the Patriot Act and similar Orwellian legislation. I have participated in UCLA teach-in events and external political meetings.

211

Those political activities are similar to many of the protests I participated in during my student days. The difference is that in late middle age, I have both the public speaking skills and the personal gravitas from many decades of agitational activity that I have become of the featured "leaders." I welcome the role. It reflects a lifetime of political activism and it seems like a natural progression at this stage of my life.

Like many other politically active academics and others, I joined the opposition to the war in Iraq from the inception. I actually spoke out publicly before George Bush used the cover of "weapons of mass destruction" to justify his grotesque "shock and awe" attack on Iraq without a Congressional declaration of war as the Constitution required. My opposition to both the war itself and to the wider perfidy of the Bush presidency has been a substantial focus of my recent political life. I marched in numerous anti-war demonstrations and I made a point to weave my critique into my scholarly presentations in my own classes and throughout the world.

In 2003 and 2004, Los Angeles experienced a major strike of supermarket workers. Ruth and I had come to know and like our local supermarket checkers and others during our weekly grocery shopping excursions to Vons. They received relatively low pay, but had reasonable heath benefits that grocery executives were threatening to reduce. I have been pro-labor my whole life, but here I felt a closer connection to the battle. When picket lines went up, I joined thousands of others in supporting the workers by refusing to cross the lines. It was easy for us to find alternatives by shopping in supermarkets and others stores without labor disputes. Any inconvenience was trivial.

I felt that merely observing the union lines was not enough. This was a protracted battle and I decided I had to join the picket line at least once a week. I drove to Vons, put on a cap from the United Food and Commercial Workers Local, picked up a picket sign, and marched for an hour or so in front of the supermarket. I observed the union requirement to remain peaceful, but I also joined my fellow picketers in yelling "scab" at the replacement workers the companies brought in to break the strike.

I found some of my students' reactions to the strike puzzling and disappointing. Many confessed to crossing the lines regularly, claiming that they had little or no alternative to buy their food and other necessities. I replied that I thought that excuse was nonsense, often using the more appropriate word "bullshit," depending on how well I knew individual students. It reinforced my sense that many of my UCLA students had a powerfully entrenched sense of entitlement that often transcended their public proclamations of progressive politics.

In recent years, human rights issues throughout the world have occupied my attention both as a citizen and as an academic. The military regime in Burma, with its unspeakable record of human rights abuses, has been a source of considerable student attention throughout the United States. I have spoken publicly on this issue, including a presentation to the University of California Regents about the need to eliminate their investments from corporations doing business with that oppressive regime. Likewise, I have participated vigorously in the campaign to end the genocide in Darfur, Sudan. At the University of California, student and faculty efforts for divestment have been successful and I have been gratified to play a small role, especially as a speaker on this compelling and urgent issue.

Another human rights issue has touched me even more viscerally. I have continued to be outspoken on the continuing Turkish denial of the genocide it perpetrated on the Armenian population in 1915. As the son of a Holocaust survivor, this issue has special emotional resonance for me. I have been honored at invitations to speak at the annual genocide commemoration in April each year on the UCLA campus. Each time I have spoken, I have again felt that I have entered a "zone," where the passion takes over and leads me to a feeling of extraordinary transcendence. I always note my Jewish identity on these occasions, indicating my view that Jews have a special obligation to support the formal recognition of the Genocide. A huge Armenian student population attends UCLA and my role as a non-Armenian advocate of genocide recognition has augmented my personal visibility on campus and in the wider community.

For many years, I have added the Armenian Genocide to several of my classes. Like my commitment to bringing in the Holocaust at least once every academic year, I have done the same with this topic, if not quite as extensively. Reactions from my Armenian American students are always gratifying but dismaying. Each time I even mention the genocide, students come up to me after class and thank me, sometimes profusely, for mentioning the topic. That reveals how little it occurs in many other classes and my impression is that the vast majority of students outside the Armenian community know almost nothing of the grisly events of almost a century ago.

One more highly controversial topic has been a source of considerable public and student interest in the early years of the 21st century, especially in California. Like every large university, UCLA has a substantial gay and lesbian student population, many open and some still understandably closeted. I have addressed these issues in some of my classes for years and I regret that it has not been a major focus of my art-related research. The controversy over gay marriage has erupted on campus and in the state,

213

especially with a California Supreme Court decision that first ruled that gays had the right to marry and then with an odious public initiative that outlawed it in the 2008 election.

I have been an active partisan on this issue. As usual, the best use of my talents politically is my public speaking. I have addressed the issue several times, identifying myself as a straight man with a long term marriage that is not even remotely threatened if my gay and lesbian friends are legally entitled to marry. In fact, I argue passionately that most public objections to gay marriage reflect a deep homophobia often reflecting religious biases stemming from family backgrounds. But of course, in these settings of political oratory, I usually speak to audiences who already agree with me.

More problematic is when I raise issues of homosexuality with African American audiences, many of whom bring strong religious biases to this topic. I try to acknowledge their sincerity of their faith, but I never back down in my support of gay rights. I articulate the view firmly that gay rights are civil rights and I will, even bluntly, tell black individuals and groups that they have no ownership to the label "civil rights." I have made similar comments to Jewish audiences about the term "Holocaust."

All of this political activism reflects my personal vision of living a morally engaged intellectual life. As a teacher, it fosters my drive to connect theory and practice. For my students, it provides an opportunity to study with a faculty member who refuses to stay isolated on campus and who brings his personal political experiences into classroom discourse. Throughout my academic career, I have found that even many students who disagree profoundly with my views and with my activism appreciate my passion and willingness to share those experiences with them.

Some, of course, are appalled at my political activism and outspokenness and I have found myself attacked in conservative student newspapers, fully within these students' First Amendment rights. Among other things, they object to my clearly articulated view at the outset of every class I teach that *no* instructor is neutral or objective and that my professional responsibility is to be candid about my biases. I suspect, too, that some students, not necessarily consciously, also object to my style. I am loud, I am energetic, and I am relentless in pursuing my intellectual objectives, no matter how touchy or controversial. In short, I believe, it's a very Jewish style. My student evaluations have remained exceptionally strong for more than 40 years, although I know well that my views are well to the left of the vast majority of my students. My recent political activism returns me to the origins of my maverick academic life. Since 1967, this approach has been the hallmark of my academic identity.

In the contemporary electronic age, I have found myself on at least five right-wing websites. Most are rehashes of familiar conservative complaints about liberal professors seeking to indoctrinate unwitting college and university students. I found one especially repulsive. Calling itself "Masada 2000," it targets academics and others who oppose the ultra-Zionist and racist views of the site's creators. Although the site was removed in 2007, web surfers can still access it and find the names of the 7000 "traitors" and "self-hating Jews" identified and posted on the web.

"Masada 2000" seeks to identify Jews who "despise Israel" and detest their own Jewish identities. Its 7000 targets are specifically labeled the "Self-Hating and/or Israel Threatening LIST," known more commonly by its acronym, the S.H.I.T. list or sometimes the "Dense and Israel Repugnant Traitor's List," or D.I.R.T. The list is extremely broad, including Noam Chomsky, Woody Allen, Gloria Steinem, Michael Lerner, and other luminaries. Not surprisingly, American Jewish academics are well represented. Viewers can access their "favorite Jew" alphabetically, where they can find brief or fuller descriptions depending on the target. My own reference is comparatively slim, identifying me merely as teaching African American Studies at UCLA—itself, presumably, a suspect category for the site's sponsors.

I have no idea how people merit inclusion on the S.H.I.T. list. It may be that targets have been active in progressive Jewish organizations, published books and articles critical of various Israeli policies, or simply signed petitions in favor of peace and ending Israeli occupation. It could also be that inclusion results from informers, perhaps even right-wing Jewish college and university students spying and reporting on their suspect professors.

Accusations of religious and cultural self-hatred are especially repugnant; my father's escape from Hitler's Germany and its personal psychological consequences make me share the anger of many other S.H.I.T. list targets. Many on the list are amused and even proud of their inclusion. But others legitimately worry about the implications for their professional and personal lives. Extreme Jewish elements, including a small subset of the Jewish student population, may well seek to isolate listed faculty members and even seek to damage their careers through invective, innuendo, and outright falsehoods. Organized religious extremists are often dangerous. "Masada 2000" designees are more vulnerable to threats and reprisals, even physical harm, than their less politically outspoken and active faculty colleagues.

Of all the venomous websites available, "Masada 2000" most closely resembles the worst character assassination elements of McCarthyism. But even less strident websites that accuse Jewish and other academics of hostility to Israel present serious dangers by equating legitimate criticism of

Israeli policies, especially its continuing occupation of Arab lands, with Jewish self-hatred or anti-Semitism. I categorically refuse to retreat in my public views and I have no fear whatever of retaliation. Quite the contrary: my response is an article, accepted but not yet in print as of this writing, entitled, "The Old McCarthyism and the New Media: Contemporary Threats to Academic Freedom," robustly defending academic freedom generally, my own engaged pedagogy, and even my critics' First Amendment rights.

Chapter 24
Final Reflections: It Was Worth It

People regularly say that they have no regrets about the way they have lived their lives, perhaps especially in the summations of their memoirs. This is a ritual incantation; it is expected and it provides a final rationalization for their basic life choices. But of course everyone has regrets, some minor and some major. I am certainly no exception. I can think of plenty of things I would do differently, especially in areas of life that would have had a less onerous impact on my immediate family, especially my daughter. But no one can repeal the past. All anybody can do is to figure it out as honestly as possible.

I make absolutely no apology about the political direction of my life. It reflects a serious 60s sensibility, although its origins go much deeper historically. For all its flaws and irrationalities, that era in recent American and world history did much to elevate the moral consciousness of hundreds of millions of people. It also provided millions of others the opportunity to combine their work and personal lives with a deeper commitment to their moral values. I'm extremely fortunate to be one of those millions.

My own summing up is necessarily incomplete. In my late 60s, I probably have a few more decades of life to add more chapters to this narrative. I don't fear death at all. In fact, I rarely think about it. Indeed, as I frequently tell my students, I prefer the usual human denial on that score and often note that when it comes to mortality, I'm happy to be retarded.

My story has several parts. I'm generally happy with the personal direction, although I made a dumb choice with my first marriage and a magnificent choice with the second. I'm extremely satisfied with my carefully constructed secular Jewish identity, one that takes into account the agonizing impact of the Holocaust on my father and therefore my childhood. I have been fortunate to have an extraordinary array of personal friendship and travel experiences in my life, all of which have informed both my professional and political work for many decades.

As this memoir has revealed, my life as an unorthodox academic has been central to my story. It is a huge part of the summing up. Its joys and its pains and frustrations make me ask constantly whether it has been worth it. This question has no simple answer. Doubtless, the benefits have far outweighed the difficulties. I have never ceased to enjoy the work itself, especially the classroom teaching with approximately 40,000 students to date, the extensive personal contact with so many thousands of them, and the marvelous opportunity to transform my ideas and research in to published writings. Each quarter, in the final class session, I tell my students that I hope that they find professional or occupational opportunities to provide comparable satisfactions to my own as an academic. They recognize, I believe, the passion and sincerity of my remarks. I can think of no other professional life that would have rivaled my own. Neither legal practice nor solitary writing nor political activism alone could possibly match the intellectual and personal excitement of my strange but successful career.

But candor also requires that I acknowledge the massive emotional toll of my faculty odyssey. Decades of turbulence, uncertainty, and insecurity have had their effects. They have exacerbated the anxiety I frequently experience and above all, they have had significant and sometimes enduring consequences for my family life. Living under a state of seemingly perpetual siege can and does wreak havoc; I have no doubt that both my wife and daughter have paid a substantial price. My academic battles are emotionally comparable to the lives of committed political activists in the early cold war. Their encounters with McCarthyism and their obsession with their political objectives left permanent scars on themselves and on their loved ones. Still, my marriage has endured for almost 40 years and my daughter is making her way and establishing her identity in a precarious world.

Throughout my long years of financial insecurity, even while my hustling brought me a decent living, Ruth continued her own idiosyncratic professional career and always brought in sufficient income, usually more than mine, to alleviate most of my anxieties. From 1982-1984, she led a team at UCLA that developed one of the very first computer-based writer's aides for English composition. For eight years after that, she was the Director of Science at two private companies, developing educational software in biology, geology, and physics at the middle and high school levels. Then, in 1993, she shifted her focus and became a professional evaluator of pre-kindergarten to university science and mathematics education projects, usually funded by government agencies like the National Science Foundation and the National Institutes of Health. For the past 15 years, she has operated her own evaluation company, *Mar Vista Research*, evaluating science education projects funded primarily by NSF and NIH grants to UCLA, California State Universities at Long Beach and Fullerton, and the University of Washington.

Nevertheless, I continue to harbor strong resentment even now against those university officials who stymied my work, threatening both my livelihood and sense of self in the process. I have similar feelings about colleagues whose arrogant sense of entitlement encouraged them, however unconsciously, to look at me with disdain because of my job title or

218

unorthodox formal credentials. I could always tell. These feelings will not swiftly dissipate.

During my temporary faculty service at the University of California at Irvine, the Dean of Social Science, a consummate "insider," told me directly that, after all, I could have made other decisions in my career, opting for a more conventional trajectory instead of a maverick one. Perhaps he was correct, but I suspect that my basic temperament would make a conventional academic approach unlikely or impossible. I am more comfortable as an outsider, a function of a life of political opposition to a racist, sexist, and unjust capitalist order. This is why, in my "Agitational Communication" course, I indicate my emotional identification with those who challenge power rather than exercise it. Moreover, I dislike and distrust authority and I follow orders and regulations with extreme difficulty, especially when I find them foolish or malevolent. The conventional path, I think, is a personal psychological impossibility.

The cost has been high. In 2004, I received a promotion to Senior Lecturer, a rarely granted title in the UC system that required minimal salary parity with full professors. Though I have regularly received merit pay increases during my UC faculty service, this remains my sole academic promotion in my entire academic career. In 1978, in the midst of one of my Berkeley struggles, I spoke with celebrated anthropologist Gregory Bateson. California Governor Jerry Brown had recently appointed him to the UC Board of Regents. Bateson told me that he had taught at the university level for many years and had never had tenure and that I could possibly do the same thing. He turned out to be correct, but if I had known that I would do it for 42 years, I might well have quit on the spot. I sometimes recommend academic careers to my students, but I would *never* suggest to anyone to try to emulate my specific path.

Throughout my struggles, I always thought that I would win if I made it to age 65. I passed that mark on March 30, 2008. I have acknowledged that many people have helped, especially my wife Ruth and a few courageous academics like Paul Rosenthal and some others. Any way that I decide to continue, at this point, will reflect my decision about how to live the final stage of my intellectual and academic life, probably some combination of modestly reduced teaching, guest lecturing at other locales, more writing, and special projects of great personal appeal. I plan to maintain as much classroom vigor as possible, indeed using my personality to motivate (even *entertain*, to employ the pejorative label I have so frequently encountered) my students as a deliberate pedagogical strategy to encourage critical thinking and active public citizenship. My commitment to public intellectualism remains a constant in my academic career. I will continue to speak out on public issues and write for popular as well as academic publications.

I hope also to continue my personal research, eventually producing the first comprehensive book on the history of American Jewish political art—a return to my personal origins and family heritage. Continued work on the still neglected tradition of African American art still commands my enthusiastic interest and will likely generate more research in this field. Whatever the research, it will remain engaged and partisan, fully in the tradition of C. Wright Mills and all the other intellectual giants who influenced me many years ago and provided a firm and admirable rationale for my own research and publication.

"What if" questions are fascinating but irrelevant to actual human experience. If Judge Luther Hussey had not interfered with my plan to earn a Ph.D. in political science, I might have made a successful career within that discipline. But I doubt it. Sooner rather than later, my disillusionment would have surfaced and I imagine I would have sought some innovative interdisciplinary academic home. If some academic supporters had come earlier to my rescue, I might have had better job security and been spared the scars of battle and the resulting emotional fallout. But then I would not have been able to teach 42 separate classes and enter fields I scarcely knew existed when I was an undergraduate. I would not have had the dozens of invitations to conferences and universities throughout the nation and the world to speak about subjects I found fascinating. I would likely not have helped pioneer the subfield of political art and become a respected scholar of African American art history. I would not have had the chance to travel so widely and meet such fascinating people. I would probably have not extended my research into South African politics and culture and would have missed the opportunity to experience the emergence of a modern nonracial democracy there. Above all, my travails in academia have augmented my personal intellectual development and made me a more effective political organizer and activist.

My life, of course, has been more than my work. All lives represent a *gestalt*, a comprehensive accounting of a person's complete identity. That is always a work in progress, to be sure. Since my teenage years, I have thought that life's meaning depends on people's deepest personal values and their abilities to implement those values in as many aspects of their lives as possible. Often, that requires breaking away from the negative predictions of others, especially from those in positions of power and authority. This is so even when those predictions are well meaning, although in my experience, they are often intentionally malevolent.

My sister Aimee recalls one especially painful example. In junior high school, one of her teachers or counselors told her to forget trying for any kind of higher level academic achievement; perhaps she should settle for being a maid. When she received her M.A. and went on to a successful special education teaching career, she demonstrated the absurdity, even the meanness, of her teacher's comment. Many of my African American students have reported similar experiences: "Why not try community college? UCLA may be too frustrating for you." They also defy these patronizing remarks, challenging the odds to live autonomous and multifaceted lives.

I have had all too many similar comments throughout my life: "You'll wind up in San Quentin!" "You can't really be a lawyer with your grades and your attitudes." "You need to choose between activism and scholarship." And my favorite, which a senior Berkeley faculty member told me in 1977 or 1978: "You can only teach at the university level with this passion and energy for a maximum of 10 years." There were many more, most of which are thankfully repressed deep in my unconscious mind.

Earlier in the text, I wrote briefly about my lawn cutting gig for a right-wing retired doctor in La Jolla. He asked me what I thought of the 1960 trial in the Soviet Union of U-2 spy pilot Francis Gary Powers. I gave an honest answer, replying that the United States had no business spying there and that the trial was legitimate. Patronizingly, he told me that because I was so young, I couldn't really understand such things. He also said that when I grew up, I would have more mature political views.

When I put the lawnmower away that afternoon, I thought about his remarks. I knew intuitively that he was wrong. With all the earnestness of a 17-year old, I began writing down some of my passionate political beliefs. Later that evening, I called in to one of the early talk radio shows in San Diego. The host asked listeners to discuss their views on whatever topics they wanted. When I got on the air, I proceeded with my list: support the Negroes in the south; establish socialized medicine in America; fight capital punishment. I got no further. The radio host cut me off and then said something about the garbage that college students are learning these days. This was an early introduction to mainstream media political orthodoxy, but it was also deeply instructive.

I still hold those views almost a half century later. And this memoir reflects my passionate involvement in multiple issues and causes throughout my life, starting when I testified against the Ku Klux Klan in Bucks County, Pennsylvania in 1957. My commitment to fighting racism has been a constant in my life. I have proudly opposed arrogant and destructive American military actions from Vietnam to the present. I have fought for gay rights, for women's rights, for workers' struggles, for recognizing the Armenian genocide and for combating anti-Semitism wherever I have encountered it. Above all, I have tried, with marginal success, to change university life to make it a place for serious undergraduate education and critical thinking—and to be welcome to students, faculty, and staff of all racial and ethnic backgrounds.

This is who I am. Many people who were active during the 1960s have moved on to successful careers in various fields. Many have become accomplished professionals: doctors, lawyers, professors, and others. Some have entirely abandoned their youthful idealism and others retain a rhetorical cover even while making all the compromises that grown-ups must make in all societies, especially in the advanced capitalist society of 21st century America.

I'm glad that I have never grown up.

Epilogue

Much of this memoir concerns my lengthy struggle for academic stability over the course of my long career as an academic maverick at the University of California since 1968. When my union, the American Federation of Teachers, finally negotiated the status of "continuing appointments" with seniority provisions for long term lecturers, friends and colleagues assured me that I had gained the job security I had sought for decades. For several years, I concurred with this assessment. I assumed that even in the worst of times, my personal academic record and my collectively bargained seniority rights would protect me from the loss of my job. This job security would, presumably, permit me to make any subsequent retirement decisions on terms that would meet my personal needs and any travel, intellectual, political, or other opportunities that might become available.

But I was always nervous; I fantasized that I would somehow be in for one more fight before I was through with this protracted academic (mis)adventure. Everyone assured me that this merely reflected my paranoia and that no one was out to get me. After all, my academic enemies were gone, retired or dead, and I had garnered a strong internal and external reputation. Moreover, UCLA officials constantly reiterated the need to protect instructional functions even in the face of severe cutbacks owing to the major recession of 2008/2009.

Everything changed dramatically when I arrived on campus on August 3, 2009. My recollection is that I came in early to work with one of the students in the UCLA Ralph Bunche Center Summer Humanities Institute, a special program for students from historically black colleges and universities. My plan was to review a student's research paper prior to his conference presentation. Absentmindedly, I gathered my mail from the faculty mailbox and casually opened a letter from the College of Letters and Science. At the top, in bold, were the fateful words: NOTICE OF LAY-OFF. I barely read the remainder of the letter, signed by the newly appointed dean of social sciences. The final paragraph, noting that the lay-off reflected no negative judgment about my teaching and scholarly stature and that the College hoped that the layoffs could subsequently be rescinded, only exacerbated my rage.

I felt as though I had been brutally sucker punched. To say that this final indignity was the worst psychological moment of my academic career is the understatement of this entire book. That is the case *especially* because the action was not personal. In all my previous battles, it was actually easier to formulate resistance strategy and tactics precisely because the institutional hostility was so personal. This action was directed against an entire group of second-class academic citizens, approximately 70 Lecturers throughout the college of Letters and Science. UCLA, an institution (like many others) with a bloated bureaucracy and a huge athletic program, decided to fix its budgetary problems by cleaning house through dismissing its most vulnerable academic employees.

This body blow caused me considerable emotional distress, a reality that has diminished but scarcely disappeared many months after its occurrence. Even now, this epilogue remains the most emotionally problematic feature of the book to write. But my political instincts swiftly came to the forefront. Almost immediately, I joined my union in fighting the layoffs, speaking at rallies on campus, attending protest meetings, and supporting the formal grievance that the AFT commenced against UCLA. As of this writing, my colleagues have had their jobs restored, as a result of university rescissions, but also as a result of union and student pressure.

I also realized that I had to work individually to preserve my personal academic future. My long record in the University of California ensured that I could claim my retirement pension, which, along with social security benefits, made me far less vulnerable financially than most other faculty members who received these pernicious notices. But that, of course, is not the major issue; for most academics, professional work is a key source of personal identity. Money, of course, is crucial, but is scarcely the only factor when devastating events like lay-offs occur.

Along with my general advocacy for my laid-off colleagues, I began informing my students about my precarious situation in light of my lay-off notice. To my considerable gratification, many of these students, predominantly but not entirely African American, began mobilizing on my behalf. I supplied them information and made some tactical suggestions, but they undertook the campaign on their own. After decades of university struggle, I really had little stomach for daily political battles with university officials concerned with bottom lines and personal advancements. About 30 of my present and former students gathered strong letters of support and demanded and arranged meetings with the social science dean. Some of them also arranged for support letters from their parents. These activist students also generated support in the larger Los Angeles African American community, where I had done extensive research on art and culture and where I was known and respected.

I also sought support from various senior faculty colleagues from several departments and programs on campus. This was strong in African American Studies and from my Communication Studies Chair, Paul Rosenthal. Other ladder faculty, however, ignored their less fortunate peers (and me); apparently they assumed that this administrative action was acceptable in times of budgetary stress and in any case, they seem relieved that they themselves were spared. This was disappointing but not surprising in the narcissistic universe of the modern American research university.

I also used this time to explore other academic opportunities in the Los Angeles area. UCLA is not the only game in town and I realized that in future years I could provide my teaching services to several other local institutions, especially after retirement. It could be gratifying to teach on my terms while ignoring the debilitating internal political struggles that pervade colleges and universities. One of my most promising leads is the Annenberg School of Communication at the University of Southern California. I know several faculty members there, whom I respect enormously. The possibility of joining a vibrant intellectual community, even on a part-time basis, is an exciting prospect, especially in light of some of the frustrations I have encountered over my long odyssey at the University of California.

After months of pressure and emotional distress, I decided to propose a deal that would be advantageous both to the university and to me. Specifically, I offered to retire as long as UCLA would hire me back on "recall" so that I could continue to teach one course per academic quarter — one-half of the course load that I have carried throughout most of my lengthy academic career. After some administrative delay and continued pressure, the university accepted. The social science dean and his staff acknowledged the strength of my teaching, noting that my students had spoken eloquently about my impact on their educations at UCLA and on their lives in general. This means that as of August 2010, I will formally be retired and become "Emeritus" (one of my conditions; lecturers are rarely accorded this title after retirement), but I will continue to be in the classroom each term and will have more time for writing and related pursuits. For the past several years, I had thought about such an arrangement anyway, reflecting that it made sense at the age of 68 or 69.

Teaching over 1000 students each academic year had become somewhat tiring. I had grown accustomed to classes of more than 300 students. I could, with strenuous effort, get to know many of them individually over the course of an academic term. But this arrangement is far from ideal, pedagogically and personally. The prospect of losing teaching assistants in my large enrollment classes because of budgetary cutbacks meant that I would need to eliminate or at least substantially reduce my commitment to student writing requirements. This is simply not acceptable; indeed, it is educationally preposterous in an age of decreasing verbal literacy. This retirement deal accelerates my timetable, but not by very much. I noted earlier in this memoir that I felt victorious when I turned 65. My deal solidifies that perspective.

Adversity also generates creativity. Before I received the lay-off notice, I had begun writing this memoir. In August and September 2009, I wrote furiously, seven days a week, sometimes 11 or 12 hours a day, resolved to complete the work. I deliberately channeled my rage into productive intellectual work, a strategy that has served me well over the years. In fall quarter, 2009, I taught my two courses as well as I could, generating positive student feedback even though I felt understandable hostility when I walked onto the UCLA campus and passed the administration building. I also managed to research and write two additional art-related articles, again transforming personal aggression into intellectual effort. I experienced plenty of restless nights, but having meaningful outlets like teaching and writing proved especially valuable under these trying circumstances.

When I finally concluded my deal with the UCLA administration, I felt compelled to note the substantial psychological toll on my colleagues and on myself of the previous six months. I have no idea whether those comments registered or not, but candor required me to make that statement regardless of its institutional impact. I have no illusions that the university is any different from other institution; the needs and feelings of employees are as irrelevant to universities as they are to banks, insurance companies, and car manufacturers.

Throughout the great recession of 2008 to 2010, millions of American workers have found themselves laid off, facing precarious financial and emotional situations infinitely worse than my own. In light of my own recent experiences, I have resolved to remind my students that these women and men deserve not only our empathy, but also far more governmental assistance than they have received, especially in the administration of President Barack Obama. Although I have regularly addressed these human concerns as an integral feature of my pedagogical and political vision, I have resolved to intensify my efforts along these lines in light of my brush with corporate-style managerial treatment. I expect to carry on with this educational lesson for many years to come. My most recent adversity will also, I hope, make me an even more effective university teacher.

INDEX

231